LIVERPOOL TALES FROM
THE MERSEY MOUTH

Second Edition
published in 2004 by

WOODFIELD PUBLISHING
Bognor Regis, West Sussex, England
www.woodfieldpublishing.com

ISBN 1-903953-74-7

Cover photograph by Guy Woodland

Liverpool Tales

from the

Mersey Mouth

A collection of stories from the 'pool of life'

JOHN WILLIAMS

Woodfield

To Marian, Stephen and Jonathan

*and fond regards to just some of the people
who willed this book into existence*

**Sonia Lazaruis,
Angela Nicolaou-Wright,
Christine McElney** (The Red Rose of Texas)

Guy Woodland, Jacqui Peleg, Donald Kunze, Steve Woo, Amy Friedman, Sam Leach, Carolyn Perkes, Robin Hurst, Steve Howe, Ron Formby, Ian Southam, Andy O'Hare, Karen Alkalay-Gut, Marylin Knapp, Mike McNally, Peter McCormack, George Lloyd, Gordon Tumber, Gerry Jones, Tony Siebenthaler, Iris Weir, Neil Pettit, Tim Kelly, Patrick Wallace, Cathrine Moore, Mary Lynch, Yvonne Child, Joan Harper, Alastair Ward, Jo-anne Pyke, Cathy Connelly, Chris Jones, Babs (Daxie), Audrey Canning, Marj Bennet, James Roughley, Bob Taylor, Brian Seddon, Ron Rainford, David Conlin, Viv Blythe, Naomi Phillips, Stephen Banfield, Mike Hayes, Thomas Rome, Trixie Waddell, Jan Tucker, Andy Gray, Andy Ellis, Ann Hory, Tom Brady, Paul Rainey, Anneke Pereboom, Arlene Zirkel, Robert Ward, Carmen Shulman-Zohar, Catherine Butler, Chris Bell, Chris Carrafang, Clive Warner, Paula Casper-Mercury, Dorothy Bebbington, George Clukas, Gerry Clenton, John Finnegan, Kay Davies, Sheila Graham, Sylvia and Jim Foster, Lynne Williams, Margaret Dempsey, Mike Markowski, Pam Cotton, Peter Suchet, Phillip Tootill, Ruth Nuss, Dorothy Scott, Graeme Hammond, Mike and Barbara Speakman, Pat Keshavarz, Diana and William Leece, Sylvia Foster, Sylvia Mitchell, Amanda Roberts, Trae and Pamsy.

Contents

About the Author

I was born in Liverpool in January 1945, on the cusp of the atomic age. Among other things I have been a sailor, a tailor and latterly an English teacher.

My interests are football, computing and gardening. My obsessions are my family, my love of Liverpool and staying alive.

John Williams, October 2004

Foreword

John Williams writes in the language of Liverpool, a Scouse scribe who brings to life the people and places, inner thoughts and outer images, the vigour and vitality and essentially, the iron humour of a unique city.

It is not only expatriates in Africa and Asia, Australia and America, in every little corner and cubby hole of the globe where they have finally settled who hunger for more of his wit and wisdom as they bookmark his internet site. Surfers who have never even visited Liverpool find themselves hooked on tales that astonish, of people who get under their skin, all related in that special Mersey vernacular, erudite, funny, sad, but ultimately extremely rewarding.

John displays a talent for a lovely turn of phrase which place firm visual images into the imagination: i.e. The laughing girls, in their stiff lampshade skirts, hung from the soldiers' arms like tipsy Fuchsias' or 'I can see those shoes even now, lurking in their nest of tissue paper like sharks in the surf.'

There have been wonderfully gifted writers from Liverpool who have enhanced the theatre and television with their work – Neville Smith, Alun Owen, Willy Russell, Alan Bleasdale, poets such as Roger McGough, Brian Patten, Adrian Henri, even masters of the horror genre such as Ramsey Campbell and Clive Barker. Now John can join that august company as the Scouse master of the internet, feeding over 100,000 eager global readers with his tales of fascination and acute observations of Liverpool life.

In 1960, when John Lennon, Stuart Sutcliffe, Rod Murray and I decided to utilize our efforts in promoting Liverpool as the Dissenters, it was because we were aware of the vitality of our own city and the people in it. We wanted to promote the talent that existed but, in those days, didn't have a voice.

I was delighted when John Lennon used to show me his poems in Ye Cracke in Rice Street and I asked him to write about his group the Beatles in the very first issue of Mersey Beat, a piece I called 'Being A Short Diversion on the Dubious Origins of Beatles.' I was delighted with its unusual and unique style and published it, much to John's surprise.

It was with equal delight, while surfing the net, I discovered the work of another John, whose writings evoke such memories for me with his talent for painting pictures with words.

Now, with the publication of the first of what I suspect will be several collections of his tales in book form, an even larger audience will experience the world of the Mersey Mouth!

Bill Harry, founder of *Mersey Beat*

1.   Sitting on the Dock of the Bay

In 1955, live entertainment in Liverpool was not only a possibility but was an absolute necessity, as the broad net of television had not been universally cast. For free entertainment the old Pier Head was unbeatable. On Sunday evenings in summer its approaches were thronged with milling crowds returning from day trips to New Brighton or Seacombe on the snub-nosed ferries that butted their way through the sullen currents of the river Mersey.

There were often GIs from nearby Burtonwood airbase, sporting a girl on one arm and a cuddly toy on the other, both delightful creatures representing a prize for the soldier's prowess with a rifle. The laughing girls, in their stiff lampshade skirts, hung from the soldiers' arms like tipsy fuchsias.

At the entrance to the boarding tunnel sat an old woman. She sold miles of pink rock candy, all of which bore the legend, 'Liverpool'. I thought it odd that Liverpudlians would want to travel to the Wirral and then come back to buy a souvenir of their own town, not realising that strangers to the city might have purchased a bar or two.

Most Sundays my mother and I would take a bus from Huyton, about seven miles from the Pier Head, and either go direct to New Brighton or, if funds were short, spend the evening taking in the sights at the truncated pier. The entertainment fell into two broad categories, the religious and the secular. The secular group was made up of buskers, spoon players, drunks and escapologists. The religious contingent was almost always lay preachers, some of whom seemed to relish the cut and thrust of the heckling infidels as much as the prospect of saving sinners.

I used to stand on a seat and watch the preachers on their homemade pulpits that were mounted on legs so that the divinely inspired orators could exert maximum crowd control. They always wore a kind of wrap over made of waterproof materials overprinted with texts from the bible, lending them the appearance of half-armoured warriors. Given some of the comments that flew their way they really needed those oilskin flak jackets.

I vividly remember one man, who was as much a scourge to the local religiosi as Attila was to Rome. He must have been about seventy, tall, straight-backed and with a patriarchal shock of white flyaway hair. Winter or summer he always looked as if he was outfacing a gale. His comments, delivered with a military gruffness, were either sarcastic or droll.

One unfortunate victim of the elderly Attila, was a totally bald, bespectacled little man, whose broad Lancastrian accent invariably undermined his attempts to appear profound before the cosmopolitan strollers of the Liverpool waterfront. One hot and sultry evening the itinerant preacher decided to make a frontal assault on Satan's white haired shock trooper.

Perhaps it was because the veteran Hun had disdained even to heckle the ineffectual yokel that the preacher unleashed his attack. He pointed dramatically at the old man, who was ostentatiously reading the 'News of the World', a gutter tabloid, and bellowed, "Behold, the text of idolaters and sinners! Repent your backsliding for the lord repays the wages of sin with eternal death!"

The crowd buzzed in anticipation, and the preacher laid both hands on the sides of his lectern with the air of a captain who had knowingly piloted his vessel into stormy waters. The scourge looked up and said mildly, "Calm down, Curly. Yer can have it back in a minute." The onlookers hooted with laughter as the preacher's scalp turned a dull red and it seemed to me as if the sun had set in the wrong place. He struggled for words, but they clung tenaciously to his throat and all he could do was gasp as if the retort had penetrated his being through the solar plexus.

Sensing abject capitulation, people began to drift away. Just then I saw the resident escapologist writhing on the ground about twenty yards away and, apart from a pale looking young man in a raincoat, his Herculean struggles had gone unnoticed. Suddenly he broke free, stood up and bowed to his audience of one. I turned to my mother and said plaintively, "We missed the escapologist, Mam!"

Before she could reply, Attila's adjutant stabbed a finger at the preacher, who was by that time wrestling with his portable pulpit, and said, "When yer've seen one escapist, son, yer've seen them all!"

His remark was too cryptic for me, but it brought a smile to my mother's face.

2. The Green, Green Grass of Home

I can never picture my Aunt Alice without seeing her against the backdrop of the crumbling farmhouse in which she acted out her many roles. Throughout my childhood she was, by turn, a robust foster mother, a spring of endless mischief and a raven-haired gypsy whose glittering eyes deflected all glances from her hard life as a caretaker cum tenant to a rich farmer. The latter only wanted her services as an animated scarecrow to protect his precious crops. His name was Jackson, and he lived in a well kept, albeit cheerless, house about a mile away. Jackson allowed Alice, her husband Stan and my cousin Tommy to live rent free in the ramshackle 'Coxhead' farm, as long as they kept an eye on his secondary barns and fields. I still refer to it as 'my auntie's farm', but it was never hers, nor was it by then a working farm. Nonetheless, its many outbuildings, orchard, fields and dramatic Victorian interior furnished me with all of the ingredients that made up my golden age.

I lived with my mother for most of the time, on a large council estate in Huyton, and even as a child I was appalled by its uniform dullness. Green door after green door opened onto myriad lawns hemmed in by Privet hedges that bordered seemingly endless tributaries of grey-blue tarmac. Eventually the streams of asphalt found their confluence in Prescot Road, which carried buses into Liverpool, ferrying the locals along the river of traffic that flowed from our cold new suburb into the warm, war ravaged heart of the old city. Those surroundings filled me with a sense of oppression the like of which I would only ever again experience in the khaki jungles and rivers of the Cameroons. So, whenever my mother suggested that we make a foray to Coxhead farm my heart would sing a hymn to difference.

Two buses were necessary to reach the farm. The first would drop us off on the outskirts of Prescot, an ancient market town, where we would wait for the number 8l bus to Wambo Lane, an eroded sandstone path skirting a small estate of grey pre-fabricated houses, like a beach edged with slate cliffs. From there it was a short walk to Sandy lane which was a serpentine mixture of sand, pebbles and potholes that probably started life as a stream.

Then, just before the farmhouse came into view, a pond could be seen, its algae-blanketed surface resembling a pristine lawn that had sunk below the level of the surrounding earth under the sheer weight of its own verdant perfection. Next came the pigsties, low and squat, constructed entirely from great slabs of local sandstone. The slabs had shifted and inclined at angles as if still resting in their original bedding planes. Overgrown with weeds and reeking of decay, it might have been an ancient burial ground. Finally, a left diagonal past the skeletal barn and a few steps to the kitchen door which appeared strangely dead amid the sheen of blooming lichens which looked as if they had been sprayed onto the walls.

For six glorious weeks of every summer, and every holiday in between, the farm was my fortress against the vicissitudes of a life that was often ruptured by my mother's overwhelming need to escape the confines of an unhappy marriage. The farm was a monument to decay and wilful neglect, but for me it was a haven, where I could breathe freely, like a duckling amid the muddy debris of its egg.

At the rear of the house sprawled an orchard the size of a football pitch. I loved it with a landowner's lust, watching its seasonal changes with sharp interest. In winter, the frost transformed the rampant grasses into silver filigree that crunched noisily underfoot, sending its resident hare bounding from its nest beneath my favourite pear tree. I remember, too, a huge owl, which perched in the lower boughs of an apple tree; unless one approached too closely, whereupon it would lurch into space; its first slow wing beats synchronised to the gently reverberating branches left disturbed by its flight.

Then, the arrival of beloved spring, when the sun would massage life into the stiff grasses and uncoil the wrought iron brambles and the gnarled fruit trees ushered in the sun with tiny bouquets of green leaves and red-flecked apple blossom. Spring, the fragrant foot soldier to Summer's golden army and the promise of six weeks of rustic bliss with my wonderful country mother!

3. In With the In Crowd

I was a teenager long before the denim age dawned. In those days, to be seen in Liverpool wearing denim, or 'dungaree', as it was called, was to declare oneself a member of the merchant marine. Only sailors had, or even wanted access to Wranglers, Lees or Levi's, which they picked up on America's eastern seaboard.

Far from being fashion conscious, those men chose denim for the same reasons that Mr Levi's originals took off among the Forty-Niners. They were made to withstand the elements.

On dry land, we were still aping the fashions that filtered down from the American pop idols via Cliff Richard, Wee Willie Harris and Marty Wilde. The look, inspired by America's Dion Di Mucci, was Italian. If you weren't sporting a striped, single breasted, three-buttoned suit, with enough back lift to freeze a Polar bear's tush, then you were a square, a terminal cube.

As a post-atomic child, I quite naturally picked my own first suit. My mother went with me to pay the bill, you understand. So it was that I found myself in a large draper's which went by the name of Burman's and which specialised in deferred payments. Rather like Prince Charles' arrangement with Burberry's.

It wasn't a shop so much as a warehouse. Suits, shoes, shirts and ties hung everywhere and they catered for every kind of taste, from Teddy boys with their velvet drapes to riders of the purple sage in cowboy boots and jackets, straight off the cover of a Hank Williams album. They also sold the garments that would accompany my initiation into urban adolescence.

My mother remained stoically silent as the outfitter introduced me to the arcane mysteries of jetted pockets, single vents and trouser bottoms that had a 'v' cut-out at the seams. I chose a blue and black striped job that had my mother silently mouthing 'monkey suit'. I ignored her ill-informed remark and proceeded to purchase a blue and black striped handkerchief, with tie to match.

Then came the shoes...

Now my mother had suffered with her feet all her life, so much so
that even before I'd started school I could spell the word chiropodist.
So you can imagine how she felt when the warehouse man, sorry,
sales assistant, brought me my first pair of fashion shoes – black
winkle-pickers. I can see those shoes even now, lurking in their nest
of tissue paper like sharks in the surf.

I was entranced. The way to the 'in crowd' was spread out before
me! My mother pleaded with me to buy some 'sensible' shoes, but I
earnestly convinced her that the grammar of clothing was like the
grammar of toys; everything came in sets.

I never outgrew that suit. It lost its shape within a week and the jetted pockets, simply slits with seams, no longer met, but gaped open as
if I had a pair of terrified eyes either side of my tie. The stripes, once
straight, waved their way down the length of my body so that I felt as
if I was standing in front of a distorting mirror.

As for the shoes, well they lasted most of the summer, until an in-
clement cloudburst revealed to me the limitations of tat.

By Christmas of that year I had abandoned the Italian look for a
duffel coat.

The greatest blow came a year later when I started work for Solly
Abrams, one of the finest bespoke tailors in Liverpool. I had had my
Italian suit put into the dry cleaners in the hope of obtaining its renaissance, but when I started work even the youngest punters looked at
me with disdain as they recognised the shmutter I was wearing.

And the worst of it was that Solly wouldn't even begin to measure
me for a suit until I had the cash in hand, since that was how he operated. There followed weeks of shame as I gradually retreated to the
rear of the shop, anxious to avoid the looks of open disbelief that
came my way. Even my jetted pockets seemed to be winking crook-
edly at me.

Incidentally, Solly's suit lasted me into my late teens when it was
attacked and partially eaten by Fifi, my mother's pathologically insane
poodle.

4. Desperado

This is a cautionary tale, telling of my only foray into world of disorganised crime. It was in 1963 and I was working at the time, but because of my nomadic lifestyle during childhood, and my relatively brief career as a sailor, I didn't know many people of my own age. In short I was bored.

I happened to meet two blokes who were in their late twenties and were affable enough to arrange to meet me again. Because of these two I would depart the straight and narrow for the first and only time in my life. I remember only too well their real names, but in the interest of anonymity I will henceforth refer to them as Smash and Grab.

Smash was a heavy-set man with reliance on obscene language the likes of which I had never known, not even at sea. Almost every other word was punctuated by one of the four letter words. Even common phrases were often punctuated with the 'f' word. So you would often hear amazing constructions such as the immortal sentence he once uttered while bemoaning his lack of life opportunities:

"I wanted to join the Royal fucking Marines, but I 'ad flat fucking feet!"

Grab was a quiet, gentle, person, who worried incessantly about his children. I had arranged to meet them in Huyton at a pub called the Eagle and Child. The 'Eagle', as it was widely known, has long gone, but its legendary status as one of the roughest pubs in Liverpool remains. It was one of the last pubs before the city of Liverpool merged with the county of Lancashire and had a lot in common with the frontier saloon bars in Tombstone and Dodge City. One looked too closely at another's face at one's peril, because it invariably invoked the snarled question, "Who the fuck are you lookin' at!" followed by an invitation to partake of a knuckle sandwich.

That night I simply affected tunnel vision and stared fixedly at my pint of mild.

Smash and Grab seemed a bit uneasy … and it was nothing to do with the close proximity of the largest fighting force ever assembled in one place since D-Day. It transpired that they had been invited to earn some easy money and in turn they invited me to join them. Friends are like that, even those of bare acquaintance.

The deal was that one of their mates, we'll call him Moriarty, after the fictional criminal genius, worked for a firm that installed and maintained burglar alarms. According to Smash and Grab, Moriarty had access to 'inside knowledge'. Apparently, his firm didn't bother to send payment reminders to clients, but instead, simply cut them off if they didn't keep up their instalments. So, at any given time, Moriarty knew which shop or warehouse had no working security alarm.

Smash assured me that we would be okay as Moriarty was a good feller who 'knew his stuff'. I was reluctant as I was working and money did not hold the same pressing need for me as it did for Smash and Grab who, as far as I could gather, hadn't held a responsible position since they were school milk monitors. Sadly for me I was bored and vaguely anxious to remain friends with the two erstwhile thieves.

I should have baled out after Moriarty made his entrance, because his first words to me after being introduced were:

"Giz a cigarette will yer?"

A criminal mastermind who didn't have the price of a packet of Woodbines! Like a fool I agreed to accompany them and so we piled into Moriarty's two-door van. We headed up Stockbridge Lane and before long were parked outside a shop facing my old school of St. John De La Salle.

We were about to break into my old tuck shop! It only sold cigarettes, bread and crisps and was generally perceived as a facility benefiting those pupils who were on a low protein diet of Woodbines and loaves stuffed with potato crisps. I couldn't believe what was happening, but stupidly made no attempt to leave.

Smash climbed over the yard wall armed with a screwdriver and attempted to lever off the window grill. The November air was rent with the shrill yammering of an alarm. Moriarty literally jumped into the driving seat with the alacrity of a formula one driver at the starting grid, while Grab and myself competed furiously to get into the van through the sole remaining door. Smash was still navigating the barbed wire and leaking expletives in a flood of abuse. After an age of dithering we sped away.

Moriarty, without a trace of irony, remarked:

"They 'aven't cut that one off yet!"

Not simply a master criminal but a master of understatement too!

Plan B then came into operation. Moriarty knew of a fancy goods shop in Lodge Lane that was a 'cinch'. Now I lived just off Lodge Lane and was puzzled as to why anyone would find it profitable to rob from a shop that sold swan-shaped ashtrays made of glass and coasters bearing images of the Mersey Tunnel. You don't argue with a criminal mastermind however, and we were soon parked in a side street unloading the tools of the trade, which in this instance consisted of a large crowbar and two fourteen-pound hammers.

As we unloaded the precision tools, in full of view of any passers by, I noticed that Moriarty was still in his seat. He explained that he would be 'keeping Dixie' on the off-chance that we would be rumbled. As we trudged up the alleyway to the rear of Aladdin's Cave I turned and saw Moriarty's face lit by the flare of a match as he attempted to light a very small cigarette stub.

After scaling the wall at the rear of the shop, during which operation the crowbar fell from Grab's clutches and clanged loudly onto the pavement, we found ourselves confronted by a steel shod door barring our way to infinite riches. Smash and Grab took this as an affront to their ambitions and promptly set about removing the offending obstacle by dint of hitting it with their hammers. The door remained obstinately intact and I was appalled by the noise they were making. They seemed oblivious of the racket and just redoubled their efforts.

Bong!... Boing!... Bong!... Boing!... Bong!... Boing!

The more the door resisted the more insistent they became.

Bong!... Boing!... Bong!... Boing!... Bong!... Boing!

I was suddenly in need of a toilet, but although I was bold enough to attempt to rob the shopkeeper I was too shy to take a leak in his yard and so I was reduced to jumping from one foot to the other.

Smash turned to me and snapped, "Keep the fucking noise down will yer!"

I could only stare at him in disbelief as he returned to his Herculean task.

Bong!... Boing!... Bong!... Boing!... Bong!... Boing!

It defied belief that they even imagined nobody would hear them. I was aware that lights were being switched on in the surrounding houses and the sound of sash windows being raised was adding to the cacophony made by the duo of dedicated campanologists as they tried in vain to ring the changes.

I pleaded with them to try at least to muffle the sound by wrapping a coat around the hammers, but to no avail. They continued giving it the Bells of Shannon with all their might.

Bong!... Boing!... Bong!... Boing!... Bong!... Boing!

It was like being on a stag night with the Hunchback of Notre Dame.

The sound of a vehicle slamming to halt followed by the unmistakable crackle of a walky-talky and the barking of a dog brought the performance to an abrupt end.

As one man we panicked. All the artfully forged tools were abandoned to the night as we scrambled madly over the dividing wall. I landed in a knee-high mound of wet mortar and found myself a poor third in the inaugural race of the Lodge Lane Steeplechase. As we clambered over wall after wall I became aware of the fact that the pursuing policemen were casually sauntering along the adjacent alleyway.

We were suddenly faced with an insurmountable wall, and still in a high panic I noticed that there was light on at the rear of the last shop. Hope rose in my heart, there might be a way out, and I opened the door to the shop, closely followed by Grab.

Inside I saw an old man in the process of pouring milk into a teacup. When he saw the gasping mortar-splashed apparitions the bottle dropped from his fingers and sprayed milk all over the floor. It wasn't a storeroom, it was rented accommodation! I saw a door and was convinced that it must have opened onto Lodge Lane. I dashed forward and opened it. It was a staircase leading up to the man's bedroom! I flew up the stairs.

I hid under the bed. In my panic I was reverting to my childhood, playing hide and seek. A patently frightened policeman shone a torch under the bed and said pleadingly, "Come on out lad, you'll be okay."

His fear was matched by mine, and so I got out from under the bed. I was covered in roughly a year's worth of the householder's dead skin. Ugh! Served me right for ruining his cuppa.

The young policeman and I faced each other in a silent fear-filled stand-off. Then the sergeant entered the room, whereupon the younger policeman jabbed his truncheon hard into my midriff. I was still gasping when I was taken downstairs where another policeman was trying to persuade the old man to press charges over loss of his milk. The man declined. If I didn't know by then that Smash and Grab were totally useless I was made aware of their ineptitude when the senior policeman greeted Grab by his christian name, and then said, "Christmas coming up eh lad? You must be gettin' your shopping list together then?"

Grab nodded. I looked for Smash but he had obviously escaped, or so I thought until we were all going out of the back door when one of the policemen opened the door to the outside toilet to reveal Smash sitting there in his overcoat. The smile on the policeman's face showed that he had known all along!

Moriarty had disappeared into the night and I never saw him again.

We were taken first to Lawrence Road Police station, where a young policeman actually bought us some cigarettes with his own money! I nicknamed him PC Sweet after a character in the popular television police series, *Z Cars*. After signing our confessions we were driven to the main Bridewell in Dale Street where we spent seven hours sharing a cell with other miscreants.

Among the assembled felons was a West Indian called Linton. He was six feet six and built like a well-honed racing snake. He had been arrested for loitering with intent to burgle. Later, as we waited at the bottom of the stairs leading to the dock, we overheard a policeman informing the court that a worried householder had alerted him, to Linton's presence in his backyard. The policeman related how when he arrived at the yard he found Linton attempting to conceal himself in a dustbin!

We were convulsed with laughter as we visualised Linton's six-foot-six frame trying to insert itself into a dustbin like a self-retracting Jack in the Box! We were still chortling when we arrived in the dock, which probably explains why Grab copped for three months in jail, thus missing his family's Christmas for the third year in succession, and Smash got a suspended sentence, while I got a year's probation.

Looking back on it I realise that Linton was as much a victim of an all embracing panic as we were.

As we left the court I was surprised to see PC Sweet and asked him why he was there. When he explained that he had been present in another courtroom as an arresting officer I replied that I found it incredible that such a nice man could arrest anybody.

He actually blushed.

5. Ain't Gonna Work on Maggie's Farm No More

I used to spend most of my summer holidays at my Aunt Alice's while my mother worked to supplement my father's maritime allotment, but there were days when I was at home and so find myself with loose ends which my mother would bind together as best she could. This usually involved her losing a day's pay while she took me on some outing or other.

I vividly remember one glorious July morning when I was about nine years old. My mother had risen early, thanks to my unsolicited assistance, and had taken me to the sweetshop at the corner of Finch Lane and Princess Drive. A knot of men and women were congregated on the pavement. Some of them were near neighbours and as my mother exchanged pleasantries it emerged that they were waiting to be picked up by a farmer who wanted to harvest his crop of peas.

I immediately implored my mother to take me. Now pea picking had as much place in her plans as a round the world solo flight, but she finally agreed, as she could never resist my wheedling. At a very tender age I could well have written the world's first manual on pester power.

Within minutes we standing shoulder to shoulder on the back of a violently swaying farm lorry, looking very like those wretched refugees I'd seen on *Pathé News*. The lorry, smelling strongly of silage and slurry, meandered through the countryside toward the farmlands that would one day be known as 'Bird's Eye country' after the frozen food giant had sunk its ice-pick deep into the rich black alluvial soils of South West Lancashire.

A heat haze shimmered above the endless pea fields, rendering them a Renoir in green, as the lorry finally pulled up at the farmyard. The farmer addressed our flock of sheepish looking townies and explained the drill.

"You fill the hampers to the top, with peas ... not stalks ... and re-member, we don't pay for stones!"

He shuffled back into his house while we milled around, collecting the large wicker baskets or 'hampers' before traipsing to the field where the crop lay green and pearlescent with condensation.

The picking was straightforward enough. We simply uprooted a plant and, holding it above the yawning hamper mouth, stripped the pods from it and dropped them into the wicker baskets. It was an incredibly slow business filling the seemingly bottomless hampers, as each plant yielded barely a few handfuls of the precious pods and it seemed an age before my mother and I had picked enough to enable us to drag the hamper to the weighing station, where a bored-looking farmhand lugged the basket onto the scale and adjusted the weights to ascertain whether the basket was full or not.

To my dismay our first attempt was deemed to be underweight, so we had to drag the hamper back through the yielding soil and pick enough to satisfy the demands of our rustic accountant. Happily, it wasn't too long before I was in possession of a brass tally, which regis-tered our first full basket.

Among that merry band of harvesters was one of my neighbours. He was the father of fourteen children and possessed of an acerbic wit from which few escaped, including the members his enormous family. However, crops are impervious to even the wittiest of invective and so Tommy was forced to rely on labour alone to achieve his tar-get. Like everybody else he was working in tandem with friend, and work he did. All day long he and his mate toiled like a pair of armour-less Trojans, with only an occasional pause to swig from a much-needed bottle of brown ale.

As my mother and I steadily accumulated a respectable tally I thought it odd that I hadn't once bumped into Tommy and his mate at the weighing station. At the end of the day the puzzle was solved when it transpired that Tommy and his pal, those inveterate towns-men, had shelled the peas from every pod he picked before he deposited the peas in his hamper, and not only had he only filled a single hamper but he didn't get paid for it!

Tommy took his disappointment like a true stoic. "Thieving bastards!" he roared, and then clambered aboard the lorry, repeating the phrase ad infinitum.

With my genius for exploiting my mother I happily took the lion's share of our joint earnings, leaving my mother with an aching back and badly sunburnt arms. There must have been times when she thought I was the biggest hamper to her life. Such philosophical considerations cut no ice with me though as later that evening I sat in the stalls of the Granada Cinema tucking into a tub of Wall's vanilla and watching Jeff Chandler smoulder his winning way through the Wild West.

We never again danced at those particular rites of spring, but every time I see fresh pea pods I remember that day when I ate almost as many as I picked. In the eighties the Bird's Eye factory, which had been one of the mainstays of the local Kirkby economy, closed down … in spite of protests and the Herculean efforts of 'Tommy the Pod'.

6. Send in the Clowns

I never really saw the appeal of the circus, but that might be because in my childhood I only ever saw two of them. My Aunt Alice took me to the first one, at the old boxing stadium next to the Liverpool Cotton Exchange and it was about as exciting as watching Frank Bruno shadow boxing.

The only thing I can really remember is the clown's empty water bucket routine. You know, the one where he carries the bucket on a pole and pretends he is going to spill it on the audience. The next one I saw, Billy Smart's Circus in Sefton Park, was slightly better, if only because we went boating after the matinee performance.

Decades elapsed before I was to witness another parade of the circus arts, and that was only because I had free tickets. My girlfriend was still young enough to want to go and so we did. The big top was in Newsham Park; I say 'big top' but it was more of a bloated marquee. The ringside seats were simply a row of canvas and tubular steel office chairs. The cheap seats had been salvaged from scrapped buses, and came complete with knife slashes and a hand written sex manual, courtesy of Boggsy, in collaboration with his semi-literate friend 'Keny'.

As we sat through various routines I became aware of something odd. The knife thrower, the snake charmer and the juggler were one and the same man! He was an Asian who must also have been something of a quick-change artist, as he never wore the same outfit twice. When I pointed him out to my girlfriend the whole evening took on a new and intriguing slant. We began watching closely, to see what else he would do. Even in the murky light of the big top he was quite distinctive because he was the only one in the circus with anything like a physique. The rest of the crew looked as though they'd had to fight with the monkeys for their share of the peanuts, and lost.

The mystery man, who we nicknamed the Prince, appeared again, this time to hammer in a loose peg, and another time wielding a spade to clear an abundance of horse droppings. He certainly got about, and was providing us with an unexpected but highly welcome diversion.

Throughout his various acts the Prince had called for young volunteers to help him. I don't know whether it was the effect of the bright lights or over inhalation of the ammonia-rich atmosphere, but almost every child present volunteered at some time or other. Sitting right next to me was young boy who had volunteered at every call, only to be ignored by the ubiquitous Prince. I felt sorry for him.

Then the ringmaster announced the ultimate act of the evening. Again, the request for volunteers was made, and the kid to my right frantically thrust his hand into the air. The lights went down, and, to the accompaniment of his own war-whoops the Prince, dressed as an Indian chief, bounded into the ring, illuminated only by the glare from the fistful of burning brands he was carrying in his left hand. Still issuing blood-curdling whoops, the Prince cast his eyes around for a likely candidate…

The raised hands fell, like a forest levelled by a freak storm – except for the boy next to me. He was covered in confusion and his hand was still going down when the Prince's baleful glare alighted on him. In a series of terrifying leaps the Prince reached the cringing child and, in fireman fashion, slung him over his shoulder.

As he galloped around the ring, his war whoops quite drowned the sound of the boy's screams, who by then was openly crying and nigh on traumatised.

When the Prince finally deposited the boy onto the floor the youngster tried to bolt, but he was in the grip of a man who could wrestle a fully-grown Indian Python, and so he was forced to stand his ground. To the child's eternal credit he recovered sufficiently to help the prince finish his act. He would have learnt a salutary lesson though, never volunteer, especially for something you know nothing about!

The circus over, we decided to pay the additional entrance fee and visit the 'zoo' which was immediately adjacent to the 'big top'. As we walked up the pronounced slope into the zoo I was surprised at the sponge-like surface under our feet. Then I looked down and saw that the floor was composed of a two-foot layer of assorted animal droppings. The smell was overwhelming, and all around us people were gagging, and I don't mean telling jokes. Some of them were being sick and one poor woman unleashed projectile vomit that cleared the Zebra pen by some distance.

As if the smell weren't enough I found myself gaping at what must have been the world's only case of Lion Mange. Honestly, the poor lion's hindquarters were so bereft of hair that for a fleeting moment I thought I was looking at a baboon's bum! As I staggered out, desperately pushing women and children aside, I noticed the Prince nailing up a sign that read 'manure for sale'. Poor man, he really believed that someone would want to purchase instant nausea!

A year later I was passing the site of the departed 'zoo'. Not a thing was growing in the circle of bare earth where the 'floor' had been, the concentrated ammonia had killed everything, leaving behind a miniature desert. If anybody had bought the manure they would probably be specialising in cacti by now.

Several years later my lady and I, footloose and fancy free, decided to go on a camping holiday to Ireland. We were going on my motorbike, which wasn't her idea of travelling in style. Indeed, one of her favourite songs concerns 'Geronimo's Cadillac'. However, she cheerfully helped me load the tents and assorted bin bags onto the Honda and, looking like urban refugees, we took off.

We left Dublin and headed west to Tralee, where she had relatives. They greeted us with open arms, and I am still touched by that, because if someone turned up at my house looking the way I did, I would have hidden behind the door. John and Mary, however, were hospitality personified and everything was going swimmingly until I mentioned that we were camping. They were scandalised.

You see, it rains so much in Ireland that Irish architects spend the first three years of their training building waterproof huts in the Brazilian rain forests. For an Irish person the idea of someone wanting to live exposed to the elements, in an oversized nylon shirt is simply absurd. Within an hour they had dropped us off at their caravan that was parked in the nearby holiday town of Ballyhague.

We had been there for about two days, enjoying the delights of Guinness and the pitch n' putt course, when we awoke one morning to find that a Big Top was being erected near the caravan-park.

I looked for the name of the circus. It was an Irish circus, which explained why the Big Top was really big. It was huge in comparison to the one in Newsham Park. We decided to go and see it, as my lady-love was bored of looking for golf balls. I was especially impressed by the seats, which were in high tiers, like all the pictures of circuses I had ever seen.

You won't believe this, but who was in the ring testing the safety nets? That's right, the Prince himself! Now I wouldn't blame you if you thought that this was a cock and bull story, because it wasn't until he had been through several of his acts that my companion believed me. We awaited the finale with bated breath, and sure enough the call for young volunteers was made. The hands went up. The Prince, whooping and screaming, entered and the hands went down, except for one that remained defiantly rigid. The Asiatic aristocrat then raced toward the one remaining volunteer, who stood up to reveal the bulky frame of an enormous farm boy, whereupon the Prince blinked, faltered, and came to a stumbling halt before offering the boy his hand to help him into the ring!

After the show I saw the Prince talking to some roustabouts. I was anxious to tell him that I had seen his performance before and enjoyed both occasions, so I approached him and said, "I saw you once in Liverpool!"

The Prince, that noble survivor of Pythons, fires and Indian wars, shrank back in fear.

As I walked away, deeply puzzled, my lady ventured the idea that he might well have been an illegal immigrant.

Farewell sweet Prince, and sorry if I startled you.

7.   Down by the Riverside

It's only lately, through writing about Liverpool, that I have become aware of the part played in my life by the River Mersey. It is my fluid umbilical cord, forever connecting me to anyone who was born on or even simply visited its all-embracing shores.

As a small child I used to gaze at it and wonder where exactly in the world my father was and when would he next sail, homeward bound, across the Mersey bar. I can remember accompanying my mother to Garston docks to collect my father's 'allotment' – his monthly allowance to her.

It was just after the Second World War, when austerity refused to abdicate its dominion and many everyday things were impossible to obtain, so you can imagine my shock when I saw, on the quayside where the Elders and Fyffes boats discharged their cargoes of bananas, tons of the precious fruit lying heaped in a tangled mass of red, green and yellow, like a funeral pyre for the victims of some dreadful plague.

My mother told me that they were to be rendered into polish, and while that may have been true, the sight of such conspicuous waste took the shine out of that day's outing.

The Mersey was the point of departure for my short career as a seaman; a career that despite its brevity took me to some fabulous places. The river was also the means by which I was able to enjoy the delights of the Wirral, with New Brighton and Moreton our most frequent destinations. However, the most life changing effect of the river's nurturing flow occurred when I was in my mid-twenties.

At the time I was working in an engineering firm on the Dock Road where the working conditions where, quite simply, dangerous. You see, after I stopped working on the buses I trained as a fitter at a government training centre and left there equipped with some questionable qualifications, which would always be derided by those engineers who had served *bona fide* apprenticeships. Nevertheless, I had worked in enough places to know that having iron girders stacked higgledy-piggledy in the middle of the working area was not conducive to safety.

Whenever somebody wanted a piece of metal he had to drag it out of the precariously balanced pile. It was like playing the children's game Ker-Plunk! with one's own life in the balance. The firm's nickname was 'the bus stop' – because everybody was waiting to move on.

I had been recovering from severe depression even before I got the job in the 'bus stop' and one morning I found myself staring at its near windowless facade, filled with an overwhelming sense of despair. After a minute or so of internal debate I turned on my heel and walked towards the Pier Head and the Woodside ferry. I know it was an irresponsible thing to do, but I couldn't face another day amid the rusting gloom of Vulcan's enclave.

As it turned out it was the best move I ever made, because when I got off the ferry I wandered into Oliveira's Café and met a man who shouldered a boulder into my life-stream and diverted its course forever. His name was Alan Kendrick Hughes, a.k.a 'Yozzer' and on that beautiful May morning he signed articles as helmsman to my foundering craft and steered me away from the doldrums where I might have been forever becalmed.

Yozzer was tall, bullish, self-confident and, to use his own phrase, 'As rough as a bear's arse.' However, his gruff bearing disguised an innate generosity and that morning, after he'd heard my tale of leaving the 'bus stop' without benefit of a bus or even a valid ticket, he determined to find me some work.

I don't know what he would have said had he known that my qualifications were shaky to say the least, but that very evening he knocked on my door and told me to meet him at a bakery in Anfield the following day. The extraordinary thing was that he lived in Moreton, miles across the River Mersey and had made a detour just to let me know.

The bakery job, known as a 'shutdown' because the work had to be done while the normal workforce was on holiday, was only temporary, but within weeks of working with 'AK' – as Yozzer sometimes referred to himself – I had gained enough confidence to find a reasonable job working for John Smith and Bob Crawford, who had a contract to maintain plant at the Bidston factory of Pilkington's Fibre Glass division and who were decent enough employers.

A few months later Yozzer walked onto the site and started working for the same firm as me. He was, without doubt, one of the most wickedly funny men I've ever met. Even people who didn't enjoy his lacerating brand of humour rarely objected, as he was an old fashioned hard case too. One day we were working together, preparing the way for John Smith to remove some Platinum bushes, which helped spin the fibreglass and which were worth a fortune. As we 'surveyed' the job – or to use Yozzer's expression 'gave it a good coat of looking at' – a security guard sidled onto the platform where we were standing. His demeanour spoke, or rather droned, of self-importance and pomposity. Clearing his throat noisily and pointing to the platinum bushes he said: "They don't arf swell up with the heat yer know."

Yozzer, who was a trained engineer, asked deadpan: "Oh really? And what's the co-efficient of the linear expansion?"

The furiously blushing guard gestured like a fisherman estimating the size of the one that got away before scuttling out of sight. I don't know if he has ever recalled Yozzer's question, but every word has been etched into my memory ever since.

Incidentally, a few weeks later ten of the platinum bushes, worth £120,000 at 1970 scrap prices, disappeared, and were later found in the house of an old age pensioner! Perhaps there is a case for raising pensions to a decent standard.

Yozzer's bullish outlook came to my aid months later after the job at Bidston had panned out. He called to tell me that Cammell Lairds were taking men on and said that I should get over to their shipyard the following day at 8 o'clock.

I duly turned up and was ushered into an office where the hirer asked me if I had been sent by the dole, as that was the main criteria for this particular intake. Befuddled by nervousness, as I knew I had no real place there, I replied that I hadn't and I was dismissed.

When Yozzer found out what I'd done he went berserk and told me to get back inside and say that I *had* been sent by the dole. More afraid of upsetting AK than of being rumbled as a 'dilutee', which was what government trainees were scathingly referred to, as they diluted the strength of apprenticeships, I did as he said and was taken on.

The three years that followed were among the happiest of my life as I worked with some of the funniest and cynically worldly-wise people I have ever encountered.

In ancient Greece a philosopher called Diogenes was so appalled at the tyrannical state of the world he decided that since most people were being treated like dogs he might as well live like one and promptly went off to live inside an empty barrel. Since the Greek word for dog was *Kunikos* he and his followers were called cynics, and it is a shame that his noble sentiments have, over time, become distorted to mean something bitter and mean-spirited.

My reference to ancient Greece is not entirely misplaced, given the historical dimensions of Cammell Lairds shipbuilders. Even before I'd ever set foot within a mile of the yard I'd come across a mention of it in Thomas Armstrong's *King Cotton*, a saga of the suffering that Liverpool and Lancashire people had endured when the American civil war closed down the cotton industry. I had been surprised to read that the Confederate Gunship *Alabama* had been built in Birkenhead at Cammell Lairds. Lairds had also built the world's first all-welded ship, and then, ironically, had been virtually wiped out when the Japanese appropriated the technique to build super tankers. The *Ark Royal* aircraft carrier had also slipped out of Lairds and into the bosom of the Mersey.

In 1939 a submarine called *Thetis* was built there and on its trials, just 40 miles away off the North Wales coast it sank and ninety-nine men were lost, the overwhelming majority of whom were civilian workers from the yard. Men who were just like my new comrades, Billy Audley, Yozzer, Jacko, Roscoe, John Poole, Davey Garlic and Paul Flynn. Between them they introduced me to a camaraderie I had never known, even in the close confines of a merchant ship.

Audley, an ex-Merchant Navy engineering officer was clever, funny and singularly eccentric in that he moved in his own orbit without regard for the frantic circling for position practised by most of his peers. He wore his thick curly hair short, at a time when even grand-fathers felt somehow compelled to ape the contemporary fashion for long hair. His clothes – blue check shirts, jeans and denim jackets – were worn winter and summer, year in year out, regardless of trends toward loons, kipper ties and platform soles. Like the steel of the ships he helped build, he was mentally tough and impervious to the fickle winds of change.

One day as we were sitting in the dinner hut, made available to us by the desertion of the rats who refused to endure its shabbiness when there were perfectly good sewers to be had, a young livewire of a kid called Brian began reading aloud from a tabloid.

"D'yer know," he asked in amazement, "that the *Thetis* holds a world record?

He was of course referring to the fact that more men died aboard the ill fated submarine than any other similar tragedy, but before he could make that point, Audley, his jaw muscles working with indignant rage at the tabloid's trivial treatment of the event, snapped, "What for? Staying down the longest?"

Nobody laughed.

On another occasion, as we waited for a pub to open its doors, young Brian almost swooned in admiration as a flash sports car sped past us and gasped, "Did you see that!" to which Diogenes mark II, pointing to the pub railings, replied, "It's only that iron fence in an-other shape lad." A commonplace remark but it was the first time I'd heard a man question material values when he had the wherewithal to buy his way into consumer heaven.

By complete contrast Paul Flynn was a quiet, easy-going young man who simply laughed when I nicknamed him 'the oaf' because of his oddly medieval hairstyle. I remember one night taking him and his wife to the old boxing stadium to see David Bowie's first Liverpool concert. That night Paul met the other, underground, side of Liverpool and he loved it. His delight was obvious from the way he kept dancing, even when there was no music playing.

I suspect such activity would have been frowned on by Roscoe, who was intensely politicised and the possessor of a piratical beard as well as an appetite for Emile Zola. I remember the first time I met him, it was on the morning I started working at Lairds. We were walking along, after having slipped out of the yard to have breakfast at a cafe in Green Lane, something that astonished me but certainly not the proprietor, who was apparently well used to guys scaling the perimeter wall simply to build an appetite, when Roscoe said, "If only we had bread!"

I was taken aback because he'd just demolished a plate of toast smothered in bacon and eggs. Roscoe, a.k.a. Keith Ross, simply smiled and explained that he was quoting from Zola's novel, *Germinal*. Now I'd read a lot, but not what you'd call classic literature, and I was so intrigued by his enthusiasm for Zola that I later got hold of a copy and read it myself. You could say that Roscoe pushed me in the direction of great literature and ultimately university. I have heard since that he owns a delicatessen. I hope he has plenty of bread in both senses of the term.

Although I only spoke to him once, old Jacko will always represent to me the old Merseyside spirit before it was bludgeoned to death by Thatcherism and voodoo economics. I first saw him when I was going with 'the Aud' for an evening aperitif in the Queen's in James Street. He was about sixty and was wearing a flat cap and one of those silk scarves that conjure images of the great depression. As we passed him, leaning against a wall, Billy asked him how things were going on a particular job that Jacko had been lumbered with. Jacko's expression was one of utter contempt as, on one of the few occasions I ever heard him actually speak, he conveyed his hatred of the bosses.

"They keep tellin' us to work 'arder, but if they spent some friggin' money on modern gear we could work more efficiently!"

His wisdom is indelibly printed in my scrapbook of scrapped working class heroes.

Soon after that I was given a job for which I was not at all suited. It involved the installation of some rather delicate looking valves. As the charge-hand dispensed the job, my heart sank, but I needn't have worried, because Jacko, apparently as part of some unspecified punishment, was allocated to show me the ropes. The job was on a ship that was in the fitting out basin and was due to embark on sea trials in Faslane near Glasgow. Tucking his silk scarf into his boiler suit, Jacko led the way. When we got to the engine I enquired of him what we were supposed to do with the gleaming, stainless steel valves. By way of answer he simply placed one of them in the locating hole and hit it with a Lairds' issue two-pound hammer. He then repeated the process eight times, four at either side of the engine, pulled out a pocket watch and indicated that it was knocking off time. Not once did he utter a word to me.

When the ship returned from its sea trials I enquired of one its complement, a fat unpleasant bastard who had insinuated himself into our hovel, how things had gone. He replied that, apart from the fact that none of the injector valves worked and had undergone emergency repair at sea, everything had gone well.

It was then I decided to go back to school and learn something well enough to be confident when I was working with it. I wanted to be a *bona fide* anything with no more hiding from exposure as a fake. It was at that juncture that Davey Garlic, a self assured young man who would have looked equally at home in a student demo, assured me that I would be alright as I had 'a good head on my shoulders'. How he divined that from our hovel-bound discourses about ale and football I'm not at all sure but I was a grateful for his encouragement nonetheless.

When I look at what has happened to Cammell Lairds, recently swindled out of £40,000,000 by some Italian crooks that reneged on a deal, I am almost glad that John Poole can't see it. I say almost because John, whom I barely knew but who possessed one the friendliest and dazzling smiles I've ever seen, went progressively blind. He was a good man and a conscientious worker but now he is almost sightless.

Perhaps Jacko was right. There is no point in working yourself to death when all most people can expect is a cheap burial in an over-crowded cemetery when perhaps we all deserve a Viking funeral on the Mersey.

I will end with a story which sums up the character of the shipyard workers. Some time in the seventies an ex-British submarine, which had been sold to the Chilean navy, was being refitted. It was berthed in a huge basin and one day an unarmed torpedo was accidentally fired. The missile streaked the length of the basin before leaping a quay wall, where it demolished a workman's hut. There was a deadly silence all around, but then a huge wave of laughter and relief echoed on the water as, from the debris of the hut, a white shirt was raised and waved in surrender.

Funny yes, but yet another example of the workforce being torpe-doed by their friends.

8. Mother Nature's Son

Until I was in my late twenties I thought country life was an oxymoron. To me, the countryside was a place where city dwellers went to sample the various delights of muddy lanes, nettle rash or the experience of simultaneously hearing, smelling and feeling the squelch of a fresh cow pat through the gaps in one's sandals.

It's true that I had loved spending summers on my Aunt Alice's farm, but that was situated well within the boundaries of urban civilisation. The countryside I am referring to is the one where bus stops are so well camouflaged with moss, lichens and creeping things that by the time they have been spotted the damned bus has pulled away; the same countryside where silence is nearly as loud as the beating of bird's wings; the countryside that sends one screaming mad with boredom!

My introduction to the niceties of rural England came about when I met a young woman who plucked me from the comforting bosom of inner city Liverpool before depositing me in the wilds of the Fylde, that area of Lancashire so wild and uncharted that it is designated on maps by the legend, 'Here be ferrets!'

I hadn't known her very long and so when she suggested we go and stay with her parents for the weekend I was a trifle dubious. I mean, apart from wind burned cheeks and frozen fingers, farmers don't have much in common with Scousers who work in Cammell Lairds.

On the Thursday before our proposed visit, during the only shipyard strike I participated in, I was co-opted onto a picket line. Picket line duty is a bore, and often coldly so, but it was midsummer and I was relaxed as I stood at the entrance to the yards. I wasn't even disturbed when the BBC television team turned up to take no doubt defamatory pictures. Indeed, I was quite looking forward to the evening news and was mildly disappointed that my idiotic grin was only visible for marginally longer than that possessed by the Cheshire cat.

The following evening I was ensconced on a Ribble bus bound for Poulton Le Fylde. Now, long before then I had circumnavigated the planet and thought myself well travelled, but as I sat in the Olde Tea Shoppe, surrounded by laid back country folk for whom the word 'strike' was restricted to the bowling alley, I felt oddly alienated and realised that I knew almost nothing of the country of my birth.

After another bus journey, during which we crossed over the River Wyre via a privately owned bridge, we arrived in Stalmine, a tiny village on the road to Knott End, itself a tiny village on the road to nowhere. On alighting, Rosie led me to the gate of 'Trays Cottage' and I couldn't help notice that it was located in what can only be termed 'Suicide Alley'; smack dab at the junction of a B road that, almost within knocking distance of the cottage door, turned abruptly right. I suspect that the cottage was built long before the road. In fact, I know it was, as it is a reference point on maps dating back to 1601. After the road had been built it must have been a bit like living in the path of a moving glacier.

Anyway, Rosie's mum, a woman so kindly and self effacing that she reminded me of my own Gran, gave me a warm welcome and invited me to sit down to supper which was hot from the oven. As I tucked into meat and potato pie and savoured the sweet taste of pineapple and grapefruit 'Quosh' – charmingly referred to by the gentle Peggy as "orrible" – I was aware that Rosie's dad was candidly staring at me through light blue eyes that seemed to reflect the skies under which he spent most of his life as a dairy farmer.

With a faint smile on his ruddy face he asked, "Are you a communist then?"

I almost choked on a mixture of potato, onion, corned beef and short crust pastry as I wondered what it was about my appearance that made my political leanings so transparent. As it turned out the answer to my wondering was simple: Dick had seen me on the bloody BBC news!

How the hell he remembered my face from its brief exposure on the small screen I'll never know, but from that moment on my relationship with his daughter seemed somehow destined to slip away as slowly and inexorably as a ship on launching. Not because Dick gave a monkey's toss about my politics, you understand, as he was a yeoman farmer who didn't care who was playing at political masters, because he knew they all needed his milk, but simply because when worlds collide people sometimes get dislodged and drift into space.

Later that evening Rosie and I were taken by her sister Janet and her brother-in-law Chris to a pub called 'The Shovels' in nearby Hambleton, where, under the bright lights of the pool table and the dazzling smile of Janet, I played eight ball with Chris. The newly married couple made me feel more at home 'in't Shovels' than I sometimes did in my local in Liverpool.

I stayed at Trays cottage many times in the following years and only ever experienced kindness from both Dick and Peggy. Peggy actually made the long journey to Liverpool to visit me when I was clinically depressed. I can still see her bewildered distress as she tried desperately to cheer me up, but the perennial glint of a smile behind her glasses was temporarily dimmed.

Many years later I was watching the BBC northern news and almost choked when I saw footage depicting the rear end of a crashed car protruding from the downstairs room of Trays cottage. Suicide alley had almost become a reality, but miraculously the occupants of the cottage and the driver were spared any serious injury.

I occasionally entertain a vision of Dick smiling and asking the driver, "Are you a communist then?" while Peggy tuts at Dick's boldness and asks the man if he'd like some "orrible".

9. Reelin' and Rockin'

My two boys share the quaint notion that pop music began sometime between Robbie Williams and Shania Twain. If I make any kind of contribution to their conversations about music they immediately taunt me with cries of, "Oh yeah, the Beatles, John Lennon ... we know Dad, we've been to the museum!"

It's the museum bit that gets to me. The salutary truth is that I was in at the birth of Rock and Roll – but only because of my mother! You see, in 1954 my 'old girl' was a young dude of 26. She liked going out with her friends, especially on the big local fiesta days like St Patrick's day or the 12th of July. To her it just meant wearing something orange instead of green, something you could do in Liverpool without getting kneecapped. She had been a teenager during the be-bop years so her progression to pop and rock was as natural as shamrock.

In Kensington High Street, Kensington Liverpool that is, there was a record shop, which was permeated with the smell of sheet music and the cardboard sleeves of 78s. Music and magic all in one lock up shop. (Go to HMV nowadays and you need a tour guide to take you round the odourless, soulless, pile-carpeted warehouse they call a store.)

One day my mother gave me the money to go and buy a record for her. It was Bill Haley's 'Rock Around the Clock' and I would like to say that my musical conversion was made on that day, but truth to tell I was still untangling the lyrics of such classics as 'Gilly gilly ossen feffer katz and ...' I still haven't figured it out!

In those days rock was synonymous with Teddy boys and violence, because of their antics in the cinemas during the screening of Bill Haley's movie. Apparently they were dancing in the aisles, thus holding up the more sober patrons who were queuing patiently for Kia-Ora and choc-ices. Inconsiderate thugs!

We only had one Teddy boy in our street, and I never saw him fighting anybody, except his mum when she was dragging him to school. Even as a nine year old I found his Edwardian drapes and enormous sideburns – 'louse ladders', as my grandfather called them – outlandish, and I suppose, by inference, threatening.

I don't know why that should have been the case, because Rudolph Valentino and Victor Mature (a.k.a. Sideburns Inc.) never intimidated anyone. Let's face it; Victor was such a pussycat that when he starred as Samson his most violent act was to strangle a dilapidated lion skin that was so poorly stuffed it was little more than a glove puppet. As for poor Rudolph, apparently the worst he could do to anyone was to throw the lips on them, because he was reputed to reek constantly of garlic.

Our local Ted, Eddie (yes, his name was Eddie) used to frequent a pub in Low Hill called the Blue Ball which was almost adjacent to a police station and directly opposite Sacred Heart church. It was a focus for the Teds and their girlfriends as it played, at such a volume as to be heard on the street, all the rock and roll that was available at that time. Everybody who lived within a mile of the place knew those three songs off by heart.

The police station and the pub are long gone and the church is under constant threat of demolition to make way for roadworks. Perhaps the Jeremiahs were right; Rock 'n' Roll *is* the devil's music!

The pub was just a crepe-soled hop skip and jump from the Cavern, for an unusually athletic Ted that is, but if the Cavern was in business those days it was for the beatniks and jazz freaks, not exactly the Teds' bosom buddies.

I have heard that John Lennon was a bit of a Teddy boy. I wonder if he ever went to the Blue Ball?

Did I mention John Lennon? God I hope the kids don't read this! (I wish ... as far as they're concerned my memories of Liverpool are about as relevant to them as the fine print of the Magna Carta.) Their *laissez-faire* attitude toward Liverpool's heritage and somewhat lamentable lack of civic pride is partly understandable when you consider that successive Liverpool politicians have, in their finite wisdom, demolished the Cavern, razed, or rather lowered the Overhead Railway and so transformed the Pier Head and Mersey Ferry service that you can't even stroll on the landing stage without some officious pillock asking for your boarding pass. Boarding pass! God, when I think of the days I spent sagging school and ceaselessly voyaging the golden triangle between Seacombe, Woodside and the Pier Head – all for the price of a single ticket.

Oh I know that strictly speaking it was illegal, but at least the ferry was full of like-minded people. The last time I went on a ferry there was a smattering of tourists and the sound of a Scouse accent was as rare as the mating call of a Dodo.

By the way, yesterday a pair of self-employed scrap metal dealers made off with the gates of Strawberry Fields! They were found today, intact. Shame we can't say the same of that place in Mathew Street or the 'Docker's Umbrella'.

At least – thanks to John, Paul, George and Ringo – whatever else the gormless politicos do to diminish our heritage, Strawberry Fields will *always* be forever...

10. Granddad

Whenever I see an advertisement for Kellog's Cornflakes I am instantly transported back to my infancy and my earliest acquaintance with my grandfather, who looked after me when my mother was at work. He was a lean and saturnine figure with thinning and severely brushed back dark hair, who was irascible in a way that was truly democratic, because his irritability encompassed all within his reach. Everybody I knew feared his acerbic wit, his weapon of choice, which he readily wielded as he demonstrated his unwillingness to suffer fools, gladly or otherwise.

His relationship with me, however, was always characterised by a muted gruffness as he attempted to come to terms with the daily needs of a four-year-old boy. It would be fair to describe him as embittered by his experience of life, but now when I recall what little I know of his upbringing, I am amazed that he was not even more of a martinet.

Born in 1896 he was little more than a baby when his mother died. His father, who was a baker, placed my granddad in an orphanage. Small wonder that in his teens the army seemed welcoming to him and by the start of the First World War he was a private and on his way to France and the carnage of the western front. Wounded at Mons he was taken prisoner and spent four years in a German prison camp before being exchanged for German officers in April 1918. I have often wondered what the exchange rate was. I mean, what is a partially disabled Scouser worth vis-a-vis an officer *und* a gentleman?

During the thirties he worked as a labourer for the electricity board. Part of his job involved cutting the power supplies to people who had defaulted on their payments. My granddad was sacked when he was caught going back to the powerless householders and, under cover of darkness, re-connecting their supply. He won no medals for those exploits but I can't help feeling that there was a certain honour in his actions.

By the end of the second war his oldest son had become a veteran of the Murmansk convoys and my granddad had been diagnosed as having Tuberculosis. After that here was a definite shift in the balance of power, and not just in world politics. Until his death in 1955 my granddad was largely housebound, apart from his weekly foray to the Hillside pub, which was just up the brow from his home. Occasionally, as if by way of a change from my Sunday pilgrimages to various churches with my grandmother, he would take me to the pub, where I would sit outside on the low encircling wall, eating crisps and drinking lemonade.[1]

My granddad was an early riser and so was I. Sitting at the table, which was the focal point of the small council house living room, I would watch him kneeling in the hearth and setting about lighting the fire. Like a chef, he would assemble his ingredients before transforming them into a tried and tested recipe. With precise strokes he would take a hand axe and reduce a medium sized block of wood to slivers and put them to one side. He would then take the previous evening's 'Liverpool Echo' and, after delicately tearing the double pages into single sheets, methodically screw the pages into tight balls before laying them in the grate with the tenderness of a man packing rare bird's eggs into a crate, before covering them with a layer of kindling.

Finally, he would sift the ashes of the last fire through a garden sieve and carefully scatter the residual cinders on top of the pyre.

There then occurred that Promethean moment when he would weave a lighted match in and out of the newspaper crevices. The flame would lick at the paper eggs and my granddad would lean back on his heels and observe a moment's quiet satisfaction before leaning a shovel against the grate, onto which he would spread a double sheet of newspaper. The resulting draught would suck the newspaper hard

---

[1] Opposite the pub, nestling among the hazels, was C.F. Mott Teacher Training College, an innocuous-looking place which in the 70s would inspire the name of a visiting rock band, Mott the Hoople, who are best remembered for their hit song, 'All the Young Dudes'.

against the Zebra-blackened[2] grate surround and a lion-like roar would fill the air.

This was a critical time, as the paper could easily catch fire, and so my granddad was always a model of concentration as he scrutinised the paper for tell tale signs of scorching. By then the black newsprint was almost obliterated by the fierce orange glow that emanated from the small inferno behind it. Just when it seemed that the paper must succumb to the law of Fahrenheit 451, Granddad would snatch it to safety and take the shovel away to reveal a bed of glowing cinders, so hot it would have been possible to shape horseshoes in them. Then he would anoint the fire with a layer of fussily selected pieces of coal.

One day his collarless shirt slipped over his shoulder to reveal a four inch wound on his upper arm which was as blackened and twisted as the curling splinters of wood which had fallen, charred and brittle into the hearth. To this day I can still see that indelible reminder of man's madness.

As if by magic my uncles would appear and get ready for work. My grandmother, Rose Ann, had already left for her job, which was, ironically, in Adam's Bakery. After the men had left for work we would have our breakfast. Granddad would heat some milk and then pour it over a bowl of cornflakes. To this day I can't relate to cornflakes with cold milk and shudder when I see my wife enjoying them as a summer snack. Granddad never referred to them as cornflakes; to him they were simply 'Kellogs'.

Now you would think all that remained was to eat them, but you would be wrong... Granddad, as methodical as ever, insisted that I 'box' the cereal. By this he meant that I should stir the cornflake and milk mixture until it formed an orange-coloured mush. Then, with addition of a spoonful of sugar it was deemed fit to eat.

After that came the toast course, and that too was a ritual. In those days, before the advent of sliced bread, people took a pride in being able to slice a loaf evenly. Indeed, leaving a badly-cut loaf looking like

---

[2] Zebra is a polish applied to grates to keep them shiny black. It gets on one's chest something wicked.

an Alpine overhang was a breach of etiquette on a par with sticking discarded chewing gum under the tabletop.

Granddad was a bread sculptor, a veritable Donatello of the loaf, and his slices were always even and straight. When he had toasted the bread he would spend what seemed like an age spreading what was always refereed to as 'best butter' onto every millimetre of its scored and golden surface. Burnt toast wasn't only inedible it was wasteful of bread and fuel, both offences representing mortal sins in his eyes.

After breakfast Granddad would settle down to reading the *Daily Herald* while simultaneously teasing out a block of rolling tobacco, from its oblong and compressed shape, into a hillock of brown and twisted strands which always reminded me of the tuft of horse hair which obstinately refused to be re-inserted into the small tear on the seat of the chair I sat on.

Then, when he had devoured every inch of the large and incredibly black typeface of the newspaper, he would perform the most baffling task of the day. At least, it was baffling to me. Taking a mixture of ash and potato peelings he would smother the fire until it was just a dull red and emitting less warmth than a dole clerk. The 'fire' would remain in this parlous state until about four o'clock that day, when he would unfold the scorched piece of newspaper and fan the flicker to a flame with which greet my gran on her return.

He called it 'damping down the fire' and I suppose it is as good a metaphor as any to describe the vicissitudes of his life.

My granddad's methodical approach to almost every aspect of life even extended to advice on how I should eat a pomegranate. Handing me a needle, he would instruct me how to harpoon each individual crimson seed, exhorting me to be *extremely* careful to avoid any of the pith, as it was poisonous. It wasn't until I was an adult I realised that the 'toxic' nature of the pith was just a ruse, Granddad's way of ensuring that I would be occupied for at least an hour while I ate the precious seeds one by bloody one. Nice one Granddad!

It wasn't until long after he was dead that it occurred to me that as a survivor of both prison camp and the thirties' slump, my grandfather had learned that there was no point in rushing things. Each day was calibrated by tiny rituals which, added together, filled an otherwise empty existence, much like those housewives, who, imprisoned in their homes, used to cultivate repetitive and often useless tasks, such as carefully indenting the edges of a pie, as if the stomach had aesthetic sensibilities, simply to relieve the boredom of their unfulfilled lives.

11. Carry That Weight

Throughout the early fifties the 'Cold War' was chilling hearts throughout the world. In Liverpool we were having our own war with the cold. Fuel was at a premium, and people were like so many old men gathering winter fuel, without the benevolent gaze of King Wenceslas. Anything that could be burnt was burned. Rubber tyres, railway sleepers or coal dust mixed with something resembling cement, coyly described as 'Briquettes'; which burned a dull red, like a drunkard's nose but without the heat. One desperate family in our road sought to warm things up by burning all of their interior doors. When the doors had been finally consumed the house had a lot in common with an igloo; no doors and icicles everywhere.

In the nearby town of Prescot there was a gasworks, which sold coke (to burn, rather than sniff up one's nose, you understand). People used to arrive there with all manners of vehicles to carry away the precious fuel, which looked like cinders that had been dusted and then sprayed silver-grey. There were wheelbarrows, home made go-carts (or 'steeries'), handcarts, bikes, prams – all groaned under those bulging sacks. We – my Gran and I – had a pram; none of your modern buggy nonsense mind! If there was any resemblance between our pram and a McLaren, it was with the racing car, but heavier.

One day, as we slowly perambulated up the long hill from our house to the gasworks, we noticed two men in front of us, similarly engaged. They each had a grip on the handle and were struggling just to stop the pram from rolling back over them. I just thought that they must have had a big baby on board. Gran looked at me in bewilderment as a small black police car passed us at about three miles an hour, before settling in roughly twenty yards behind Sisyphus and his mate. Poor Nin, that's what we called Gran, was terrified; but then, almost any form of authority left her quaking. I don't know why, because she was so innocent she made the driven snow look shifty.

Ahead of us, the two toilers were still striving to reach the brow of the hill, which was about sixty yards off. The police car stayed tucked in behind them like a beetle stalking a pair of unsuspecting ants, until they reached the crest, whereupon they leapt out and arrested the poor bastards for stealing lead, which they'd hoped to sell in the scrap yard.

Nin was disgusted; not at the fatigued and signally failed felons, for she rarely had a bad word to say about anyone, but at the sadistic attitude of the police, who had let the men sweat blood when they could have stopped the backbreaking ascent much earlier.

I've sometimes wondered what her reaction would have been had she known that the lead came from the roof of her beloved church.

'Praise the Lord and pass the umbrella', no doubt.

12. Shelter from the Storm

My first school, St Dominic's Primary RC, known locally as 'The Doms', was built to cater for the children of those people who had fled the slums of old Liverpool for the new housing estates on the fringes of the city. In 1939 it was flanked by a fungi-like explosion of air raid shelters to protect the infants against that moment when the sirens shrilled a warning of the Nazi's advance. By 1950 the curved shelters, buried under soil, were overgrown with grass and at lunch-times scores of children would play at being cowboys and Indians amid a miniature replica of the black hills.

We infants had a permanent leader. By universal consent, he had the sole right to call himself Hopalong Cassidy or Chief Sitting Bull. He was of African descent, but that made no difference to the authenticity of his leadership. He treated everyone the same and we were all his willing minions. He was the only Anglo-African in the school and perhaps that's why we acquiesced to his rule, but I suspect it was mainly because he had an unflagging energy that refused to let a game die simply because the Indians were all shot or the cowboys stuck with arrows.

I met him at a bus stop thirty odd years later. He looked tired, like so many working men whose lives are such a burden that only sleep or alcohol offers relief. Time, and the forked tongue of the white man, had finally disarmed the great war-chief of the Ogallala Sioux.

I still shudder at the contrast between the grassy slopes of the shelters and their nauseating interiors. They stank of urine, excrement and other bodily secretions beyond our ken. Tins, cigarette packets, 'French letters' and even discarded sanitary towels littered the floors. One visit was enough for most of us, although there were some who found an allure in the detritus of desire. I have met people since who remind me very much of those shelters, wholesome on the outside, dank and putrefying within, a perfect metaphor for the Catholic vision of the soul.

The school was a different story. Its bosom of common brick contained some uncommon teachers. Miss Campbell was, is and always will be, my pet teacher. She was the only one I ever met who honoured the phrase *in loco parentis*. She taught us about God and the Seraphim, and in the process became my own personal guardian angel. One day my mother was unable to get home in time for my lunch and when Miss Campbell found out she got the canteen lady to find me a left over raspberry sponge cake and custard, which I ate at my desk while others drew pictures of the annunciation ... or was it the feeding of the five thousand?

Her ministrations didn't end there. When we finished school I quite often had to walk the two miles or so to my Gran's and wait there until my mother had finished work. Miss Campbell would sometimes accompany me and buy me a sweet potato from the bakers. No, it wasn't an acknowledgement of an ethnic presence, just a sugary imitation of a common or garden potato.

The last time I ever saw her was on the day I received news that I had passed the eleven-plus and was going to grammar school. I had just told my mother and was carrying my immediate reward, a huge bag of sweets, when I saw her further along the bus. When I told her she just smiled fondly and said, "I always knew you would do well John, ever since the time you argued that God had only lived in the olden days."

I was five at the time, and the memory caused us both to smile. I have wondered since whether or not my precocity was misplaced in a Catholic school. I knew that she had been genuinely amused by my remark, but teachers talk about their charges and perhaps one, more pious than her, had 'marked my card' so that subsequent teachers might have perceived me as rebellious.

Had my heavenly angel inadvertently laid the foundations for the hell I was to endure at De La Salle Grammar School? I hope not, but the doubt is now more real than the long-forgotten taste of that sweet potato.

I mean, who else but a heretic could have merited the ferocious beatings I received at the hands of the brothers? One of the most severe beatings was delivered by a brother Alban, for losing my lunch money. Not only was I thrashed, I went hungry too! Perhaps in their celestial setting all angels were women, but after Satan's Luftwaffe failed to win the battle for the commanding heights they became merely men with a grievance.

****

Pet Teacher

Why this, why that, why the other?
My darling boy I am not your mother
I am a lonely, tiring, ageing matron
not a mine of information.

Though if that is true, and I am free,
why should a stranger's child so worry me?
Yet you do, I must confess,
alarm my long sought happiness,
sounding danger to my citadel my peace,
like old Rome's sacred screeching geese.

I am sorry, I was thinking out aloud.
Button up tight, I see an ominous cloud.

****

13. School's Out

Until I attended, or rather non-attended, St John De La Salle Grammar School, I had never played truant in my life. Truth to tell, I had never really been in one school long enough to develop the loathing for learning that the religious brothers were to nurture in my hitherto willing soul. For one thing, I had never been physically punished at home, and only once in school, as on the occasion when I was despatched to Mr Walsh, the nature study teacher in St Dominic's, for being in possession of a matchbox containing six decapitated cabbage white butterflies. I was seven at the time, and as ecology itself was in its infancy some hard lessons were no doubt in order, so I received six strokes of a painfully thin cane.

De La Salle had its own perspective on the survival of the fittest. The phrase, 'red in tooth and claw' springs to mind... In 1957 anything and everything, it seemed, was punishable. Lateness, defined as a minute past nine o'clock, was punishable. The offenders, often as many as ten, sometimes twice that amount, were lined up with their hands out and palms up. One of the teachers would then move along the line, wielding a short leather strap, flailing away like a sadistic automaton.

For me, punishment was routine, as I had to connect with two buses every morning –and one was invariably late, or full. Thus the day begin as it usually ended, with me entering the class with red palms and leaving with similar. It wasn't altogether the fault of the teachers. As I discovered many years later, they were told by the head brother that every pupil came from a stable background and so any problem pupils were simply problems *per se*. That, of course, was simply untrue. My best mate was an orphan!

One teacher, Phillip Neary, while teaching the virtues of Latin, was inexplicably kind to me in a gruff sort of way. He later wrote to me from Canada, where he and his family had emigrated. I've never forgotten that he took the trouble to write to someone who was regarded by the rest of the staff as incorrigible. I discovered many years later that he worked for the United Nations. Nice to think that some of our human problems are in humane hands.

At the time of my induction into De La Salle, my mother was not only in the process of a protracted divorce, she was being treated in St. Paul's eye hospital. She would be there for months, after an electric light bulb had exploded just as she was passing under it, whereupon the shards had homed in on her pupil like heat-seeking missiles. Strange thing was, she thought for several days afterwards that she had a cold in her eye, because it kept watering. The milky white scar left by the beautifully-performed surgery can still be seen quite clearly, like a distant constellation in the night sky.

So, when I needed some assistance with the novel subjects of Algebra and Latin, I had to turn to my Nin, who was not exactly *au fait* with the finer points of this Arabian/Roman inspired torture. I was not surprised. After all, Nin was one of the many working class women who by cruel irony lived in streets named after famous Greeks, about whom they knew next to nothing.

When she told me stories of her upbringing in the Scotland Road area of Liverpool she would refer to the names of streets, like Great Homer's Street, or Iliad Street, while all the time being utterly blind to the origins of their namesake. No doubt the day will dawn when the children of John Lennon Drive will shrug in bewilderment when asked of the origins of their street name.

School, for me, was simply too daunting, so I took the easy way out, thus setting a pattern for much of my adult existence. Be it a ship, a girl or a job, whenever things got too rough it seemed that I could find neither the courage nor the sticking spot. Or perhaps I had missed out on the most conventional lesson of all, which exhorts us all to simply 'grin and bear it'. Who knows?

Instead of my experiencing the joy of education, derived from the Latin *educare* (to lead out – i.e. release that which already exists), I found myself hiding in the shadows of cafes, parks and the forests that in those days fringed Liverpool like the coral reef which once surrounded Bikini Atoll. I lost months, even years at the shrine to

Huckleberry Finn, the patron saint of truancy. One school report noted that out a possible ninety half days in a term I was absent for seventy. Other comments referred to my dishevelled appearance – the result of days in the hedgerows, no doubt.

Those years were quite simply and utterly wasted. If there was any glamour in truancy it passed me by. To me it was simply a routine, like school or work. Every day I would leave home with my dinner money. Every day I would spend it on five cigarettes and a copy of the *Hotspur, Wizard, Rover* or *Adventure*. Oddly enough, those comics were the only saving graces, since they eschewed pictures and instead narrated their tales through yards of densely-printed text. Thus, as I sat in the damp undergrowth of the forests, accompanied by the birds perching in the ubiquitous rhododendron, my reading at least was always up to scratch, and the adventures of 'Wilson the Wonder Runner' kept me in touch with some aspects of geography. (He always seemed to train in remote and savagely inhospitable terrain, clad in the only homespun body stocking I'd ever seen.)

For the rest, it was merely banality and the terror of discovery. My mother once bumped into me near Sefton Park. I blurted out some lie that the headmaster, Brother Oswald, had passed away and we'd been given a day's holiday. She simply rang the school and unearthed my silly lie. She didn't remonstrate. She only had one good eye, but she could see which way the land lay.

A year later I found myself in St. Bernard's Secondary Modern. No shrine to Academia, like De La Salle, but by the same token no sanctuary for devotees of the Marquis De Sade.

Dark Angel

They said she would watch over me
And protect me from all harm,
So I wore my guardian angel
As if she were a charm

In a dark and anxious hour
I offered up my prayer,
But as dawn distilled the silence
I knew she could not hear

I walked alone that morning, and,
For the first time in my life,
Sharp terror scored my screaming soul
Like an avenging angel's knife

14. Summer in the City

I was in town recently, having taken my family on our first car trip to the big city. My fear of making a fool of myself by parking badly was running high, and so I had opted to seek the sanctuary of a pay-and-display car park called Blakes, facing the Royal Liverpool Teaching Hospital. (Incidentally, while there it was deeply scarred after a surgical strike by a swine that must have been hunting specifically for a car that was parked in so much empty space that it could have been named the Rover-Mir.)

As a result of my parking phobia we had to walk down London Road and cross over to the fountains at the foot of Wellington's monument, where I beheld a sight I had not witnessed for almost half a century. The fountain was not only operating, but dancing in and out of its fragile-looking cascade was a gaggle of boys and girls, the oldest of whom was about seven while the youngest was a tiny tot, who, in full view of Napoleon's nemesis, was completely *au naturel*.

I turned to my wife and told her how I had done exactly the same thing when I was a child, fully clothed of course, and in possession of a summer concessionary tram ticket which was priced at one penny for all day rides. It was thanks to that pecuniary freedom that I, and thousands like me, had been licensed to roam the city in search of diversion.

The response from my family was one of complete and utter astonishment mixed with revulsion and my boys chorused almost in unison, "But Dad, the water must be full of pee and vomit from all those drunks looking for somewhere to go!"

I was dumbfounded as such possibilities had never occurred to me. I was about to deride their observation when I noticed the abundance of pubs in nearby London Road and had to admit to a feeling of queasiness, as I remembered dunking my head beneath the fountain's waters. My sense of unease was suddenly compounded by the sight of the toddler insouciantly performing a fair impression of Le

Manikin Pis, wholly oblivious of the giggles of his fellow fountain-eers.

Water, in the shape of swimming pools at the Harold Davies Baths in Dovecote, was, apart from my sojourns with aunt Alice, the mainstay my childhood summers. The entrance to the pools consisted of foot baths so as to remove the traces of summer dust and any stray pollen from the feet of the bathers, but there must have been another, secret, entrance used by the smaller children because I can still see and smell the water in the infant pool, which was so murky that had it been distilled would have made a reasonable ink substitute.

It was there I learned to swim, after a fashion. My technique was so poor that when my schoolteacher took us – to complete a length of the main pool in order to be awarded a certificate – I was allowed to abandon my attempt after three quarters of the distance, on the premise that I would return in my own time and complete the task.

I did return but once again I was completely knackered by the same point. However, I claimed the certificate nonetheless. *Mea culpa, mea culpa, mea maxima culpa* (or should that be 'gulpa'). As a smoker I still end up wheezing after swimming a length of the pool, but I do at least make it, gasping, to the end. My children, who could swim Marathons if called upon, are utterly contemptuous of my aquatic shortcomings.

Yet I did enjoy my time as a summer swimmer. I don't think I ever went once in the winter, when the pool appeared to be the preserve of people training to be Arctic seals. I used especially to enjoy the après-swim of hot Bovril, and Jammy Dodgers, a biscuit that provides one of the few childhood links between my children and me.

My one major achievement in the sphere of the amphibians was when, at the age of fourteen, I decided, heaven knows why, to attempt a one and a half somersault dive from the high board. My first attempt was perfect as, after tucking myself into a somersaulting ball, I straightened up and cleaved the water with barely a splash.

Thereupon an older youth encouraged me to do it again and I did, but something went awry and I hit the surface full on my chest. It hurt horribly, and I was about to limp away when the man insisted that I must try again or else I would never do it. The result was the same, a torso that looked as if it was in dire need of basting. If *Weissmuller* means 'White miller' then I was definitely Johnny Rotmuller, the ruddy Tarzan of the urban jungle!

A less hazardous pastime was collecting pictures of footballers that came inside packets of bubble gum. They seemed like a bargain at the time, as the pink strip of gum was the same size as the photograph of the brilliantined heroes of the beautiful game. The only drawback as far as I was concerned was that while there must have been thousands of footballers in Britain, I invariably ended up staring at the police type mug shots of Ivor Allchurch, who was apparently some kind of Welsh Wizard; Alf Ramsay, later the most successful manager the English national side has ever had, but who possessed what was, even to a child of the fifties, the most ridiculous hair parting I've ever seen, which went straight down the middle as if he'd been attacked by Lizzie Borden; or the Birmingham goalkeeper, Gill Merrick who looked oddly dashing with his Gablesque moustache.

Those dextrous skills necessary for unwrapping my candied disappointments came in useful during those long summer evenings when television was still in its own childhood.

As the swallows soared high above us in their interminable quest for insects, those amongst us with access to books would tear pages from dilapidated volumes to make paper aeroplanes. I possessed quite a knack for making them and enjoyed countless hours perfecting them so as to make them glide in widening circles before they settled on the patch of grass we called 'the square' and which at other times was our cricket pitch. Children's television, and the joys of *Blue Peter* were still only blips on the radar and so we had never heard of 'Origami'. On Merseyside we were simply getting on with it. It was a form of exercise too, as we jumped and stamped on the noses of the planes in order to flatten the many complicated folds in the paper, which would otherwise have had a deleterious effect on the aerodynamics.

As an adult who has been repulsed by the images of book-burning in Nazi Germany, and similar scenes in the anti-Beatle Bible-Belt of North America, I have some slight regrets over my vandalism of those tomes. My only excuse was that it could be said that it was done in the furtherance of our scientific understanding of aeronautics, or even to enhance our manual dexterity. The truth, I suppose, is that on those long hot summer nights, while seeking entertainment that didn't cost anything, those books provided us with a type of textual healing.

15. Three Times a Lady

My aunt Alice never had much money but it never seemed to bother her the way it bothers most people, including me. Now I don't want to give the impression that Alice had anticipated hippie-ism and abandoned materialism, it was just that she had an irrepressible sense of humour and spent most of her life laughing at the slings and arrows of outrageous fortune until they were rendered impotent. She laughed at all the missiles fate launched her way, and believe me, Dame Fortune deployed some of her most spiteful weaponry against Alice. I imagine there was a degree of jealousy, because Alice was so vivacious and attractive. I've never met Lady Luck, but I wouldn't mind betting she has a wart on her nose and a five o'clock shadow.

However, beneath Alice's apparent gaiety she nursed a deep sorrow, and I mean literally nursed. Just after Guy Fawkes' night in 1953 Alice gave birth to my cousin Stanley; he was profoundly disabled and for the next fifteen years Alice and Stanley's father, Stanley senior, raised him at home.

Her love for baby Stanley was overwhelming and she fiercely resisted the attempts of well-meaning doctors who pleaded with her to allow her then two year old baby to be hospitalised in Alder Hey Children's Hospital. She responded to their pleadings by asserting vehemently, "They are not getting him in there to let him die!"

Given the current scandal surrounding the hospital perhaps she knew something nobody else did.

Such was her innate optimism that she bore three more boys, Antony, Mark and John but when Stanley died Alice was devastated. She once said to me, as her forever baby sat on the floor, lost in the creations of his innocent mind, "He can hear the grass grow, you know." She noted this with such pride that I knew she believed it, and, equally, that she was right.

Alice's personal heartache never intruded into my relationship with her. She was always my madcap aunt who saw the passage of time as something to be punctuated with fun and games. I remember one occasion when she hung bunches of gooseberries from the wooden trellis that served for a porch at the rear of the house so that the trellis looked as if it was supporting a grape vine. The mock vine had a purpose because the insurance agent, 'the clubman', as he was usually called, was due. Informed by Alice of her intention to see if the poor man noticed the grapes, Tommy and I eagerly looked forward to his arrival.

When he arrived he probably never noticed two small boys staring at him intently as attempted to write his entries. Come to think of it he probably never noticed Alice either, as his gaze was fixed on the gooseberries and their leaves, which festooned the trellis. I have often wondered what he thought about it. Perhaps he thought Alice was a pioneer of sun-dried produce.

The most vivid example of her mischievous nature concerned a shopping visit made by my cousin, Tommy and me. The nearest shop was a decent walk down Sandy Lane, up Hedgefield Road and then along Wambo Lane to the sandstone farm buildings that incorporated a grocery store. Alice, fully occupied with Stanley, persuaded me and Tommy to go to the shop for supplies, promising us that on our return she would take us on a picnic.

Tommy and myself went to the shop, after making a detour to see if there were any frogs in the pond, chattering gaily about the impending picnic. When we got home Alice led us into the orchard where our lunch was spread on the grass!

We fell for it every time. When The Who sang 'Won't get fooled again!' They must have had Alice in mind.

Alice's fostering of me didn't end when I attained maturity. Once, when depressed after the break up of a love affair, I had thrown myself into the task of decorating the living room of my *pied a terre*, a small red brick terraced house in Low Hill. I was determined to paint that gal right outta my hair. Unbeknown to me I was to have an assistant. Saying that she was 'just passing', Alice bustled through the front door with a bag of groceries and then insisted on wielding a six-inch painting brush, which I had 'won' from my Uncle John and have since denied all knowledge of in spite of his repeated enquiries that stretched over many years.

Yes, Alice cut a fine dash with that 'Wally' brush, which was what we call such brushes as they were usually deployed for use with Walpamur emulsion. Just passing indeed! After receiving a telephone call Alice had responded to my mother's concern for me in the only way she knew how, by feeding me and being there.

Thanks love.

16. Sweet Talkin' Gal

Until 1954 sugar in Britain was rationed and could only be purchased if accompanied with a coupon. Sweet confections in Liverpool, therefore, were at a premium. There were few cakes, few sweets and, as a direct consequence, fewer tooth cavities. The latter circumstance didn't really bother me as, like so many children of the 40s, I thought oral hygiene meant not swearing. I wasn't too badly off for sweets as my seafaring father used to bring home tins of Welch's fruit drops and Uncle Joe's mint balls. For those without a direct supply, window gazing at jars of variously coloured sweets was the tragic alternative to the heavenly delight of sucking tangy sherbet lemons or sharp edged pineapple chunks until the roof of one's mouth was sore and sometimes lacerated.

My Gran used to tell me tales of when she was a child and often stood in front of Ligget's Rock shop in West Derby Road and made imaginary purchases, consisting of four farthing bags of assorted candy, which transaction accounted for her imagined penny.

The nearest I can relate to that was when I was once in possession of three pence, a gift from my Uncle John, but was unable to buy any of the tempting goodies as I had no ration coupons. To this day I can still recall my bewilderment.

In those dark and bitter days birthday parties were something to get excited about, especially when they were hosted by Auntie Alice. It must have been about 1952 and the occasion was the birthday of Alice's son Tommy, an event that is indelibly printed in my mind.

Alice's invitation was answered by all of my cousins, and the large living room of the farmhouse was fairly crammed with expectant youngsters. After we had eaten the sandwiches, jelly and cakes the games began. Alice produced a tin and began to lay sweets out on the mantelpiece. All eyes were focussed on the long necklace of blue tinted cellophane wrappers that contained the unmistakable dull sheen of treacle toffee. I was puzzled, though, as to exactly why she had decided to place the toffees on display rather than simply hand them round. Alice quickly provided the solution.

Holding aloft a sweet so that it glinted like an overlarge Sapphire she said, "The first one to speak won't get a treacle toffee."

There was a collective gasp of horror but no words were uttered. The only sound in the room was the ticking of an old alarm clock and the crackle of logs on the fire, which was necessary even in June as the old house was stone flagged and could have been used as a training camp for the Russian Special Forces.

Eventually, about six logs on from Alice's edict, one of my cousins cracked. I think it was Tommy Kelly, who could have talked the legs, head and tail off the proverbial donkey. Tommy's dismay was soon matched by that of his cousin Keith. His older sister, Sheila, glanced at me and her look of steely determination made me quail. However, after another four logs had been consumed to white ash neither of us had broken the silence and Alice had grown bored with the game.

Of a sudden she declared Sheila and myself joint winners. There was no applause as we victors stood up to receive our bounty. Ungracious winners that we were, we slowly and teasingly unwrapped the crackling reward and, in slow motion, slipped the contents into our mouths.

I will never forget Alice's squeal of delight as the realisation crossed our faces that the toffees were in fact lumps of coal! Moreover, even we two victims of her wicked humour were forced to echo her madly infectious laughter. I still like to believe that she was only preserving our milk teeth from the ravages of sugar.

Oh Alice!

17. Too Much Monkey Business

Liverpool had survived the blitz but then, ironically, had fallen to the planners and Lego-trained architects. By the end of the swinging sixties the old market, the heart of the old Liverpool, had been razed, and in its place a concrete monstrosity of quite hideous aspect had been thrown up, and I mean literally thrown up.

The facade of the old market was a beautiful crescent-shaped Georgian terrace, which housed offices and bars in its warren-like interior. Behind, nestling inside the sickle-shaped enclave, lay the market, which to me was as exotic as any eastern bazaar. Inside its vaulted passageways there were butchers, bakers and though I never saw them there were no doubt candlestick-makers too. But the shop I will always remember was the pet shop. I didn't have a pet, but like every other child I was drawn to the window, where there were always animals on show. Puppies, rabbits and guinea pigs held us spellbound.

One day I went to look in the window and saw a youngish and terribly appealing chimpanzee. It was staring at us and chattering, the way they do, and then it turned away to pick up some fruit. As it turned its back on its admiring audience it revealed a large expanse of its red and naked buttocks. I took one look at its raw, bald and swollen rear, and promptly vomited. Perhaps that's why they replaced the cobblestones with tiles.

Years later I would again be sick on the very same spot, however the cause of my nausea would not be a primate's bum, but an over indulgence in what was known locally as 'jungle juice' (Yates's white wine topped up with lemonade), a drink so potent that I used to get a blinding headache just ordering it.

Yates's Wine Bar in Charlotte Street was situated on the periphery of the market, but my favourite pubs were in the market proper. My mates and I would have a drink in as many pubs as our stomachs or wallets could stand before setting out for the Temple club, just off Dale Street. The crawl went something like this: the Duckhouse, which was a spit-and-sawdust pub with a great juke-box, then every bar in Casey Street and onto the gay pubs, the Old Dive, the Dart and the Magic Clock. We thought we were really daring drinking in those notorious haunts of gays, though in truth they weren't called anything quite so civil then.

The head barman in the Old Dive was a famous queen called Sadie. His real name was Tony and his fame stemmed not solely from his sexual preference but from the fact that he had once severely thrashed a man who had thought a gay barman would be a pushover in a fight. Sadie served time in Walton gaol for his contribution to that episode of community learning. For the most part he was a tolerant man, whose genuine wit and biting repartee made him popular with most men, regardless of their general prejudices. He could make the most jaundiced person laugh and our Friday nights were enlivened by this stand-up guy in the spotlight, who was out front when so many of his peers were hiding backstage.

Talking about stages, I remember when I made my first Holy Communion and my Nin took me to the market. I was still kitted out in my white shirt and shorts, wearing my holy medal of some sort and as we passed a toy stall the proprietor stopped me and handed me a model cowboy mounted on a horse. I was thrilled and thought seriously about taking my first communion every week thereafter!

The market that replaced the old one hardly has a store that boasts an individual owner. Most shops belong to a nationwide chain. In any case, I doubt if a child would go anywhere without his designer outfit, so unless they embroider a Lacoste logo onto plain white shirts nobody in that market will ever again see the participants of one of the most innocent rites of passage.

Now the upstart market, which had usurped an institution that had been there for over a century, is rumoured to be earmarked for replacement, after 35 years.

Someone is making a monkey out of us all!

18. If I had a Hammer

I am, much to my family's dismay, an inveterate do-it-yourself enthusiast. It's not that my constructions don't work, or collapse at the sight of a book, CD or cup. It's just that while I am big on function, I am a little lacking in aesthetics. For example, my homemade computer workstation was solid but somewhat plain. Well, truthfully speaking, it was downright ugly. You see I found nothing untoward in having a cup hook screwed into a shelf to support a modem cable; after all, it was porcelain coated, not one of those common brassy looking types... My wife, however, could hardly bear to look at it, which was unfortunate as it resolutely occupied a fair sized portion of the living room. Replacing it involved a trip to Ikea, where I reluctantly purchased a soul-less but well-made Swedish equivalent.

I remember the first time I ever saw a shop that sold tools and wood. It was in Lodge Lane and it bore as much resemblance to modern DIY centres as cave dwellings do to a Californian condominium.

The interior of the shop was dark and unbearably foul smelling. The latter circumstance was due to the fact that the poor proprietor was forced to wear a colostomy bag and even the pungency of creosote and paraffin signally failed to mask its pervasive odour.

He was a nice old man whose quiet air of defeat did not prevent him being ready to discuss the merits of pine over oak with a fourteen year old whose only prior attempts at carpentry had resulted in a raffia strung footstool which my Gran claimed for herself, more out of encouragement for me than any real desire to rest her size fours.

It was with the advice of the proprietor that I tried to build a clothes' horse for my mother, who had become immersed in the laundering of my baby brother's essentials. Needless to say, my attempt was a dismal failure, because my clothes' horse was hobbled by design faults and when one of its legs buckled under the weight of drying nappies it had to be put down.

My urge to mimic the achievements of Sheridan and his ilk subsided until I moved into an old house, which, according to the estate agents specification was 'in need of modernization'.

I'll say it was! It was 1967 and my house still had a huge concrete and brick air raid shelter hideously attached to the rear wall, where it remained until 1972, when the council decided to pay for the removal of all such monstrosities. Until then I had used the shelter to house a workbench and my collection of antique and largely rusting implements. The only modern tool I possessed was a Black and Decker power drill that I had obtained courtesy of Players Number Six cigarette vouchers. It was barely out of the prototype stage and used to terrify me as the ventilation slots in its thin shell revealed blue sparks furiously whizzing about the motor. Every time I used it I would sweat profusely even before I'd started drilling, as I was treated to my own personal sighting of the Leonid meteorite shower.

With the shelter gone I had to move my bodging kit to a cupboard on the hall landing, where I was forced, due to lack of space, to pack my tools into an old suitcase. This had unfortunate ramifications, because whenever I tried to extract a tool from the tangled heap of metal I would invariably end up with a cut. It was as if the spurned tools were resentful at being ignored and so, with malice aforethought, would either snag, scratch or stab my jilting hand. One of the first jobs I had to do was to make a first aid cabinet.

The years passed and my skills improved, as did my collection of tools, which had grown to such an extent that I had to store the newcomers in a tomato crate.

In 1979 my wife had joined me in my terraced shoebox and I had to commence a serious campaign of house improvement. One day I was sitting at the dinner table sharing a drink with my mate John Mcintyre when I decided to replace the ugly fifties-style tiled fireplace with a Victorian cast iron job that my next-door neighbour had just thrown out, thereby missing out on the rewards of the antique fireplace boom that was just on the horizon.

Taking a Cammell Lairds' issue two pound hammer[3] I smashed away the plaster surrounding the tiled carbuncle. As the dust and dislodged soot began to settle, my bemused drinking partner became more and more unsettled and before long he made his excuses and left. I continued my architectural heritage campaign with a vengeance and by the time my spouse came home from teaching her sometime hooligans she found her personal Vandal had created a voluminous blackened cavern where there had once stood a shining edifice.

In retrospect, her calm response to my impulsive orgy of destruction was typical of her stabilising influence on my life.

Ironically, the cast iron grate that I so abruptly installed became a selling point when eventually I sold the house, but that's another tale.

One day, shortly after my son was born, in 1986, I decided that it was imperative to repair a faulty electrical point lest we inadvertently end up with a barbecued baby. My wife took the baby for a walk so as not disturb Isembard Kingdom Brunel at his labours.

When I took the faulty cover off the electrical point I discovered that I had to re-drill a hole to take a firmer Rawlplug. This presented a logistical problem in that I needed the electricity on to power the drill. Typically impulsive, I decided that it would be safe to use the drill, as the hole didn't appear to be close to any wires. As I drilled into the brickwork a blue spark leapt between the exposed wires and my drill. The Black and Decker flew from my startled grasp, or perhaps I hurled it away, and I sat on my haunches shaking violently.

Until that day I had always thought that the cinematic images of electrocuted comics such as Buster Keaton were just hoary stereotypes, but when I stood up and caught sight of myself in the mirror I was forcibly reminded that they were, in fact, true reflections of victims of non-lethal electrocution. My hair looked as if it had been freeze-dried and then attacked with a wire brush, while my eyes stared back at me with that wild, uncomprehending look which characterized Steve McQueen's shell-shocked expression in the movie *Papillion* when he was punished with solitary confinement.

---

[3] Also known as a 'Yankee Screwdriver'.

Just then the mother of my child rang the doorbell and in my mind's eye I can still see the sooty streaks on the back of my trembling hand as I opened the door. Her horrified expression also remains with me to this day, quite literally scorched into my memory.

When I explained what had happened she suggested, with impeccable logic, that I buy a cordless drill. I still have it, but it has been superseded by a state-of-the-art all-singing-all-dancing multi functional drill/screwdriver, which allegedly doubles as a cable detector cum egg timer.

P.S. My boys nicknamed me 'Daddy fix' which isn't a bad testimony to my bodging skills. You try replacing the arm on a Teenage Mutant Hero Turtle and make it watertight!

19. On the Good Ship Lollipop

At the age of sixteen I joined the Merchant Navy. Like most teenagers I desperately wanted to be regarded as manly, so going with the prevailing wind I opted to be a deckboy as opposed to a steward. The latter were regarded, by those in the know, as effete and subservient.

Before long I found myself at the Merchant Navy training school at Sharpness in Gloucester. We were billeted in brick-built barracks but our 'training' took place on the SS *Vindicatrix*, an old German merchant ship captured in 1918. Looking back at it now I don't imagine it put up much of a struggle. It was permanently moored in a canal next to the river Severn, and we never saw so much as a rowing boat in the ten weeks we were there. The wily stewards only had to endure this slackest of backwaters for six weeks. It was then that I began to question the wisdom of deciding to become a sailor rather than a despised 'piss pot shaker', as the stewards were scathingly referred to by us rough, tough, creampuffs in our manly blue pullovers.

When I arrived at the camp I was immediately picked for the boxing team. My inclusion had nothing to do with any prowess on my part but more to do with the fact that I was born in Liverpool. Its reputation for producing hard cases had preceded me. More to the point, the date of my arrival meant that I would get in a solid eight weeks training, enabling me to take part in the annual boxing competition between Sharpness and the other training school in Gravesend.

One of our budding boxers was a big lad called Billy, who used to enthuse about a beat group he regularly saw performing at the Walton Co-op – Gerry and the Pace Makers. Billy fervently maintained that they would be the biggest band in England before long. It now strikes me as ironic that The Beatles were at that very moment playing in Hamburg, from where the *Vindicatrix* probably sailed many times in her chequered career.

Eight tedious weeks later, during which time I had discovered I possessed something of a knockout punch, we piled aboard a canvas topped lorry and rolled eastward to Gravesend. After the mind numbing boredom of Sharpness, where the only relief was to be found at the Seaman's mission, which had a juke box and a smattering of local girls, who had apparently formed the world's first mutual chaperone society, the Thames-based training camp was a revelation. For one thing, the lads were allowed to go out at will. For another there were girls hanging about all over the place. I had a clear idea of how biblical yokels might have felt on their first visit to Sodom and Gomorrah. Oo-arr! Oo-arr!

Eventually my bout was on and I was matched against a Scots boy called Jimmy Rhinds, who hailed from Corby. He was about eight inches taller than me and wiry, like a muscular hairpin. When we entered the ring I was just a little apprehensive. Scared stiff, actually. The bell rang and in a panic I bounded into the centre of the ring and literally ran onto a left jab that reduced my brain to mist. The next thing I can consciously remember was the referee pulling me away from the prone figure of Jimmy who was lying still on the canvas.

The contest had lasted 19 seconds, including the count. In my fog-bound panic I had hurled punches like a manic parent throwing confetti at the wedding of a lumpish child. Later Jimmy came and shook hands, with his right hand, as his left wrist was fractured and in a sling. He was a nice lad, but had, I suspect, about as much place in the ring as me. When we got back to camp I placed my trophy in my locker. It was the last time I ever saw it.

My first ship was the *Cape York*, a tramp belonging to Lyles of Glasgow. Now the sea is its own unique world and my baptism into it was a disaster. The reasons for this were twofold. Firstly, the crew managed to breach the cargo – whisky and export Guinness – and so drunkenness on a Bacchanalian scale was the norm; and secondly, one of the crew fancied himself as a hard man and picked fights with everyone in the seaman's mess, except for me, as I was below even his sadistic horizon. Between the hangovers and the one-sided fights, the atmosphere on board that ship was stygian in its gloom, all brought about by a cretin who fancied himself a pugilist, but was, in essence, a sociopath. Even I managed to get drunk and challenge someone to a fight, only to shamefacedly withdraw my offer in the cold light of day. One of these hard drinking hard men was killed during a brawl in Australia.

It was this immersion into the font of life at sea that ensured I would only make three or four more voyages before becoming a landlubber forever. My penultimate voyage was on the cruise ship *Empress of England*, and it was aboard that floating hotel that I finally realised the foolishness of my initial decision to be a sailor rather than a steward. You see, the stewards had access to the best food, they were always dry and they pulled female passengers with the same ease that Sebastian Cabot's sailors had pulled in cod off the Newfoundland coast. My choice of roles could be described as having gone for *Macho* over *Mucho*.

You see the problem for 20th century sailors is that they are largely redundant. This phenomenon is summed up in the aphorism, 'There used to be wooden ships and iron men, now there are iron ships and wooden men'.

The ship steered itself with what was called an 'Iron Mike', there were no sails to make, mend or hoist and so the only thing we had to do was act as maritime charladies. We cleaned and washed the gleaming white superstructures and kept the wooden decks spotless by dint of scrubbing them with lumps of sandstone on the end of a stick, which was misnamed a holystone. I curse it still!

The worst and most frequent task was 'sujeeing'. This consisted of washing down the paintwork with handfuls of cotton waste soaked by soapy water that we lugged around in buckets. Now it was a shit job at the best of times, but in the North Atlantic winter it was hell on water. We used to have to wear old disposable rags that would both keep us warm and financially solvent.

Thus it was that one freezing cold day in the Belle Isle Straits I found myself wearing an ancient overcoat, tied around the middle with hairy string, clutching a bucket of water in one hand and a lump of icy cotton waste in the other, all the while staring into a porthole that revealed the 'effete' stewards gliding round the dining room where the eyes of admiring females followed their every movement.

Those so-called 'piss pot shakers' were having a ball as they sashayed about, unencumbered by anything heavier than a snazzy-looking waistcoat, while I stood shivering in my hairy overcoat like the runt of Bigfoot's litter!

20. Sailor Stop Your Roaming

Ships are like houses, some are cold and uninviting, while others make you feel entirely at home. When I joined the MV *Cape Grafton*, my second ship, I had expected it to be like her sister ship, that ocean going gladiatorial arena known as the *Cape York* that had been my first taste of life at sea. However, the *Grafton* turned out to be a home from home. My change of ships in mid-stream came about because of a mystery illness that swept through the crew of my first vessel, the *Cape York*, like wildfire while we were en route from Australia to Japan. I was the last to contract the sickness, which caused symptoms of a mild fever, and when we reached Osaka the captain insisted that I should see a doctor in the hope of identifying what it was that had laid low so many of us.

However, before that we had time to go ashore and enjoy the delights of Osaka. I went ashore with two of the nicer members of the York's crew. One was a Londoner from Enfield and the other a farmer's lad from Suffolk. A taxi, so highly polished that its gleaming dashboard bore reflections of the white anti-macassars carefully draped over the seats, took us to a place known as 'the Fuji bar'. I remember the name because I still have a souvenir of the place. It is a dog-eared card, depicting two toddlers, a boy and a girl, inspecting their private parts and bearing the legend, 'There is a difference!'

As bars go it certainly was different from the pubs in Liverpool. It was fairly heaving with some of the loveliest women I'd ever seen, and apparently they were all available, at a price. I was the youngest in the party and, after several large bottles of Asahi lager, the older men began to gently tease me by telling the women that I was a 'cherry boy' – a virgin. I wasn't, as it turned out, and said so, forcibly. My denial only served to spur my shipmates to make more accusations, and before long every girl in the place believed that I was a 'cherry boy'.

In my embarrassment I was unaware that among the bargirls a virgin youth held a certain cache, which was the reasoning behind the men's merciless teasing. They knew I was broke, because when we were at anchor I had spent a month's pay buying the mandatory porcelain tea service and kimono suits from the 'bum-boats', and so they were actually banking on a young lady 'taking care of me' for the night, *gratis*. Their ruse worked, because a stunning young lady called Michiko took me back to her tiny apartment and did indeed take care of me. To this day I cannot forget her demure loveliness or her half-hearted complaint that she had been conned.

The next day, after a medical examination, I was taken to Moymoyama isolation hospital, apparently suffering from diphtheria. The hospital was in a terrible state of disrepair, as in 1962 the Japanese economy was not so much a tiger as a newborn kitten and money was tight, I suppose. The people, however, were wonderful. They were generous to a fault, often sharing their food with me, and all this took place in absolute silence as neither party spoke the other's language.

I had been there for about a week when I began to notice a young lady who was unusual in that she was not only exquisitely beautiful but also very tall for a Japanese woman. I would bump into her on the stairs or at the entrance to the bathhouse. One day she glided into my room and placed a plate on my bed. On the plate lay a fried egg melded together with a slice of Spam. Apparently it passed for some kind of hamburger. I ate it with slow difficulty disguised as relish and the lady beamed with pleasure. Perhaps I had misunderstood something and the egg had been a symbol of fertility, because later that night she came back and stayed for quite some time. She was discharged the next day and I never saw her again, although I thought I saw her often when those first images of the extraordinary and beautiful Vietnamese 'dragon ladies' began to filter through the smokescreen of the war.

The following day a nurse came in to my room and asked me if I would talk to her husband who was keen to learn English. I wondered how that could be done with me in hospital, but it transpired that he was a patient too. His name was Ryuichi Ogino and he was a traffic policeman. He and his wife more-or-less adopted me. I don't even begin to understand why, but the ordinary Japanese people treated me with a kindness I never experienced again until I visited Israel and enjoyed the generosity of poor Moroccan and Yemeni Jews.

Ryuchi was keen on guns and motorbikes, and insisted that the Germans made the best of both. At the time I thought he was relating to the other defeated member of the Axis powers, but now I realise he was just being discerning in his choice of manufacturers.

One night he asked me if I wanted to go for a drink in the town. Puzzled, I agreed, and that night, under cover of darkness, we slipped out of a basement window and went to a bar in sight of the great medieval castle. It was more of a shop than a bar, but it was exciting in its own way because of the novelty of things. We went out every night for almost the rest of my stay, and it wasn't until my last night in hospital that his wife let slip that our escape route was through the mortuary! Talk about getting dead drunk!

My freedom, which was how I viewed my sojourn in Moymoyama, ended abruptly when my captain argued, logically, that if I really had contracted diphtheria, then most of his crew should have been dead. So, after three weeks of bliss, I was to join the ship of fools again at a place called Tamano, which had dry dock facilities.

The night I got back to the *Cape York* we all went for a drink, as the ship was due to sail the next day. We had only been in the bar for ten minutes when our resident psycho kicked off and challenged a sailor from another ship to a fight. Now, whether the psycho's perception had been distorted by booze, I don't know, but when the object of his challenge unwound from behind his table it was obvious that the Black-Country bully had made a dreadful miscalculation.

Within a minute, the *York*'s champion lay on his back. Then the giant of a man who had put him there compounded the boot boy's humiliation by refusing to give him the hiding he deserved, but instead, pinned him to the floor while delivering the only lecture on social etiquette I ever heard given from the kneeling position.

It was then I decided to cut myself adrift from the *York*, or more correctly, desert. I didn't want another nine months of that loser's company, because he was the type that never learned. As it happened, I bumped into him in Gibraltar two years later. He was sporting a black eye and, judging by his whining about how unlucky he had been, his beatings were by then becoming routine. Perhaps I misjudged him by thinking he wanted to beat up people; maybe he was really looking for someone to beat *him* up.

I digress. By seven o'clock the next morning I was climbing a hill overlooking the harbour, clutching a brown paper bag containing two hundred cigarettes and a blue sea-jersey. As I reached the top of the hill I heard the trumpeting of the tugs as they towed the *Cape York* toward the Inland Sea and my heart hit top C. Just then I walked headfirst into spider's web that hung from the wooden shrine at the hilltop and only by ducking at the last second did I avoid the bright yellow and black spider at its centre. I had almost left one snare for another.

At the foot of the hill I came across an old woman forlornly chasing a large pig round a tree. Now I'm not brave where animals are concerned, even a yapping Chihuahua can trigger my castration complex, but I couldn't leave her and so I stood in the pig's path as it charged around the tree. Miraculously the porker stopped long enough for the woman to grab it and guide it into a pen. She then gestured to me to follow her into her house. Once inside we sat in silence while she poured what appeared to be a large green salad into a bowl. It was tea, but to me it just tasted like musty hot water.

In the west we talk about laughter lines, but the old woman's face was deeply grained with what I can only describe as struggle or hardship lines. I had seen many faces like that in my own town of Liverpool. After drinking half of the bowl I stood up to go. She bowed her head and I attempted likewise but only succeeded in looking like a five-year old performing a wobbly genuflection. I headed for the main road and the chance of a lift to Osaka, where I would get in touch with Ryuichi Oginosan and his good lady.

First, though, I had to get a lift. My incredible run of luck in Japan continued. I was miles from Osaka and the trucks and vans passing by could have been going anywhere, yet the first person to stop for me simply nodded his head when I uttered the word 'Osaka'.

All day long we travelled in the pick-up that was carrying Oxy-acetylene equipment and again I experienced the kindness of the ordinary Japanese people as the driver bought me over-sweet rice cakes that were dyed purple and which I ate with difficulty. When we reached Osaka the driver, who was certainly not wealthy by any stretch of the imagination, gave me two hundred yen so that I could get a bus to the central post office.

Before I reached Japan I had been imbued with the idea that the Japanese were a cruel and ruthless people. After my experiences of their extreme generosity, extreme courteousness and extreme hospitality I can only conclude that whatever enterprise they are engaged in, an absolute commitment prevails. They can be extremely kind in peace and extremely wicked in war. To them, the idea of a convention that says war, the ultimate barbarism, must have gentlemanly rules of engagement, must appear absurd and half-hearted.

Within thirty minutes of my telephoning Ryuichi Ogino he had met me at the post office and taken me back to his one-roomed flat where his wife prepared a meal of meat and a kind of soup which contained cabbage and bonito flakes (dried fish shavings). I can never forget that meal, because it was so delicious and because it was also my first proper meal in freedom.

After three days of just being in the way – as we all shared the same small floor space for sleeping and eating – I decided to leave. Another factor that determined my departure stemmed from the fact that Ryuichi was terribly compromised, as he was a policeman giving shelter to an illegal alien. I can still see the man's sad expression as he left me at the entrance to the immigration office. From there I was sent to an immigration jail.

I expected to be treated badly, but I was in for a surprise. When I arrived I was given a meal of steak and salad, followed by coffee and ten 'Peace' cigarettes. They must have had the idea that westerners only ate steak, which was horrendously expensive in Japan, and so I got the same meal three times a day for a week! My Japanese luck again! And it was luck, believe me, because in the cell directly oppo-site were three women who were illegal aliens and who cried constantly, as they were being deported back to Mao's China. I hope God helped them.

One of the guards was keen to learn English and often came to talk to me. When I returned to England I sent him a dictionary. I also penned him a letter, in which I wrote: "If you ever hear of a band called The Beatles, they are from Liverpool."

I sometimes wonder if he ever received either the letter or the dic-tionary. If he did, what did he make of the reference to an obscure band that played alien music in a provincial town!

After seven days in the immigration holiday camp I was hand-cuffed and escorted to the railway station by two immigration officers, who then accompanied me to Tamano where the *Cape Graf-ton* was being overhauled in the wake of the departed *Cape York*. It was quite a journey on that train, which was a precursor of the fa-mous 'bullet' trains. I remember eating lunch from a wooden box containing rice and pickles, watched by a sad-eyed woman who no doubt wondered what a 16-year-old boy could have done to be hand-cuffed even while eating. To be fair, as far as the immigration police were concerned I was a high-risk escapee. In reality I was as anxious to get back home as any sailor who has been at sea for months.

I had come full circle and now found myself back in Tamano, aboard another ship, without having a fully defined role. It just hap-pened that the chief cook of the Grafton had attempted suicide and so his assistant was now the chief, which created a vacancy in the galley. The new chief, a young man from Falmouth by the name of Brian Kelly, was reluctant to take on a sailor in the galley, but bowed to the wishes of the captain. As it turned out, he was to become a friend and mentor, at least until we got back to Britain. The term employed by seamen for such a friend made at sea was 'a board of trade acquaintance'. Such relationships were the product of a system that men rarely saw their own families, much less ex-shipmates, who constantly moved on.

The *Cape Grafton* was an old wartime construction known as an 'Empire boat', which had at one time carried grain, and also a small spotter plane that had been employed to seek out U-Boats. The bow retained traces of its old shape as a miniature aircraft carrier, but that was its last link with glory, as it was now a battered old tramp steamer, condemned to wander the oceans to carry any cargo that its owners could arrange.

As it ferried coal from Australia to Japan, the ship's agents were already concluding a deal that would mean we had to go to Nahru in the South Pacific, load a cargo of phosphates, sail once more to Newcastle, New South Wales and pick up more coal for a return trip to Japan.

While were in Australia for my second visit we were told to expect a 'D.B.S' a Distressed British Seaman, who had left his Norwegian employers and was trying to get back to the UK. As we waited for him in case he wanted a meal, who should come up the gangway but the conqueror of the Cape York's sad pugilist! His name was Brian too and he had spent all of his pay-off in the five weeks he had been waiting to be repatriated, and so I was delighted to be able to offer him a ten-shilling note. He was worth that for putting the sociopath in his place with such a rare mix of force and reason!

While we returned to Tamano for the second time it was winter and my Japanese luck continued to flow, because I was virtually adopted by the family that owned the Mocha Bar, my favourite bar, as it was small and friendly. One bitterly cold January day the family invited me for a meal and I accepted with alacrity. When I arrived I found everyone sitting on the floor around a circular table which was draped with a heavy cloth that had a hole in the middle to allow the heat to escape from the stove underneath, which was supporting the table. I placed my cold feet under the cloth and felt the heat from the stove gently toasting them!

What followed was one of the most absurdly embarrassing experiences of my life. We were all served a bowl of soup that was almost at boiling point. I then saw everyone present crack open a raw egg and carefully drop it into the soup, which they then ate rather slowly.

Determined not to allow my squeamishness to let me down I drained my bowl and congratulated myself that I hadn't gagged on the strands of raw egg that permeated my soup.

It was only later I saw that in the bottom everyone else's bowl was a perfectly poached egg that had formed because, unlike me, the others hadn't agitated the soup while eating it. God only knows what Masumi and her family thought about the barbarian who had devoured a raw egg!

The time came to leave Japan and head for home via Nahru once more, to ship phosphates to Leith in Scotland. By then I was becoming a useful member of the ship's galley. So useful, in fact, that by the time we had reached Japan for the second time I was able to deputise for Brian Kelly, who had been 'detained' overnight in Osaka while we were still at anchor. I cooked a Sunday roast for 34 crewmen and the only complaint came from the captain because I had forgotten to make the gravy.

Brian Kelly was a generous and conscientious tutor and to this day the lessons he taught me have become some of my most important skills. He was a bit of lad our Brian, always well dressed going ashore and ready for what the world held in store. He was also a caring man and for a 26-year-old displayed remarkable concern for my welfare. The very first day I went to work for him he said in his Cornish brogue, "Jesus, I've seen more muscle on a chicken's lip! By the time we get home I want you to have put on a stone!"

So *every* day of the 67 days it took us to reach Scotland I breakfasted on four fried eggs and two medium sized fillet steaks, while everybody else got by on cereal or pancakes. When we got to Scotland I hadn't gained an ounce.

One of the quirks of seafaring is the peculiar nature of their tax system. If a ship was away from British waters for a full year from April 7th to April 7th the following year, then no taxes were payable. Now it happened that the crew of the *Cape Grafton* had been away for twenty-one months, but by cruel twist of fate were due back in the UK on April 6th. Thus it was that every so often we would develop 'engine trouble' and find ourselves drifting in the Pacific. The idea was to delay our arrival until the requisite date, thus avoiding paying tax. It was during one of these enforced halts that we caught a shark, using a meat hook tied to a rope and baited with offal. It was fascinating to see it homing in on the bait, because in the crystal water we could see the tiny pilot fish clinging to the shark's head and guiding it to the offal. This time the pilot fish were the marine equivalent of Judas goats, and like the Judas goats, they escaped the fate of their host. It wasn't a big fish, measuring five feet in length, but nonetheless it had a fearsome array of teeth. We disembowelled it and hung it over some awning spars, then queued up to have our photos taken with the monster from the deep. One man had his photo taken whilst kissing the shark on its pointed snout, so others followed suit. After about an hour we were taking it down to throw it overboard when in death's final convulsion it suddenly snapped shut its open jaws! We never again baited those magnificent creatures.

The ship arrived in Leith on April 8th and we had our first drink since Japan, as the *Grafton* was a 'dry' ship because its captain deemed it so. I sometimes wondered if the enforced sobriety of the *Grafton's* crew was the reason the voyage was so peaceful and I now have to conclude that it was.

21. The Things We Do For Love

It is a fact that every letter I have ever received began with the phrase, 'Dear John'. Happily, not all of them were from departing lovers. One of the strangest Dear John letters I ever opened was from my solicitor, a woman, and it read:

> Dear John,
> It is my great pleasure to present you with your decree absolute...

I mean, I could have felt like cutting my throat or looping a noose over the banister and she was in bloody raptures! The truth is that I too took great pleasure from the news, but you know what I mean.

During my first sea voyage I received scores of 'Dear John' letters, *all* of them from my mother. Our first port of call was at Willemstad in the Dutch West Indies, and awaiting me there were eleven of those powder-blue airmail letters ... and we had only been gone ten days! I was not only embarrassed, I was totally confused, as she kept writing things like, 'In case you didn't get the last one I just wanted to say...' and the next letter would begin almost exactly the same way. Within a year of leaving Liverpool I'd received so many letters I could have fashioned them into a large kite, tattooed *Par Avion* on my arse and flown myself home.

I don't know what it is about me and letters, but I've had some weird times with Her Majesty's Mail. Over twenty years ago I was madly in love with a young Brazilian lady. Talk about a passionate relationship – we broke up so many times I used to take super glue as a food supplement. One night, after our umpteenth spat, I was so drunk and enraged that I slumped into a chair and wrote her a letter in which I think I compared her to the star of a Stephen Spielberg's movie, *Jaws*. I staggered down to the pillar-box and posted the letter. Now, whether it was because I was stoned off my face or there was a trick of the light I don't know, but I swear its mouth turned its corners up and grinned at me!

When I awoke I was stricken with remorse. I had to somehow stop that letter from reaching the girl from Ipanema and so I leapt out of bed and searched desperately for my passport. I had no plans to go to Brazil, and in any case she was living in Mossley Hill, but I had to somehow persuade the postman to give me the letter back so I needed I.D.

I was ahead of the postman and found myself uncomfortably lurking around the pillar-box at the corner of Prescot Road and Hall Lane. When the postman arrived and I explained the problem he reacted as if meeting a barely coherent clown reeking of alcohol and waving a passport around was an everyday event and gave me the poison penned letter without further ado. I needn't have bothered because about a month later she did a Dorothy Lamour and took the road to Rio.

The following year I met girl from Gloucester who was so fiery she made the departed Carmen Miranda look like an aloof version of the Ice Maiden. She was a student at my old college and I met her while having an afternoon drink. Within days she had moved in with me. Within weeks she had been hauled off home by her scandalised parents who bombarded her with letters, yes letters, by the sackful, upbraiding her for her moral lapse. They didn't mind her sleeping with a man, as long as he wasn't from Liverpool, that latter day Sodom and Gomorrah.

When she left to go home I was devastated, and so when I received a letter from her inviting me to go and meet her folks I was ecstatic. I phoned her and we made arrangements for her to meet me at Cheltenham Station. She mentioned that I would have plenty of time as I would have an hour's wait between trains at Birmingham.

Imagine then my sense of surprise, nay panic, when, after arriving at Birmingham New Street I saw the Cheltenham train preparing to leave. I leapt aboard and settled down with a can of beer. I met a group of Royal Navy chaps who were bound for Plymouth. Their wives accompanied them and they were all of them extremely affable. I told them my story and they wished me good luck. After about an hour one of them said, "I recognise this place … I reckon it's Cheltenham next stop."

I was fairly quivering with excitement as I got my bag down. However, my excitement was suddenly tinged with alarm as I overheard the conductor inform nobody in particular that the train would shortly be passing *through* Cheltenham. My worst fears were confirmed when I asked him what he meant. In my haste I had boarded the through train and it wasn't stopping until Plymouth!

I took the blow as best I could and was instantly reprimanded for using bad language on a public conveyance. The sailors were as upset about my plight I was, and one of them suggested that as the train always had to slow down when passing through a busy station I might be able to make a jump for it. I didn't need persuading and so I opened the carriage door, cheered on by the sailors and their wives, one of which held my bag in readiness to hurl it after me.

I was so excited at the prospect of meeting my darling gal that fear was not a factor as the train approached the station and did indeed slow down – to about twenty five miles an hour. I leapt for the platform and my momentum was such that it carried me forward unrelentingly so that I was running alongside the cheering sailors for what seemed an age until I reached the far end of the platform and was forced to run down the ramp into a wasteland where I fell and rolled over and over, causing the release of masses of wispy seed pods from the dense ranks of Rose Bay Willow Herbs.

I could still hear a faint cheering as I attempted to make my way up the ramp, so it was with a bizarre feeling of dread that I realised something was terribly wrong with my left leg, which suddenly buckled and collapsed under me. My heart sank as I thought of being in hospital instead of being with my West Country woman. It was only when I noticed that I was not in pain that the truth dawned on me. I had lost the heel from my cowboy boots. The relief!

My elation was short-lived, as there was no sign of my lady, and so with a growing sense of foreboding, I phoned her. When I told her what had happened she went into hysterics, not because of my shattered heel but because in my haste I had jumped aboard the early train, which was why I ended up on a through train. That was the reason why she wasn't there to meet me.

We spent the rest of the afternoon looking for 'dabs', her name for plimsolls, while the local cobbler repaired my boots. I spent a lovely week with her, visiting the remains of my old sea training school at Sharpness, where we stayed at a local pub.

Needless to say I eventually ended up with a broken heart, which no cobbler could repair, but fortunately another lady could, and did!

22. Albatross

I read today that the Albatross is in imminent danger of extinction and realised with horror that, as an ex sailor, I might be among the last human beings to have seen one of these magnificent creatures majestically gliding across the southern oceans.

Of course, at the time I didn't perceive the big birds as being anything other than outsize seagulls as they scavenged in the ship's wake, swooping greedily on the garbage we daily hurled over the stern.

Whenever I think of the lone Albatross that tailed our ship I have an image of the bird's silhouette merging with the curling crests of wind-driven waves beneath unrelenting grey skies. It must have been present on fine days too, but I was only really aware of it when, in spite of adversity, the big bird demonstrated its marvellous skills in its daily pursuit of survival. How ironic, it seems to me now, that it should seek to feed from the hand of man, its unthinking Nemesis.

Waste seems to go hand in hand with my memories of our Albatross. For some reason it will always be associated in my mind with potato peelings, bacon rinds and loss. The reason for this peculiar association lies in my role as temporary galley boy on the MV *Cape Grafton*. Every day one of my major tasks was to peel potatoes – enough to feed thirty four crew members. Now, prior to going to sea my only experience of peeling vegetables was on an aborted camping trip, where I had managed to reduce plump carrots and potatoes to matchsticks as I sliced the peel so thickly it could have been used to thatch the roof of a dwelling in the rain forest. So, when Brian Kelly first pointed me in the direction of a huge mound of potatoes my heart sank, because I was well aware that I was to paring what a combined harvesting was to lawn trimming.

You can imagine my joy, therefore, when he opened a drawer and handed me a Swiss made swivel-bladed peeler, of the type that is now commonplace but which in 1963 was as revolutionary as Sputnik. The alpine sharpness of the blade reduced the daily mountain of potatoes to a relative molehill of effort. I can recall its smooth handle fitting into my grasp so easily that it felt as if it had been a natural development in mankind's evolution.

One bright morning as I sat outside the galley, de-skinning the equivalent of a smallholder's output, I was aware that a high sea was running and out of the corner of my eye I could see our avian stalker hurdling the swell. I was immersed in a reverie concerning a young lady from Newcastle, New South Wales called Bettina Owens, with whom I had enjoyed a brief and regrettably platonic friendship some weeks previously. Like many a lovelorn young man I was indulging in mawkish sentiments and singing to myself, secure in the knowledge that the strains of my quavering voice would be rapidly carried away on the breeze, to take its rightful place amid the detritus of the sea.

I had just begun the umpteenth rendition of Marty Robbins popular song,

> "Out in the west Texas town of El Paso
> I fell in love with a Mexican girl...

When suddenly a huge wave surged over the gunwhales and before my horrified gaze swept away the vat of peeled potatoes *and* my precious Swiss peeler! I frantically raced after the dixie of spuds which was sailing through the open door of the galley and heading rapidly for the other door and was confronted by the sight of Brian leaping onto the chopping block with the agility of a startled monkey.

As I was caught in that midstream between terror and laughter I saw the scattered potatoes and my peerless peeler disappear over the side, the metal wetly gleaming like a disoriented flying fish before it disappeared into the ship's wake.

Our Albatross, alerted by the cascading vegetables, swooped on the unexpected spud fest and I swear it smiled as it gratefully accepted its watery manna.

That was the last I saw of the big bird, as the *Grafton* crossed the equator that day and the gliding garbage hunter turned back south. I was forced to revert to the primitive use of a knife to peel my potatoes and had to peel more of them than ever before to arrive at an edible amount.

Thus, although the bird had gone I carried around my neck, a la Coleridge's stricken sailor, the Albatross of drudgery.

The lesson of energy conservation in particular and conservation in general was driven home that day and I still harbour fears that the shining metal peeler might have acted as a lure to the bird and been swallowed whole, thus ensuring that in some sense I had personally contributed to the extinction of the loneliest of ocean voyagers.

23. Hello Goodbye

When I was a teenager in Liverpool I had a recurring nightmare, from which I would awake shell-shocked, awash with fear and foreboding. There was never any real form to the dream, just a vague awareness that I had got married and had been suddenly gifted with responsibilities for which I was unequal.

The nocturnal invasions began when I was seventeen and only ended three years later, when incredibly, given Mercury's interventions, I got married. Looking back, it is as if I had been sleepwalking and had stepped out of a nightmare before blundering into a terrifying reality, without ever waking.

It all started one summer's night when I met my bride to be. Just seventeen, she was pretty, completely innocent and entirely without guile. I was nineteen and a battle-hardened veteran of the sexual revolution. I walked her home and despite her undoubted charms I didn't pursue anything other than a half-hearted attempt at making a date for the following week.

Now it so happens that up until then I had never stood anybody up in my life. Moreover, I was always the first to arrive on a date because I was too insecure to imagine that a girl would wait for me for any length of time. However, I stood up the future Mrs Williams, with more than a twinge of remorse, as she was a nice, trusting kind of person.

Several weeks later I met her again and we had about six or seven dates over a three-month period. One night I called for her to find her in a state of great agitation. She was 'late' and she had already consulted the old wives who told her a tale about the efficacy of something called 'slippery elm'. The 'remedy' failed and it wasn't too long before I was facing the hostile gaze of her clan.

Only one of her relatives, her older brother, who was in his late thirties, even mentioned the fact that we did not have to marry, but as he was vigorously polishing the well-worn stock of a shotgun at the time I didn't attach too much credence to his words. My mother's response was a mixture of resignation and forced gaiety. She told me years later that when she was alone she simply cried.

All that remained was to approach our respective Parish priests and obtain permission to marry. Now not many couple get married in November, so when we went to see her priest his first question to my intended, accompanied by a righteous sneer cast in my direction, was:

"How many months are you?" And that was that.

My own priest spent hours talking to me about the responsibilities of marriage, while totally ignoring my girlfriend.

Thus both of our 'fathers' had, in one way or another, managed to make their children feel like lepers.

The wedding was set for November 5th, Guy Fawkes Day. The event itself was a damp squib and in the years that followed I couldn't avoid the feeling that both of our lives were hanging fire. To say that the ceremony was low key is a bit like saying hermits don't get out much. The wedding day itself began badly as, with my head throbbing from the excesses of the previous night's binge, I staggered to seven o'clock mass at St Bernard's in Kingsley Road to take communion blessing before the afternoon ceremony. When I reached the altar my mind was shrouded in an alcoholic fog. It was only when I opened my eyes to receive the host that I noticed a coffin standing on a bier less than two feet away. It was a requiem mass.

I reeled home to find John, my best man, already there. John was, in fact, my second choice, as I had fallen out with my best friend over something trivial. That sense of second best permeated the whole day.

We arrived at the church in St Domingo Road Everton. By some supreme irony it was called Our Lady of the Immaculate Conception! We found ourselves standing in the entrance, looking aghast at the dilapidated condition of that particular house of the Lord. A galvanised bucket stood on the porch floor collecting drips from the roof and I was uncomfortably reminded of the line, 'My cup overfloweth'.

John made the obligatory remarks about marriage and kicking the bucket and we entered the church proper. As we knelt in the front row my best man was seized by nerves and he dropped the ring and silver coin he'd been twisting between his fingers. It seemed to me that the omens were queuing up to shake my hand. As we stood at the altar the priest arrived wearing a grubby-looking surplice that he had either rescued from the washing bin or else always kept to hand for just such shameful weddings.

Alternating between sniffing noisily and wiping his nose on the sleeve of his surplice, he took us through the ritual. In our nervousness and shame John and I were standing in the wrong place and the priest almost joined him and my bride in marriage! Fortunately, for John, the priest rectified the farcical situation with his usual ill grace.

After the ceremony we stood outside the church and had our photographs taken beneath the grey and lowering skies. My newly acquired sister-in-law extended a limp hand to me and said:

"I suppose I had better shake hands with you."

My beloved Aunt Alice overheard her and bit her lip as she strove to remain silent in the face of such ungraciousness.

After a rather quiet meal for four in a Dale Street restaurant, where a lady insisted on buying us a drink to celebrate, we went back to my in-law's home to get our bags, as we were catching a coach to Blackpool for our two-day weekend honeymoon.

My mother and aunt Alice had waited in my mother-in-law's home until we returned from the restaurant, but since neither of them were equipped for arctic weather they left the igloo as soon as the Huskies arrived to take myself and my bride to the bus station.

We hadn't booked a hotel and so when we arrived in Blackpool we simply knocked on the door of the first bed-and-breakfast we came to. It was owned by a Mrs Jones and she made us welcome by offering us a drink of tea and an honoured place by the coal fire. Pointing to a picture of a pretty blonde girl aged about seven she gaily informed us:

"That's my little Mary. D'you naw, I 'ad six miscarriages before I 'ad 'er!"

I glanced at my wife who had turned the colour of the ashes that lay in the unswept hearth. We made our excuses and left and went for a quiet meal in a seafront restaurant before retiring gratefully to bed.

We lay in bed, idly discussing this and that, as there was no real desire on either of our parts to do anything else, when the door burst open and Mrs Jones walked in and tossed a hot water bottle on the bed. We might have been swinging from the light fittings! Or perhaps Mrs Jones was a clairvoyant, who in the summer months occupied a stall on the Golden Mile.

When we went downstairs to breakfast in the morning we noticed a woman and three children, all sunk in silence. Mrs Jones couldn't wait to inform us that the family had arrived in the middle of the night and the reason for their funereal silence was simple; they had shared a sudden bereavement. I nodded sympathetically at the widow and wondered if somebody was trying to tell me something.

In spite of the fact of two beautiful children and the dignified bearing of their undemanding mother, who just happened to have a ticket on a runaway train, my marriage ended four years later and we both lived happily, and separately, ever after.

24. Young, Gifted and Black

When, after the assassination of Caesar, Mark Antony was addressing the Roman mob, he held up the murdered man's toga and, according to Shakespeare, pointed to one of the many rents made by the assassins' daggers proclaiming, "...You all do know this mantle ... see what a rent the envious Casca's dagger made!"

Antony's oratory inflamed the mob to murderous intent and Casca's fate was sealed. Not one Roman citizen asked the obvious question. Namely, that given all those bloody slashes in Caesar's toga, how could Antony say with the slightest certainty that any particular rent was caused by Casca's dagger? Nobody asked because the mob mentality is many things, but it is never analytical.

In the early sixties the Spion Kop at Liverpool FC's Anfield ground accommodated over twenty thousand souls, but amidst that heaving sea of people, oftimes jubilant, sometimes sad, I can only ever recall seeing one face of African origin. That face belonged to a man called Ollie, and it always bore huge smile. Regardless of what was happening to him, Ollie's eyes were always bright as he maintained his raucous support of the team he so obviously adored.

He didn't appear to have any fixed position on the Kop, and so, smiling and shouting, he would bob up all over the place. It occurs to me now that he was always alone, and without the anchor of friends drifted from place to place, possibly leaving adverse remarks in his meandering wake. I used to enjoy seeing him 'perform' and so it is all the more shaming to me that one Saturday afternoon, in spite of my upbringing, which had explicitly encouraged racial and religious tolerance, I joined in the hateful chorus of abuse aimed at Leeds United's winger Albert Johannson. Albert had been uprooted from his native South Africa and was the first non-white player I'd ever seen. Every time Albert got the ball that day the terraces resounded to cries of "Ooh! Ooh! Ooh! Coco Pops!"

I can't remember seeing Ollie again. Perhaps he did attend other matches, but couldn't find within himself his old fervour and so I didn't notice him. It is ironic that in the following year, 1966, Goodison Park, just a quarter of a mile away from Anfield, played host to Pele, the greatest footballer of all.

The succeeding decades would see Anfield graced by many players of African descent, notably the majestic John Barnes, and while his skill and flair destroyed many an opposing defence, my memory of that hateful display off the pitch is indestructible.

My sense of shame was sharpened the other night when I saw a television documentary about alcoholism in football and discovered that Albert Johannson had become an incurable alcoholic, who died in such abject poverty that all he left behind him, apart from bewildered defenders, was a few pennies and a bus ticket.

There is no denying that I must have played some part in his alcohol-fuelled escape from pain. He might have been better off had he remained under the oppression of failing Apartheid rather than suffer the torment of fools like me.

25. Somethin' Stupid

The recent deaths of two of Liverpool's soccer legends, Billy Liddell and Joe Fagan, reminded me of my brief meeting with the former, a goal scorer so prolific that at one time Liverpool FC was nicknamed 'Liddelpool' in his honour. It was in the summer of 1978, when I was an undergraduate at Liverpool University.

I had been wandering about the student's union building when I recognised the grey haired and upright figure of the Scotsman who was almost single-handedly responsible for Liverpool's successes of the late forties and their survival in the fifties. He went largely unnoticed by the students, most of whom were, unlike me, too young to remember him, if they hailed from Liverpool at all. After our encounter I bet he wished I'd never noticed him either!

I had only seen him play once, and that was in his farewell performance to his beloved Anfield, back in 1960. It was during that period of my life when I supported both Liverpool FC and Everton.

Billy's last game, against Huddersfield, was memorable for many things, not least of which was that it was the only occasion I saw a ball kicked so hard that it burst, with a bang that reverberated around Anfield like a howitzer. It was, of course, Liddell, the human cannon, who had fired the ball goalward, only to see it rebound off Ray Wilson's legs before exploding.

Wilson later went on to win a world cup winner's medal with England, which many people say they were lucky to win, but on that day at Anfield he was even luckier because if the ball had hit him six inches higher he would have been singing as a member the famous 60s group, The Five Seasons!

So you can imagine my nervousness as I approached the great man, saying, "Excuse me, but I saw your last game for Liverpool."

He smiled benignly and nodded, waiting for me to continue. Now I could have commented on almost any aspect of that game ranging from Ray Wilson's brush with becoming a falsetto, to the state of the meat pies. Instead, I blurted out something about that day's other, almost unprecedented, incident, again concerning the legend himself.

"Er... You missed a penalty."

'Jesus tonight!' I thought, as he smiled, tight lipped, nodded and strode purposefully away. He must have wondered what had made him settle in the city and give his life to Liverpool football club, the magisterial bench *and* Liverpool University when there were plant pots like me around!

My only other encounter with a famous footballer went off rather better. I was having a drink in what was then the nexus for the counter culture, the Everyman Bistro bar, when I noticed Liverpool's latest signing, Kevin Keegan, quietly making his way toward the exit. He was unrecognised by the rest of the clientele, for most of whom football was completely 'un-cool'. If it didn't come in king-size cigarette papers they weren't interested.

I myself was acutely interested in both outdoor and indoor sports. Anyway, I exclaimed to my girlfriend, loudly enough for him to hear me, "That's Kevin Keegan!"

He smiled shyly and waved, and it was clear that he had enjoyed being recognised. A few minutes later my girlfriend and I decided to go back to my place and play Subbuteo ... or some similar game involving manual dexterity, luck and a reasonably flat surface.

When we got outside we stood on the pavement and tried desperately to hail a cab. I say desperately because, vis-a-vis Subbuteo, I was feeling lucky. A cab drew to halt and just as we were about to open the door that car behind hooted its horn. The cab driver looked around, nodded to the other driver and sped off. I was just about to remonstrate when out of the car window popped Keegan's head.

"Which way are you going?" he asked cheerfully.

Thus it was that a man who would one day become one of the most famous footballers of his generation dropped us off at my house. I asked him if he wanted to come in and have a coffee, or a joint, or even both, but he smilingly declined, saying that he was training the next day and felt it would be better to head back to his landlady's digs in Fairfield.

Thanks Kev, both for the lift and staying fit enough to help Liverpool lift their first European Champions cup. That cup almost became Liverpool's private property when Joe Fagan managed them to another great victory in Rome, but the Heysal tragedy destroyed his gentle heart and ripped the guts out of the club, while Hillsborough still corrodes its soul.

As they say, it's a funny old game, and I loved it because it used to be played by ordinary people who gave to me extraordinary memories.

In the light of the disparaging remarks Keegan made recently about Liverpool, and the alleged danger to his car from thieves, perhaps he would care to remember that his car was safe back in the 70s!

26. Ragamuffin Blues

With typically idiosyncratic turn of speech, people in Liverpool always referred to the rag and bone man as 'the ragman'. At least once a week the ragman's cry reverberated through our street. It went something like: "D'yerankoooooh!" and was quite unintelligible, but it didn't really matter because his distinctive yell was always the signal for housewives to gather around his handcart and exchange their rags for cups and saucers. Woollen goods were the best currency, for they would induce the ragman to part with a piece of much sought after bone china as opposed to a mug, which was the exchange rate for cotton rags. The rags were re-cycled to produce cotton waste for industry.

One day, during my summer holidays when I was left to my own devices while my mother worked in a greengrocers, the ragman came to our road and, wonder of wonders, was offering adorable day old chicks in exchange for rags. Now my mother had just paid good money to have a white wool cable stitch cricket pullover knitted for me, which I fancied that I needed rather less than a fluffy cuddly chick. No sooner had the bastard thrust a chick into my hands than he was off like a hound of hell, fearing that my mother would appear at any time and reverse the pullover/pullet swap.

As luck would have it, my mother turned one corner just as the rogue was turning the other and, on seeing my chick and immediately getting the picture, was after him like a flash. I don't know what she said, but she was back in a minute, clutching my pullover, while I was left happily clutching the unredeemed chick, which, for all its lack of years, had more damn sense than I had!

My poor Gran was far less fortunate with her encounters with these itinerant fashion gurus. On one occasion she parted with a newly purchased mattress *and* five shillings to a ragman, on the premise that he would take the bed to my mother's house. Oh dear! He probably couldn't believe his luck. I mean, it was 1952 and a complete stranger had given him the equivalent of an errand boy's weekly wage *and* a highly-saleable mattress. He disappeared into the Bermuda Triangle of horses and carts never to be seen again!

Quite the funniest encounter she had was when a ragman accosted her and offered her a bone china cup and saucer in exchange for some clothes and a decent pair of shoes. A kindly neighbour had given her the shoes but Gran couldn't even begin to wear them as they had a heel, and she had been reluctant to refuse them and so offend her benefactor.

Dangling the cup and saucer before Gran's eyes, the ragman insisted on taking possession of the items before parting with his china, and Gran, in spite of her previous experience, agreed! If ever proof was needed of her saintliness or naiveté, that was it. Naturally, he gleefully made off toward his cart with them, leaving Rose Anne stranded and utterly helpless behind a hedge. She enquired plaintively, "But what about my cup and saucer?"

To which the wall-eyed bastard, for he was without doubt both of these things, replied, "Try fucking getting them! And as for these," he sneered, hurling the shoes into the pathway, "You can stick them where Paddy stuck his nine pence!"

Just then, to my Gran's eternal shame, her neighbour, attracted by the commotion, arrived just in time to see her old brown court shoes sailing through the air and landing unceremoniously at the feet of my mortified grandmother!

You don't see ragmen nowadays, and that's not simply because of the abundance of textiles. You see, at least two of the bastards are living it up on the Cote d'Azur.

27. Down on My Knees

In Liverpool, there are no shortages of places of worship for Roman Catholics, or any other religionist for that matter, and so my maternal grandmother would often turn Sundays into an excursion of faith. Sometimes our urban pilgrimage would take us to *Our Lady of the Angels* in Fox Street, where Franciscan friars, in their brown habits and sandals, transformed the bustling heart of 20th century Liverpool into a medieval Italian retreat.

Then there was *Saint Mary's*, Highfield Street, a relatively new building wedged between the blackened granite of the Exchange railway station and Liverpool Stadium, then the home of pugilism, and most appropriately positioned next to the church since it was known throughout the boxing world as 'the graveyard of champions'. However, when bus fares were in short supply we would attend service in Knotty Ash at the nearby Carmelite Convent.

The Convent was shielded from prying eyes by a twenty-foot high wall of pressed red brick, inside which towering poplar trees stood sentinel over the huge kitchen gardens. Before this, like some war ravaged redoubt, lay acres of black cinders, crushed underfoot by the faithful supporters of the Liverpool rugby league club whose pitch had been laid around the edges of a huge bomb crater – the Luftwaffe's contribution to Liverpool's "Strength Through Joy" programme. Not that there was much joy for the supporters, because, as I remember, Liverpool RLFC rarely won a tackle, much less a match.

The broad expanse of cinders eventually narrowed to a lane hemmed in by wayward Hawthorns. For about a hundred metres my Gran and I would act out the parable of those who would seek to stay on the path of righteousness, while simultaneously trying to evade the snares of the material world and its thorny ground. Then we would have to ring the bell to gain admittance to the convent, which belonged to a closed order of nuns and so did not encourage idle visitors.

Once inside we would marvel afresh at the beauty that few eyes saw. Even Jesus' agony was somehow ameliorated by the ethereal beauty of the exquisitely sculpted stations of the cross, and the purity of the communion host was rivalled by the shimmering white altar cloths which had been hand laundered by Christ's own brides, the Carmelites.

Then, that poignant moment when the nuns, incarcerated behind a golden grill, no bigger than a handkerchief, would take communion; and as they strained their tongues to receive the Son of God, I would crane my neck in the hope of seeing a saintly face.

I never did, although many, many years later I would be given a drink of water by a Carmelite novice as, lost in a mist of grief, I sought solace in my old place of worship.

But that's another story...

Grace Before Meals
For my Grandmother Rose Anne

I remember now the gilded grille
where maiden tongues,
long shrouded in its mesh,
strained piously
for the sound of the word
made crumbling flesh

We were deaf in communion

I remember the dell and the dry wishing well
ablaze in the Dragon fly days,
where we prayed for a drink
a draught cool to sink,
or a miracle to banish the haze

We were hungry but so full of grace

I remember too the narrow path
that black cinder strewn course,
and fleeing the dust in our eyes

Brooding on hell and the bleak doomsday bell
or purgatory ringing with sighs,
among them your lover, of ancient desire
a soldier, a captive, your future, my grand sire.

We await the cleansing flames

28. Back in the USSR

Almost everybody has, at sometime or other, been involved in amassing scraps of paper that bear images of rulers and monarchs. I am not referring to currencies as such, but rather to those occasionally priceless entities which are always worth saving – postage stamps. Although stamp collecting is ostensibly a male pastime, women are deeply involved too, as mothers usually bear the brunt of their offspring's' pestering for the wherewithal to buy a percentage of the almost infinite number of stamps that are available on this planet.

I was one of thousands of kids in post-war Liverpool who was stuck on collecting those brilliantly coloured and exquisitely drawn miniature works of art. Now all art collections need a gallery and, just as the Louvre, the Tate and the Guggenheim have own distinctive style of architecture, so do the albums where stamps are hung on gummed hinges.

There were three or four categories of album, most of which were out of reach of my sticky grasp, and the difference between them was similar to that between the National Gallery and Sailor Bill's tattooing parlour. The most desirable kind of album was often leather-bound with the look, feel and smell of a learned tome. Then there was the type I had, paper backed, with the look, feel and smell of an income tax demand.

Actually, it didn't really matter to me what edifice my stamps were housed in because it was the hunting of them that generated the real excitement. I can still recall the pleasure I felt on seeing those clear cellophane packets in which four or five stamps slithered around like exotic dancers on a polished floor. They were always part of a new series, a new edition and a new desire.

I particularly remember the diamond and pyramidal shaped Mongolian stamps, of which there seemed to be enormous amounts available. Looking back on it I can't believe that there were so many Mongolians who could write at that time, much less find a convenient post box, but I can still picture those stamps with their images of men and women, wearing hats with ear flaps, engaging in the major activities of their country, which usually consisted of herding sheep or horses.

Then there were the vividly coloured Soviet stamps, which bore the letters NOYTA C.C.C.P. I never did work out what it actually meant but the sequence sticks in my mind because I used to try and read it as a complete word, just as, when film credits roll, I try to read MCMXXXIV and with as little success. The Russians churned out millions of stamps, almost all depicting their Socialist achievements, but ironically enough they were never free of charge. Still, they were lovely to behold, and whether they were extolling the beauty of athletics or the simple joys of a backbreaking harvest, the girls were always gorgeous. The Beatles knew what they were singing when they wished they were 'Back in the USSR'! Then there were the Hungarian stamps, bearing the legend MAGYAR POSTA, which to this day stir in me different, less acquisitive impulses.

In 1956 I was living with my Nin, the family name for my grandmother, in Dovecote, quite close to the Carmelite Convent and the school that was attached to it, later re-named Cardinal Heenan. In the autumn of 1956, or perhaps it was 1957, the school buildings became the refuge of hundreds of Hungarian families who had fled the carnage of the uprising.

The authorities must have decided on a policy of open access to the local community because on the night I paid a visit to the refuge I was astonished to see hordes of pretty nurses from the Alder Hey Children's' Hospital gyrating in the assembly hall to the sound of Fats Domino's 'Blueberry Hill'.

The atmosphere was very friendly and I was enjoying my taste of cosmopolitan life enormously until I overheard a conversation between a Hungarian man and a local woman, which was sobering to say the least.

He was sitting on the stairs, his calves encased in highly polished brown leather shoes,[4] describing how he had shot and killed six Russian soldiers as they were trapped inside their damaged tank.

Even at the age I was I understood that death is the corollary of war but his evident enthusiasm for killing left me feeling disturbed. I can still see and hear him as he mimicked the actions of a gunman, saying, "Russki raise hands...pouf! Another ... pouf! ... pouf! ... pouf! ... pouf! ... pouf!

The final expostulation made me feel ill as in my imagination I saw the terror frozen on the Russki's face.

However, by the following week I had recovered sufficiently to accept invitation to supper with a refugee family. The offer had been made by an English official, who had been promoting relations between the Hungarians and the locals. I duly turned up and was introduced to a middle aged man, his wife and his rather beautiful twelve-year-old daughter who was called Juliana. As we waited for the communal supper to be served they showed me photographs of their home in Hungary. On one of them Juliana and her father were sat astride a large motorcycle parked outside a neat looking bungalow. I couldn't help but think that they had been far better off than anyone I knew and wondered what had impelled them to leave what appeared to me as a luxurious existence.

The supper arrived and displaced my ruminations. It consisted of bowls of pasta ribbon noodles. Now although I was used to pasta, possibly a legacy of my grandfather's internment in Germany during the great war, I was secretly repelled by the noodles, but I ate them anyway. How strange that elongated strips of pasta, hollow or otherwise was perfectly acceptable to me but the same universal flour and egg mixture in another shape was almost repellent!

During the following two weeks I saw a lot of the family, who attempted to teach me some Hungarian. Sadly though, all I can recall is

---

[4] Decades later I would read about Hungarians who had been summarily hung from lampposts by freedom fighters because they were in possession of brown leather shoes, commodities which were apparently only available to the hated N.V.K.D. Those shoes definitely weren't made for walking!

the term for eggs, *tojaz*, which I have never really had a chance to use. Next year in Budapest perhaps!

One day my Nin said I should invite Juliana for supper and the Magyar beauty agreed. We were sitting at the dinner table in my Nin's small kitchen in her equally small pre-fab. Juliana was fascinated by the one sole hi-tech innovation in the room, which was a built in refrigerator. Nin rarely had any use for it other than storing milk as the concept of frozen foodstuffs still lay across the sometimes frozen Atlantic. I can still see the tiny food compartment that was so ice-encrusted that it resembled the winter quarters of a Siberian peasant. We used it to make iced lollies.

My Nin was delighted to find that Juliana liked drinking tea and bustled round preparing a cup for the little girl. She set the teacup before Juliana, who looked up questioningly, and said, "*Foucanel*".

Poor Nin turned ashen.

Juliana repeated the word, more forcibly, "*Foucanel!*"

My Nin looked distinctly faint. I suddenly remembered that I'd seen Juliana drinking tea by sipping it from a teaspoon and it all clicked. Turning anxiously to my Nin I said, "She wants a teaspoon Nin. Fou … it means teaspoon". So saying, I leapt to my feet and took a teaspoon from the draining board and hastily passed it to Juliana. Her grateful smile, coupled with her dipping and sipping routine, restored the fractured peace of my Nin's soul! All this had taken place in the presence of a woman who shrank in horror if somebody said so much as 'bloody'. Laugh? I nearly joined the Foreign Legion!

Refugee camps, unless they are located in far flung places such as Gaza or Kashmir, are transient institutions, and before long Juliana, she of the porcelain complexion and charming table manner, had moved on. I wonder if she ever remembers that Autumnal evening in that grey pre-fab and reflects on the fact that her linguistic contributions to Liverpool have become part of that city's decent tradition of lending a sympathetic ear to alien languages and their dispossessed speakers?

29. Bless This House

I am selectively superstitious. For instance, I don't forward chain letters; I never say 'white rabbits' on the first day of the month; I regularly cross the path of a black cat (our very own Katie) and I used to toss salt over my shoulder until I temporarily blinded my wife who was, unluckily, standing behind me.

There is, however, one aspect of superstitious behaviour that I have never been able to shake off and that is my occasional indulgence in that peculiarly Catholic habit of drenching things with H2O. I am, despite my claims to rationality, a sometime believer in HHP – *Holy Hydro Power.*

As a child, almost everybody I knew had a bottle of the *Aqua Pura,* sometimes on the same shelf as the aspirin or calamine lotion, which was appropriate as all of them were salves to body or soul.

My mother even kept her hallowed H2O in an old medicine bottle, thus rendering the connection between healing and holiness explicit. However, by the sixties, mass-produced dedicated containers for Holy Water, usually made of opaque plastic representations of the Virgin Mary, became common. Most often the Virgin Mary could be seen standing on a plastic rock surrounded by plastic snakes but some traditionalists still clung to bottles with labels indicating that it was bottled in Knock, as opposed to Lourdes.

For my mother, the sanctified water afforded many applications. For instance, a drop of it in my ear could cure the worst earache in a day. Of course, it's true to say that if the water was accompanied by penicillin or aspirin the miraculous healing could be speeded up dramatically.

Whenever we moved house, which was often, my mother was always the first to enter the house, lashing holy water on the walls and floors like a drug-crazed voodoo priestess. At times the hallways were so wet it was difficult to tell if she was blessing the house or preparing to strip the wallpaper. I vividly remember that day in 1959 when we moved into Tiber Street. I was about fourteen and thought it quite hip to follow my water-chucking mother inside, while I attempted to Limbo. My non-Catholic stepfather thought it quite funny but when she caught sight of my dirty dancing it was clear from my mother's expression that she thought her Limbo dancing son was only a two-step from Hell.

Now it so happened that the old lady next door owned an amazing collection of the taxidermist's art and invited me to look at it. Owls, foxes and weasels stared glassily at me from inside their aquarium like tombs. It was really spooky, and anticipated the Bates' motel by several years.

However, when my friend the witch doctor discovered that the old lady was trying to persuade me to become a Jehovah's Witness she promptly told her to get stuffed. I never again set foot in the animal mausoleum, but I never forgot the place.

How could I, when the wall that separated our houses was permanently sopping with Holy Water? It's a wonder my baby brother, who was born later that year, didn't develop pneumonia!

One of the saddest consequences of that episode was that for years I was rude to Jehovah's who called to my door. Then years later I read that in Nazi Germany they had opted for death in their thousands rather than renounce their beliefs. They were most definitely witnesses to the Holocaust. Nowadays, whenever they call I politely explain that I am non-religious and ask them if they wouldn't mind closing the gate after them as the local dogs wreak havoc with my flowerbeds if given the chance. The Witnesses always oblige.

Quite the most bizarre example of my mother's belief in the miraculous protective powers of Holy Water occurred in the early Sixties when I had taken possession of a Lambretta scooter. I wasn't a 'Mod'. In fact, I'd never heard of the term when I bought the scooter.

As for my mother, well, it could be argued that far from being a Mod she was off her rocker because the first thing she did on seeing the scooter was to lash liberal amounts of the anointed water on the saddle, the handlebars and the wheels. I had only travelled from St

John's Lane but it looked like I'd driven the bloody thing from Canada to California, via Niagara Falls!

At that time my mother owned a caravan that was permanently moored in a small farm at the bottom of the Horsehoe Pass in North Wales and so one day I decided to take a trip to see it for the first time. You see, when my mother was escaping into her rural idyll, where she didn't have to fret about cars and the safety of her new baby, I was living *la dolce vita*, as every weekend I had the house to myself. Nuff said.

Anyway, there I was cruising along a road on the moors just outside Llangollen when to my horror the front wheel of the scooter became suddenly stuck in a shallow rut that ran the length of the road. Within seconds I was sliding broadside towards the oncoming traffic and I could feel the burn as the friction created by road meeting my elastic sided Italian boot began to melt my Bri-nylon socks. When the ambulance picked me up the driver removed what was left of my boot-cum-sandal and threw it into the ditch!

I still can't shake the thought that without my mother's voodoo I might have been in the ditch too.

So what do I believe in ... God, Merlin or Baron Samedi?

Take your pick.

Such is the power of suggestion that when I bought my first car and the mechanic pointed out that there was a fault in the catalytic converter I thought he said 'Catholic converter' and had a surreal vision of a car running on holy water.

30. Born to be Wild

"O, for a beaker full of the warm South,
...With beaded bubbles winking at the brim,
And purple stained mouth;
That I might drink, and leave the world unseen...

Ode to a Nightingale
John Keats

The first person I ever saw riding a motorbike was an Irish farm labourer called Johnny. He lodged at my aunt Alice's farm and worked for the owner, Mr Jackson. Johnny lived in attic rooms that were cloaked in permanent twilight. Even on a sunny day a perpetual gloom made them seem somehow subterranean. Johnny was a contemplative and gentle man whose main concern in life was to keep warm in the freezing confines of the ramshackle farmhouse.

One day I went to see him, accompanied by my mother and my cousin Tommy, and was astonished by his method of keeping the home fires burning, which was as extraordinary as it was comical. Johnny had managed to get hold of a railway sleeper and had placed one end of it on the fire while the other was balanced on an old dining chair. It resembled a footbridge to the fires of Hell. Whenever the fiery end of the sleeper burned away, Johnny would simply shove the chair forward and introduce fresh wood to the flames. Talk about burning one's bridges!

Over time Johnny became like a family member and so we were all sad when he met a young lady and decided to leave to get married. He promised to come back and see us one day, and he kept his word when he turned up with his wife on a huge red Vincent 1000cc motorcycle. It really was enormous and proved to be a real handful for a gentle Irish biker. I will never forget the laughter that convulsed us all when he gravely informed us that he would say his goodbyes inside the house because he couldn't ride the monster and turn to wave at the same time!

I can still see him; stiffly upright, disappearing down Sandy Lane like an aloof knight-errant. We never saw him again and I sincerely hope it was because he was too fulfilled and happy to ever return to his draughty loft.

In the fullness of time I too acquired a motorcycle and it too was red, but that was the only point of similarity with Johnny's Behemoth of a bike, as mine was a 250cc Honda Twin, which despite its smaller engine capacity was to the Vincent what the Graf Spee was to an old fashioned dreadnought. The Japanese had lost the war, but raced away with the peace.

I had bought the bike on an impulse and didn't have a clue how to get it from the shop in Aigburth Road. Fortunately I knew a Brazilian lady whose husband volunteered to teach me how to ride it. We wheeled the machine out of the shop and onto Aigburth Road, which is such a busy dual carriageway that for part of its length it is divided by a heavy metal barrier and so, with Carlos riding pillion while shouting instructions, I managed to manoeuvre the bike into Sefton Park.

As we wobbled along the circular road that skirted the park I became aware that Carlos was sitting awkwardly. He was, in fact, poised to leap from the bike should the need have arisen!

Eventually I became quite competent at riding my machine, which is just as well because it was about that time that I met my future wife, who, as a gentle and somewhat retiring English teacher was as unlikely a biker's moll as you could imagine. But if she was terrified of riding pillion she kept it well hidden, except for one occasion when we were riding through Glasgow in the outside lane and some cretin overtook us at about 90 m.p.h. We were both reduced to tears, born of fear and rage.

When we returned from Scotland my girlfriend went back teaching and I dossed around for a while as I had just graduated and wasn't too sure of which direction I should take. I needn't have worried, because my mate Steve had it all mapped out. One day as we sat in his flat, chewing the fat (quite literally as it turned out because he was always up for a bacon sandwich from the cafe in nearby Clarence Street) he turned the conversation to my newly-found freedom of mobility.

He mentioned France and his eyes shone behind his spectacles as he mooted the idea of a trip to the continent, subsidised by French farmers, who were apparently crying out for Scousers to harvest their grapes. His enthusiasm about the joys of being an itinerant field hand brought to mind idyllic visions of gentle labour under a hot sun, surrounded by nubile and willing daughters of Bacchus and proved irresistible. My impulsive streak, fuelled by a joint or two, quickly assumed command and we were soon planning a trip to the South of France and the delights of Provence. John Keats had written the brochure and Steve had decided that we should avail ourselves of the 'warm south'.

A few days later Steve and I were sitting astride the bike, which was heavily laden with various black plastic bin bags containing our continental outfits. At the time the newspapers were carrying pictures of Vietnamese 'boat people' and much to Steve's distaste I couldn't help referring to our enterprise as 'the adventures of the bike people'. My girlfriend waved us a tremulous goodbye as we roared off towards the M62.

When we reached Burtonwood services Steve mentioned that he had forgotten his spectacles, but declined my offer to return to Liverpool and collect them. He said he didn't miss them, although I suspect he was quite relieved that he couldn't foresee any consequences of my high-speed riding. Later that night we reached Dover and before too long were safely ensconced on a Sealink ferry.

We opted to sit on deck and as I stared out at the winking lights of France while Steve built a joint with the Jamaican ganga he had stashed in his elegant biker's Wellingtons, I found myself reflecting on the wealth we'd encountered once we crossed into the south of England. The material differences between the north and south were palpable. It had been like entering another country.

We reached Boulogne in pitch dark and I had to quickly get used to driving on the right. We rode almost non-stop through northern France and didn't sleep until we collapsed in a haystack somewhere in the Champagne region. When we awoke we decided to get a coffee in a local bistro and got in to conversation with an old man. I say conversation, it was a mixture of Steve's French and my fractured Franglais with the topic limited to a discussion of the old man's pride and joy, Champagne. I never have liked the stuff, but thanks to my encyclopaedic memory I was able to rattle off famous brands of bubbly until the old man began to think I was connoisseur. He was so chuffed with us that he bought us brandy and coffee, which was gratefully received as it was cold and foggy outside.

Cheered by that example of *entente cordiale* we drove off into the mist. After about an hour's driving the grave markers of a First World War cemetery caught our attention and so we stopped and stared at the seemingly endless rows of white crosses resting on the immaculately trimmed turf, looking for all the world like the masts of a battle fleet set in an emerald sea. The spaces between the graves were very small and I remarked that they didn't seem big enough to hold a coffin. Steve agreed, observing that given the nature of the conflict there probably wasn't enough remaining of the soldiery to fill a matchbox, much less a coffin. Chastened by our encounter we hardly spoke for hours afterwards.

The weather remained cool and foggy for almost two days as we wound our way south. I couldn't believe it; we'd left behind rare English sunshine only to freeze our balls off in La Belle France! Then, just as I was despairing of ever being warm again, we emerged from the fog to see the historic town of Avignon bathed in sunshine. As we sat by the bridge, famous for its incompleteness, we began to thaw out and so were able to remove our many layers of clothing that lent us the appearance of being part of a roving advertising campaign for Michelin.

Under the influence the sun's warmth and ganga I fell asleep and had a strange dream. I dreamt that a child had run off the end of the incomplete bridge and, cartoon like, was running in mid air, while behind him his frantic mother was trying catch up with him, her shopping spilling into the river as in her panic she too trod fresh air until she grabbed him, and then they both slowly faded away. Mothers!

We were headed for Arles, where a friend of mine, a sad eyed lady of the lowlands if ever there was one, lived with her husband. Edith was an Algerian-born Frenchwoman who had married an Austrian called Giorg, whose life's mission was to ensure the survival of Teutonic gloom as a defining Germanic characteristic. He was one surly bastard, but kind in a lugubrious way.

When we reached the apartment Edith was delighted to see us, but Giorg was working in Marseilles, where he spent a lot of time, much to Edith's dismay. We hadn't been there long before Steve started chafing at the bit because he was a born earner and wanted find a vineyard ASAP. Promising to return later that evening we followed Edith's directions and within an hour we were following a tractor and filling plastic buckets with purple grapes.

Steve's romantic picture of gaily-singing grape pickers vanished from my horizon the instant I slashed my hand as I attempted to slice through the tough vines with the sharp cobbler's knife that the farmer had issued. The lateness of our arrival meant we only worked for two hours but I was already shattered and wracking my brain for answers to the sole question that occupied me. How had I fallen for the rustic idyll when the reality was backbreaking labour?

Everything about the experience was hard, from the stooping position I had to adopt in order to garner the grapes to trudging through the yielding clay while trying to catch up with the sadistic bastard of a tractor driver who was mentally racing down the winning straight at Le Mans, leaving me stumbling in his slipstream. Small wonder that there aren't any Van Gogh's depicting the joys of grape harvesting. He probably gave the vineyards a wide berth!

Steve wasn't bothered in the least, but then he hadn't spent the previous five years cosseted in Academia, because in the intervening years between his sojourn at the London School of Economics and the real world of 80s Liverpool he'd worked at anything he could turn his hand to in order to remain economically viable. A grafter he was. A grafter I was not.

The accommodation that went with the job was a shack at the side of a canal. It was far removed from my imagined scenes of well-fed and happy-looking grape pickers sipping from Keatsian beakers of wine as their grateful employers demonstrated that their labourers were truly worthy of their hire. We went inside and as I lifted the mattress from my bed in order to shake the dust from it a cloud of mosquitoes rose up and it seemed to me that they were actually hauling the mattress behind them. I turned to Steve in despair but he just beamed at the prospect of being housed so close to the job.

It was then I remembered he'd left his spectacles at home.

Ever the explorer, Steve declined my invitation to re-visit Edith, deciding instead to mooch around the nearest village and buy some candles with which to illuminate our chalet on the mosquito-ravaged marshes of the Carmargue. I sped off to Edith's flat and the luxury of a bath, before accompanying her to a Bistro where, because of the lateness of the hour, we dined on lukewarm stew.

French cuisine? ... I've had some!

Edith kept apologising for the cursory service we received, but then she spent most of her life apologising, usually to Giorg for infringing some unwritten rule of the household he dominated. She hadn't changed from when I first met her when she was an exchange French teacher who had swapped the elegance and warmth of Arles for a dingy flat in Edge Lane. Even there she had been a great hostess as she entertained barbarians who couldn't stop laughing when Giorg insisted on washing and drying the glasses whenever a fresh bottle of plonk was broached. Believe me when I say it was plonk. I know it was – it had been purchased by students.

When I got back to Chez Mosquito Steve was asleep, but he woke to tell me that he'd discovered the French word for candles was 'boogie', and then turned over and went back to the land of nod. I pondered on the possible relationship between candle and boogie, and could only come up with the idea that the dance music mimicked the flickering and unpredictable flame.

For the next two days we laboured under the hot sun and I was not only shattered by my less than Herculean efforts but my back was so bitten by the winged residents of our canal-side cottage that even Steve was concerned lest it turn septic.

Saturday morning arrived and the crop was garnered, which meant that we had to move on to another vineyard; however, before we did so we were invited by the farmer to have a drink when he paid us our wages.

Pastis, several glasses of the stuff, taken on an empty stomach, almost led to tragedy. We had decided to fly the infested coop as soon as possible, and because the Pastis hadn't visibly taken hold of me, I thought it safe to drive. It wasn't. We hadn't travelled a yard, not even a metre, when we toppled unceremoniously onto the canal bank. At that point the world suddenly became decidedly fuzzy and as I tried to right the machine Steve shouted,

"John we can't go anywhere on that!"

"It's okay," I drunkenly insisted, "I'm not that bad."

What Steve meant was that we couldn't go anywhere because in the fall the chain had come off the bike.

"Fuck it!" I bellowed, and promptly fell asleep on the grass.

We were woken by the sound of a tractor rolling along the opposite side of the canal. Still full of alcohol and equally full of myself I imperiously ordered the driver to stop and offer us assistance. Incredibly, he overlooked my Pastis-fuelled arrogance and quickly put the chain back on. We decided to postpone our departure for a few hours, opting instead to sit propped against the outside of the shack to enjoy the sun and reflect on how we might have got as far as the busy road before falling in front of a vehicle. I must have inherited the luck of the Irish!

After the effects of the Pastis had worn off, I noticed that I could hardly walk. When I examined my leg it was bleeding heavily from a massive graze which ran the length of my right leg, which I could hardly bend. Edith was both surprised and concerned to see us when we returned unexpectedly to get some treatment for my wound. She insisted that we stay the night and when Giorg came home that night on his weekly visit from Marseilles he also refused to countenance any travel on my part.

By the next day my leg was impossible to move and so it was decided that my days of trampling out the grapes of wrath were over and that Steve would continue alone. That indomitable man did too. For three weeks, on foot, he worked the last of the harvest before catching a train home. I travelled on my own until I picked up a hiker near Lyon. His name was Pascal and in return for giving him a ride to Paris he and his friends put me up for a week in their apartment. I had lovely time there recuperating and taking in the sights.

I arrived in England with my own batteries charged but with my bike's batteries quite flat and so found myself sitting forlornly on a wall by the roadside just outside Folkestone. By sheer coincidence there were some lads from Liverpool camping just the other side of the wall who sympathised but couldn't really help as they were on bicycles. Just then a flat-back farm lorry pulled up and a man, accompanied by his wife, affected sympathy for my plight, but said he couldn't help, as he had no equipment to lift the bike onto the vehicle. From his demeanour it was clear that the smug bastard didn't really give a shit and was in fact deriving huge enjoyment from my predicament.

I can still see the horror on his face when a Scouse voice from behind the wall piped up and said, "We'll get it on for you pops!"

The miserable bastard could hardly refuse and his face was a picture of resentment as the lads tossed the bike onto the lorry as if it were a bale of hay. Without speaking to me once he dropped me at a railway siding where I was able to push the bike onto a ramp before having the battery charged in a local garage.

All that remained was to get home, but that was delayed somewhat when I took wrong turning and ended up in Newcastle! By then my battery was failing again and I knew I had to get to Liverpool before lighting up time. I made it, just, to be greeted by my lady who was distraught, as I had phoned her from Birmingham seven hours earlier to say I would be home within two hours!

31. Daddy Don't You Walk So Fast

The earliest memory I have of my natural father, Andy, is of him striding purposefully up Colwell Road carrying his suitcase as he embarked on yet another voyage. I must have been about four years old and I was desperately unhappy to see him leaving. I pleaded with him not to go and he offered me what I suppose was in those days standard advice to a whimpering boy child:

"Stop crying or I'll have to buy you a dress."

He hadn't meant to crush me, but I imagine that having survived many wartime Atlantic crossings, one of which had claimed the life of his beloved elder brother John, my father found partings somewhat fraught and wanted to leave with as little fuss as possible.

The emotional turmoil I experienced on that day was symbolic of my relationship with my father until the day he died. Like so many children, caught up in the civil war we call divorce, I was a mere foot soldier; listening to well meaning non-combatants as they sniped at 'the enemy', my dad, regardless of my small presence. This happens to many children and it's hard for any child to remain aloof from the verbal attacks. Indeed, it became politic on my part to join the general skirmishing. Thus it was that I learned to disrespect my father.

The casualties of divorce sometimes have their wounds regularly opened by self-appointed stretcher bearers, all of whom appear to be in possession of ample supplies of salt. Years later, after a period of profound depression, it occurred to me that I had spent my early adolescence denigrating one half of myself.

I had no valid reason whatsoever even to dislike him, as most of my memories of him revolve around gifts and exotic animals that he brought home from far-flung places. I remember my delight when one day he arrived home leading a dapple-grey rocking horse that he'd picked up in Pakistan. It had a beautiful white mane, which I became extremely well acquainted with as I was often catapulted over the horse's neck during the course of an over-vigorous ride.

The presents he gave me were always unusual. He once gave me a Piccolo 8mm movie projector he had bought in Hamburg and I can still recall my mother's despair when I chose to premiere a Mickey Mouse cartoon ... at midnight. One Christmas, when my mother was in hospital and I was living at my Aunt Alice's farm, I was thrilled when he arranged for me to receive a fully-working model of a tank.

I spent most of that morning playing in the sandy lane that snaked around the farm and wound its way under the railway bridge towards Gateacre Brow; Montgomery for a day, courtesy of my maligned father.

My most vivid recollection of him is one that I can actually put a date to. It was when Liverpool FC were languishing in the second division of the football league and had, against all expectations, thrashed Everton, then the ruling aristocrats of football, on their own ground, by four goals to nil. My dad had been to the match but that evening he took me to the newsagents and bought a copy of the pink football Echo. For the only time in his life he read aloud to me, and the text was a minute-by-minute analysis of his team's triumph at the enemy citadel.

As in all wars, certain people are called upon to be fifth columnists. My role as a spy was brought into play when, much against my mother's wishes, her solicitor argued that I should bear witness against my father in the ongoing divorce proceedings. I will never forget the look of sorrow on my father's face as I took the stand. My mother's solicitor, eager to marshal a victory, asked me to relate an instance of my father's 'cruelty' toward me.

The only 'damning' evidence I could recall concerned the time he had cooked me what seemed an enormous meal of boiled bacon, cabbage and mashed potatoes and then insisted, not unreasonably, that I clear the plate. It is clear to me now that his pre-war childhood, lived in the harsh environment of the great depression, had impinged on mine in a most innocuous way. My own children, knowing nothing of lean times, sometimes pick at food like listless birds, and, echoing my father, I rail in vain against their wastefulness. As you can imagine, the judge was not overly impressed by my account of my father's alleged cruelty. Nonetheless my father was hurt.

So, to my old man, who never laid an angry hand on me, I make a heartfelt apology for my unwarranted betrayal. I just found it so much easier to run with the hounds, as the hare was so far out of sight.

32. Promised Land

In 1978 I headed for Israel and the fulfilment of a lifetime's dream. As a child I was a precocious reader and so I was all too aware of the Holocaust. At the age of nine I was as familiar with the depravities of the Nazis as I was with the heroics of Robin Hood. My world-view was a confusion of chivalry, where men robbed the rich to give to the poor, and barbarism, where brutes stripped the tattooed skin from human beings and made lampshades to light their victims' road to death.

I flew from Athens, whence I had travelled by coach from London, to the newly named Ben-Gurion airport, accompanied by an American Jewish kid called Howard. Howard was studying at Harvard and had the aura of stardom about him. He was tall, well scrubbed and good-looking. He spent the whole of the flight from Athens writing postcards. There must have been fifty of them! I suppose he had a lot of ladies to write to. He was also very generous and offered to help me find a place to stay. Howard was of the opinion that I needed shut-eye more than I needed to go sightseeing, but I had to press on. After a quick meal of fruit and yoghurt I was anxious to find my way into Tel Aviv.

Tel Aviv, younger than Hollywood, older than sin, rose from the shores of the Mediterranean like Venus from a concrete shell. I wanted to find the office that dealt with volunteers for the *kibbutzim* and so I was wandering around when something happened that could have come from a film script. A pert little blonde approached me, introducing herself as Rivka, and asked if I wanted to go for a swim! After what must have seemed an age to her, but was in fact a split second, I agreed.

Within minutes I was frolicking in the strong surf near the breakwater that prevented the sea from overwhelming the Hayarkon, the road that snaked its way between the shoreline and the city. Then, as we lay on the sand, eating tomatoes, which were Rivka's favourite snack, she gave me a startling insight into the social reality of Israel.

I was already aware that Israeli society was divided into two broad ethnic divisions, the European Ashkenazim and the Oriental Sephardim, but I had no idea of the antipathies that existed between all the various groupings in that country. Unprompted, Rivka soon put me right on that score. She rattled off a list of ethnic Jewish groups and proceeded to denigrate all but her own European kin.

The Moroccans, she averred, brought their Kif with them. The Yemenis drank. The Russians knew only two words of Hebrew, 'apartment' and 'Volvo'. The Argentinians in exile had not given enough money to the cause, while the Americans were seen as rich tourists and little else.

I was astonished and dismayed, because I had believed that there was a tremendous sense of national unity in Israel. Rivka's callous dismissal of her compatriots unnerved me and so I decided to cut short my sojourn on the beach and headed for the Kibbutz office.

On the way I fell in with a middle-aged man who walked through the traffic as if it didn't exist with a brisk purposeful stride. By sheer coincidence he was in charge of the Volunteer service! Within an hour I was undergoing a medical that was necessary for insurance purposes. An old doctor, who most decidedly looked like a survivor of the death camps, gave me a cursory examination, which consisted largely of slapping a very cold stethoscope onto my chest. I think the reasoning behind this was that if I didn't die of shock then I was okay. Considering where he had been I suppose my examination was the equivalent of a trip to Harley Street.

I had to board a bus to a place called Beit Shean, which was situated just south of Galilee or the *Kinnerot*, as the locals call it, because it is shaped like a harp. As I waited at the bus station in the heart of Tel Aviv I was struck by the fact that many of the women wore an excessive amount of gold jewellery, just like some of the old ladies in Liverpool's Scotland Road area. Gold, I now realise, is the hallmark of the incipient refugee. You never know when it is going to come in handy.

When the bus came there was an almighty rush to get aboard. I was appalled until I remembered that, for these people, missing the bus in the past probably had fatal consequences. It grew suddenly dark and I could no longer see where we were going, so I got into conversation with a young man who willingly supplied a running commentary on the places we were passing through. I was puzzled, because I was totally unfamiliar with the place names. I mentioned this and he informed me that he was Palestinian and that the names were Arabic.

I had a sudden vision of Israel as a beautiful woman with two lovers, each familiar with every contour of her body, but who was known to each of them by a different name. He asked me to visit his family and share their hospitality, but to my eternal shame, I never did go because I would somehow have felt disloyal to my hosts. So I missed a rare cultural experience because I didn't want to become embroiled in the politics of rivalry between two groups of people who are, by virtue of their mutual descent from Abraham, half brothers.

There are two kinds of half-brothers, those who come from the same flower pollinated by two different bees, or those from different flowers pollinated by the same bee. I suspect that the former, by virtue of sharing the same mother, are closer. The Jews and the Arabs are an example of the latter, and both, unfortunately, carry the sting of their father.

When I arrived at Beit Shean, the site of King Saul's execution, it was pitch black, and I had several miles to go. However, a kindly local took pity on me, as I must have looked very tired by then. When we reached the Kibbutz, Neve Eitan, which was surrounded by a perimeter fence because we were only few kilometres from Jordan, the Samaritan left me at the gatehouse.

The guard was a *kibbutznik* who gave me the once over and said he had to go and inform the person in charge of the volunteers. With that he gave me his rifle to hold and left me to guard the gate! He came back, took the rifle and left it propped against his chair and took me to my quarters. So then the rifle was guarding the gate! 'What a place!' I thought.

The volunteer leader was an American called Irwin, who had been a master sergeant in the Marine Corps. He looked a tough cookie but he was a very considerate man. When I told him that I had only been in Israel a day before volunteering he seemed impressed by my willingness, but because of the distance I had travelled he refused to allow me to go to work immediately as he was concerned about my health. I was only thirty-two, but years of dissolute living and my aversion to any form of exercise outside of a duvet were taking a visible toll.

The next day I wandered about, meeting the other volunteers and lying in the sun. One of the volunteers was from New Zealand. He was a mildly sardonic young man with a healthy scepticism towards all systems, including the *kibbutzim*. His name was Sol and I will always remember him with affection. He played guitar, and when the mood took him he would burst into an improvised song, inviting me to join in with a phrase I will always associate with him:

"Let's rage John!"

He would yell, a grin lighting his face, as he strummed with a furious and largely tuneless abandon.

The day after that was *Shabat* and we were all going on a day trip to the Golan Heights. I was the new kid on the block and felt somewhat shy, but before long we were all chatting like old friends. As our truck climbed the hills into the Golan I noticed that the roads were new and well-maintained – a prerequisite of a nation that has to be ready at a moment's notice to throw heavily armoured vehicles into the front line. The Golan was littered with burnt-out tanks and shattered field guns and I wondered just whose job it was to clear the detritus of war.

Our ultimate destination was an ancient Jewish settlement called Gamala, or the Camel. When I saw it rising from the middle of a valley floor I realised why it was so named. It did indeed look like a camel's hump, even to the tufted hairy-looking crown. There is a chilling story attached the place. About 70 A.D the Romans expelled the Jews from their homeland, but a few pockets of resistance remained. In Gamala the Jews put up a fierce fight and were holding out because they had an internal water supply. Then one of the Roman besiegers, a renegade Jewish historian called Josephus, betrayed the defenders by revealing to the Romans the source of the water supply. Without water it was hopeless, but when the Romans called on the Jewish defenders to surrender they refused, and every man woman and child leapt to their deaths sooner than surrender to the infidel.

Almost simultaneously, the defenders of the great fortress of Masada, which was miles to the south and utterly isolated from the events at Gamala, committed mass suicide rather than surrender.

As I sat on top of the hump I couldn't help but reflect that it was no coincidence that Armageddon lay about twenty miles away. These people will never surrender, even if it means the end of the world.

For the second time in two days I found myself holding a rifle. It belonged to an Israeli called Ronni, who was one of our armed escorts. Picnics in a war zone are so thrilling! I told Ronni that I would make a lousy soldier because I was too scared of dying to be any use. He just looked at me and said, "Fear is what keeps me alive. I keep my head down and only show myself when I have to. No heroics, just doing a job."

I thought he was very generous. He could have played the macho man and sneered.

Life on the Kibbutz was interesting but not overly exciting. It is, after all, a place of work as well as being home for many families. However, I found just being in Israel exciting. As a child I, like all Christians, had grown up with a better knowledge of the geography of the Holy Land than of my own country. At seven I could quickly find Tiberias on the map, but I'm blessed if I could have found Truro as easily. You can imagine how I felt when one day, as I was travelling to Jerusalem, I found myself sitting at a roadside in the Jordan valley opposite a signpost that pointed to two places, Jerusalem and Jericho. You can't take a step in Israel without feeling the currents of history lapping at your feet.

Jerusalem! I fell in love with it on sight. You know it's a sad thing that Jumbo jets can take people all over the world, but never gives them a sense of travelling. No sooner have you taken off for some exotic destination than you are passing through that country's customs barrier, which is just like the one you left behind.

The first time I travelled from Neve Eitan to Jerusalem it was aboard an old bus that lumbered along the Jordan Valley, hundreds of feet below sea level and stinking hot. Then, as the bus strained its way up the hilly roads I caught a glimpse of what looked to be snow-covered hills in the distance. As we crawled closer I realised that I was looking at David's city of gold. It was an age before we reached it, and I felt that I had actually made a real journey, a pilgrimage if you like.

First things first, however. The first Friday night at Kibbutz Neve Eitan I was looking forward to my first Shabbat meal. I had some idea that it might prove to be a mystical experience, but in the event it turned out to be about as uplifting as breakfast at McDonald's. Neve Eitan was not a religious Kibbutz, but I had expected rather more than the desultory prayer followed by what looked like French onion soup, sprinkled with tiny croutons, accompanied by a bottle of sweet wine, not one of which was ever opened as far as I could see. Even the Volunteers, all from drinking cultures, disdained to drink it, any more than they drank the chicken soup that was so obviously synthetic. The nearest it had ever been to a chicken was when the provisions truck passed by the chicken pens which provided a cash crop for the Kibbutz.

Chickens. Now there hangs a tale! One morning I was sent to work with an elderly Kibbuztnik who, as a young man, had been rescued from a Nazi concentration camp, only to be incarcerated by his Russian saviours in a Siberian labour camp, from which he had escaped, via China! Anyway, he asked me if I'd help out with the chickens. I didn't mind because I entertained visions of swanning around with a wicker basket filled with freshly-laid eggs. The reality was absolute hell.

My job was to take chickens, three in each hand, and carry them, squawking, wriggling and defecating, to a waiting lorry. Now live chickens are heavy, but struggling live chickens are a dead weight, and when they are spraying crap in all directions life is positively nauseat-

ing. After an hour my arms and legs were so encrusted with droppings I looked like Godzilla's twin. Six hours of working incessantly in
the shit capital of the world brought me to the point of exhaustion. So
the old man, that survivor of death in all its varieties, excused me and
I staggered to bed via the showers. When I woke up, two hours later,
he was still working!

It was during the next Shabbat meal that I had my second encounter with a strange and lovely girl called Zoah (which means golden).
Zoah was a *Sabra*, a child born in Israel, but her ancestry was such
that it caused her many problems. Her mother had arrived in Israel in
1947, along with many thousands of people fleeing the stench of the
Holocaust. Zoah's mother, however, was a German Catholic. Bearing
in mind that in 1978 Germans were still *persona non grata* in Israel, it
is nothing short of miraculous that not only was that German woman
accepted but also later became a member of the Jewish underground
army. I never met her, but she must have been some lady. Her unor-
thodox nature can perhaps be best demonstrated by the fact that
although she initially married a Jewish man, Zoah's father, she later
divorced him and married a Bedouin.

On that Shabbat evening when I met Zoah, the volunteers, who
usually shared the same table were discussing an imminent visit to
the nearby Kibbutz of Kfar Ruppin. Zoah looked directly into my eyes
and said, "Don't go… stay here tonight."

I was taken aback, but I agreed, and thus began a friendship that
lasted until I eventually decided to hit the road and see something
more of Israel than the immediate confines of the Kibbutz, and of
course spend more time in my beloved Jerusalem.

Zoah was an accomplished pianist, but would not perform for an
audience and so it was a common sight to see several volunteers
sitting slumped against the wall of the dining hall, listening to her
exquisite rendering of Mozart or Schubert. There was a tenderness in
her which was somehow screened from the world by her sense of
alienation because she was not considered fully Jewish.

It seemed strange to me that she was considered less than Jewish. I
mean, she was a member of the Israeli army and would no doubt

marry a Jewish man and produce more Sabras. However, she had fallen foul of the Jewish kinship system that had enabled Judaism to survive millennia of wars and persecution, a system that deems that only a child born of a Jewish mother is a Jew.

Israel was, for thousands of years, a virtual arena for the warring armies of the Egyptians to the south and the Sumerians, Babylonians and Persians to the North. It seems reasonable, therefore, to assume that the impregnation of Jewish women, forcibly or otherwise, by some members of these conquering armies must have been a fairly common circumstance. It follows then that had the line of descent been through Jewish males, the Hebrews would have disappeared sometime around the time of Nebuchadnezzar. As it is, by virtue of absorbing all external threats to its lineage, it has survived, in spite of the evil attempts to eradicate it. The supreme irony is that a race that is constantly accused of exclusivity possibly has the world's most diverse gene pool!

The truth of that statement can best be seen from an incident that happened when I went to cash some traveller's cheques in a local bank. The cashier, a beautiful middle-aged Indian woman who was wearing an apricot coloured Sari and a Magen David around her neck smiled at me and beckoned me to the counter. I looked at her in astonishment, both at her beauty and her appearance and asked, "Are you really Jewish?" By way of answer she simply smiled and nodded her elegant head. That kind of encounter became a frequent occurrence.

Although only a teenager, Zoah took it upon herself to sort out my confused state of mind, as on my journey I had not only walked among the remains of the Parthenon but I had left behind me a ruin of a relationship. It was during my first meeting with Zoah that I became aware of her uncanny ability to penetrate my thoughts. We were sitting on a path, near a small cluster of Pomegranate trees, when I attempted to open a box of matches to light a cigarette. I managed instead to spill the contents onto the concrete and as I tried to gather them she noticed that I was making a hash of collecting them up and said gently, "You're shy aren't you?"

Now shyness isn't a characteristic that people normally associate with me and yet I suppose that like many people I have trained myself to appear confident. I say 'trained' because I can remember going to the Locarno dance hall and approaching the prettiest girl in sight and asking her to dance, whilst inwardly steeling myself for the inevitable back heel.

Occasionally, I suppose by the law of averages, I would 'cop off', but more importantly the wilfully-sought rejections eventually lent me a Kamikaze-like confidence. The fact is that Zoah, alone of all the women I had known, had homed in on my best-kept secret, but instead of deriding me set out to bring me closer to her. Perhaps she recognised an alienated kindred spirit. I hope all of her days are golden.

My sojourn at Neve Eitan was abruptly curtailed when one day I returned from the cotton fields to find that a Kibbutznik, a woman called Shulie, had, without permission, been searching through all the volunteer's belongings looking for drugs. Although I didn't have any drugs I was just as outraged as the few volunteers who did have dope in their possession and so I decided to head North to Tiberias.

Thus it was that I went to Galilee on a sour note. I understood the need for a militaristic state to keep their youth drug-free if possible, but the whole affair smacked of totalitarianism.

I couldn't settle in my new Kibbutz. In fact, I was there for so short a time that I can't even remember what it was called. All I know is that it wasn't too far from Tiberias, a town that had all the appearance of a major resort, but without the tourists. There were strangers there though, and none so strange as the young American Jew who was a saddle-maker by trade and who had a small horse farm near the Sea of Galilee.

On my last night at the Kibbutz with no name I went for a drink in the town and fell in with the saddle-maker and his wife, who was a Sabra. The American, who was loud and ostentatiously well off, was obviously a source of irritation to the local Sephardic Jews, who were from Morocco and Yemen and therefore poor, because I could see that they observed him with ill-disguised contempt.

As the café filled with youths drinking the local carbonated grape juice the American became drunk and belligerent, informing the world at large that he was a 'champeen wrestler'. His behaviour was obnoxious by any standards, but for a Jew to behave like a Yahoo was something I'd never previously encountered.

Apropos of nothing, an ill-directed glance perhaps, he picked on a local youth, started belittling him and challenged him to a fight. The youth stared stonily at his tormentor but made no move. But the American did make a move, lashing out with his fist at the youth while the youngster was still seated. The youth fell to the ground and I thought it was all over, as did the American, who was laughing unpleasantly and jeering drunkenly at the inert boy until, like a striking Cobra, the youth sprang up on his heels and, with incredible grace and force, head butted his adversary, who promptly collapsed with a badly broken nose and had to be carried away by his deeply mortified and tearful Israeli wife.

Every city in the world likes to think that it invented the head butt, bestowing on such thuggery bravura names as 'the Glasgow kiss' etc, but when that kid unleashed his demonstration of what the Israelis call *Rosh Barosh* or 'head fighting' I couldn't help feeling, as I caught a fleeting glimpse of David and Goliath, that the act of nutting somebody has its origins in antiquity.

Oddly enough, that was the first and only act of violence I witnessed in the cockpit of the Middle East. Perhaps that is why it scorched itself into my memory. By the next day that was all it was, a memory, and I was back in Jerusalem looking up the address of the most beautiful soldier I had ever met. Her name was Noga, the Evening Star, and she was the friendliest girl I knew apart from Zoah. She was member of an army pioneer group known as the *Gareen*, which is Hebrew for 'seed'.

The Gareen was responsible for 'helping' the settlers on the occupied West bank to build fortified homes, which is ironic because Noga was so sweet and emotionally vulnerable. She 'adopted' me and during the course of our lamentably platonic relationship gave me many insights into the social stratifications that riddle Israeli society.

Once, on a visit to Beat Shean, I drew her attention to a gaggle of brightly dressed and vivacious-looking girls walking down the main street. She looked at me with her velvet brown eyes and said disapprovingly, "Chack-Chacks!"

Deeply puzzled and not a little perturbed at her remark, because she was usually so sunny and warm, I asked, "What does Chack-Chack mean?"

Noga explained that certain girls in Israel, known collectively as *Hapoakstim*, the Israeli version of Rockers or Punks, wore wooden clogs or *salops* and the noise they made when they hit the ground, chack-chack, had become associated with them. Her disparaging attitude must have been a consequence of her elite army training.

When I later caught up with her in Jerusalem we had a nice enough evening but it was clear from her demeanour that away from the Kibbutz being seen with a non-Jew was *infra dig*. Nonetheless we parted on good terms and months later I received a letter from her asking me in badly constructed English if I was 'still in life'. I never did find out if she got my reply but yes, my dear Noga, I am still in life. *L'chaim* to you.

My next tryst was with Rivka, the young woman I'd met on my first day in Israel. I'd arranged to meet her as she was going let me stay in a flat she owned in Beersheva. I'd arranged to meet her by the Damascus gate and I was there an age, thinking I'd been stood up, when I asked a man what time it was. Because his English wasn't fluent he pointed to his watch face and I was astonished to see that according to the date I was twenty-four hours early! I decided that I would find a hostel and before long I was sitting in a large room in which there were four beds. The other occupants were a Dutch couple and a very laid-back American. The Dutch couple left and the American, who was called Rick and who hailed from Portland Oregon, suggested we go for a drink.

I was up for that and I took him to my favourite bar in the world, which was located by the Via Dolorosa. There, in full view of a pilgrim staggering beneath the weight of a replica crucifix, we drank

Star lager and listened to the biggest selection of rock n' roll this side of Memphis.

Rick was one of the most amazing human beings I've ever had the pleasure of meeting. He was a truck driver for Coca-Cola and was married to an African American who every year encouraged him to explore a foreign land. The previous year he had traipsed all over West Africa, alone, taking in six countries in six weeks.

As we sat in the dusty street, drinking beer, he reached into his pocket and pulled out what looked like a bundle of fireworks. They were certainly explosive – they were composed of the finest Colombian grass! When I asked him how he got hold of the stuff in Israel he replied that he'd actually brought the joints with him from America! He took no pride in this feat, and that struck me as admirable, but what he was to tell me next was truly worthy of admiration.

It transpired that he'd spent something like eleven hundred dollars getting to Israel and was almost broke, but when I asked what he was going to do he just shrugged and said he would either find a job or simply fly home. It could have been the dope talking, but he seemed so genuinely unconcerned about the future that I found myself once again wondering why it is that while all the Americans I've ever met are so generous and charming, their leaders are, by and large, poltroons.

When I awoke the next morning Rick was already dressed and ready to take the latest steps in his casual odyssey. We shook hands and that was the last I ever saw of him. Travelling is like that, you see a bright star and suddenly it's daybreak.

I eventually met Rivka, but not before a truly remarkable episode took place. I was standing once more by the Damascus gate when I saw a pretty young redhead walking toward me, accompanied by a group of young women. I couldn't believe it, the redhead was a fellow student from Liverpool! I had always fancied her but thought she was too young for me, mature beast that I was. As she drew closer I said, "Hi there!"

You'd have thought from her shocked expression that I'd offered her a dirty postcard, but she recovered her composure long enough to tell me apologetically that she couldn't stop as she was in a desperate hurry to catch up with the main group. Her story was borne out by the anxious expressions on her companion's faces as they all scrutinised their watches. I waved her on with a smile but I couldn't help but reflect on the bizarrely 'English' nature of our encounter. Just then Rivka approached and so saved me from dwelling on it.

I spent the afternoon following Rivka from shop to shop and soon became aware that she was intent on goading the Arab shopkeepers to the point of provocation. This was a side of her that I hadn't envisaged and it wasn't pleasant to watch.

After being ushered out of the umpteenth shop by an irate and frustrated shopkeeper we met a Yemeni art student acquaintance of Rivka's who took us back to meet her family. Her family were extremely pleasant to me as, thanks to John Berger *et al*, I was able to see what their young artist was trying to express.

As for Rivka, she didn't have a clue, or indeed any interest in the girl's work, and seemed almost exasperated with them because the artist so obviously liked me. Perhaps I should have stayed with them, but in the event I went home with Rivka to meet her family and spend the night before going on to Beersheva.

It seems churlish to make adverse comments about my hosts so suffice to say that her mother was a snooty Brit and her father a successful professional who spent the evening denigrating the unemployed Moroccan, Russian and Yemeni Israelis who were a 'drain' on the country's resources. The whole conversation prefigured the Thatcherite era by a year.

The next day I travelled to Beersheva with Rivka and found myself ensconced in a block of apartments that must have been built by the British army before 1948, because they were exact replicas of the tenements in Eldon Street back in Liverpool. It was as if Scotland Road had shifted to the Negev!

A young girlfriend of Rivka's arrived, but by then I was so disenchanted with Rivka that I just wanted to get some sleep and go. Rivka informed me that her friend wasn't staying the night and there seemed to be a hint of a promise, but when the time came for her friend to leave I picked up my bag and stepped out into the street behind her. Rivka's shocked expression accompanied me to the bus terminal. It wasn't her fault entirely, as she probably thought all Brits thought like her mother. Not in Liverpool they didn't!

I have since wondered if Rivka was a self-appointed *agent provocateur*, seeking out possible threats to the state of Israel.

Before too long I was on a bus bumping along a desert road with the splendours of the Negev on all sides. That night, in Eilat, I fell in with some other travellers and decided to spend the night sleeping on the beach. As the heat of the evening dissipated in the dark an arctic chill descended and, ironically, beneath swaying palm trees, I shivered and even my army-issue sleeping bag proved useless. By daybreak I was almost frozen.

By four o'clock in the afternoon that same day I was in Sharm-El-Sheik, the resort town on the Red Sea that figured highly in the origins of the Six Day War. In 1978 Sharm-El-Sheik was still in Israeli hands. It consisted of a few gazebos, a scuba diving shop, a grocery store and a restaurant. The beach was heaven, and because the Israelis had set an enormous penalty for anyone caught degrading the coral the underwater scenery was unbelievable.

I had been told not touch anything while underwater and it was just as well that for once I did as I was advised, because while diving one day I was taken by the beauty of a feathery-finned fish swimming nearby. Just as I was about to stroke it the warning words rang in my ears and I smartly withdrew my hand. Later that day a local fisherman pointed out to me that I had narrowly avoided death as the fish in question was a Lion Fish, whose fins are deadly poisonous.

I spent a week recuperating on the golden sands, observing the ladies by day and the frenetic worship of the orthodox at sunrise. The beach was a garment-free zone and so a nice time was had by all present, although I doubt the orthodox believers saw it that way.

Funny old place, Israel.

On the evening of my departure I was walking the beach and found a pair of goggles which I just dumped in my bag, never dreaming that they would play any further part in my life.

The following morning I arrived back in Eilat and since I had no intention of freezing overnight I thought I'd just have a quick dip before hitching a ride to Tel Aviv and the flight home. As I was having a mandatory pre-dip cigarette I noticed a little man sitting next to me and indicating that he wanted a light for his cigarette.

He was wearing what looked like army fatigues and he had the engaging manner of a born rogue. That is exactly what he was. He was from Georgia, one of a batch of Jews released from the Soviet Union after pressure from the West. Apparently the Georgians thought it would be fun to include some of the rarest Jews in the world in the quota. They were rarities because they drank, fornicated, stole and fought with knives. In short they were less than kosher. However, they did have a strong sense of humour and I was quite enjoying the company of the Georgian mini gangster.

When the heat of the sun drove me back into the sea I thought I would take the last opportunity to use the goggles I'd found, and as I was swimming underwater in the crowded sea I was startled to see a gold chain lying on the seabed. I dived deeper and picked it up. Now as I had no pockets I had to take it to the rascal who was looking after my clothes and ask him to stand guard over my treasure.

I then dived again and found another, heavier, chain complete with Magen David! The rascal accepted it without any other comment than a smile and I dived again. This time I found a bundle of Israeli Liras! I decided then to call it a day. When I returned to my clothes the rascal was snoring under the brim of his forage cap.

As he gave me back possession of my booty I mentioned that I needed to hitch a ride to Tel Aviv, and that was when the Georgian revealed his favoured mode of travel, because as we were walking along the beach road he started testing the door handles of the cars. He explained that he only ever used the cars he borrowed to get from A to B and then would leave them in a prominent place, undamaged. Even though I realised I was in the company of a gentleman thief, I was quite relieved when he turned his sharp little face to me and ruefully indicated that the keys he had were not the right kind. I didn't fancy spending time in an Israeli nick.

I eventually got a lift to Tel Aviv and found that I was short of the airport tax. With only hours to spare before my flight I sold one of the chains and so was able to fly to Athens. After another arduous coach trip across Europe I found myself back home in Liverpool. Not ex- actly the Promised Land, but it was my land of milk and honeys – and they were beautiful to behold!

33. Help!

When I was about twenty-four my life changed forever. I had left school when I was fifteen and dabbled in various jobs until I joined the Merchant Navy, and then later, when I opted for a life on shore, I found myself unqualified for anything more than drifting from one unskilled job to another.

I had drifted into marriage without ever opening my mouth to question what I was doing. Worse, my mute acceptance of the situation was hardly a novel experience, as I had simply not realised that I had a voice of my own. Like so many working-class people at that time, I knew my place. At least, I thought I did.

At that time authority figures terrified me, just as they had my Grandmother, Rose Anne. Conversing with a doctor, a policeman or an employer invariably caused my voice to trail away into breathlessness and induced a tightening of my chest. I also nurtured a free-floating anxiety complex that would alight on almost any issue at any time, anchoring itself with the ballast of past failures. If I found myself in a mental conflict with any of society's mores I couldn't cope with the pressure and I always sought solutions from the received wisdom of the law, religion or that rare commodity, common sense. I was almost the perfect citizen.

Four years after completing a terribly inadequate government training scheme I tried desperately to become a *bona fide* engineer, which meant overcoming the prejudices of an entrenched apprenticeship system whereby people who hadn't spent five years as a general factotum-cum-teaboy were deemed *persona non grata*.

A friend of mine, Eddie, who obviously had little time for the hidebound attitudes of his fellow fitters, arranged for me to join the main engineering union, the AEU, with the aim of securing regular employment as the possession of union card would, *a priori*, serve as proof that I was a time-served apprentice.

The drawback in all this was that I had to present shaky proof of my apprenticeship; in other words, forgery. It worked, in the short term, I got a job, but after about a week of my Catholic conscience nagging away at me one day at work I began to cry. I told the boss I couldn't continue and left the works – Gilchrist's – with a view to seeing my doctor.

When I arrived at Dr Wolfman's surgery my face was streaked with tears and grime. Lennie calmly sucked on his pipe as I incoherently tried to explain my problem. I found out years later that he had seen it all coming, but he could no more have prevented it than he could have stopped a runaway train.

He persuaded me to go voluntarily to Sefton General and seek treatment for depression. So I went home and told my family that I was just going to the hospital for a few days. En route to the hospital I called at a friend's house and cancelled some arrangements that I had made to distribute political tracts that weekend.

When I arrived at the hospital a nurse called Karim asked me to have a warm bath and to take an anti-depressant pill. His sorrowful brown eyes were the last normal sight that I was to recognise for the next four months. The date was 6th June 1969. My own personal D-Day had dawned.

I won't dwell too much on my sojourn other than to say I experienced enough ECT to transform my mind into a unified field, and also received the odd beating from someone ironically described as a 'male nurse'. Strange as it may seem, I value that life experience above all others, because it was at that time that my world had collapsed in an earthquake recorded only by my personal psychic seismometer; yet I had been given a chance to rebuild my life, to my own rough specifications.

One day above the others is, perhaps, worth a mention. I had been in the garden, admiring the roses which were wet with rain and mantled with iridescent diamond points of liquid light. A nurse called me inside to see a psychiatrist, with regard to my going on home leave for the first time.

The consultant psychiatrist, who had been observing me from a window and who had Doctor Wolfman in attendance, sat opposite me and began asking questions. I was alright until he flummoxed me by asking what the roses symbolised to me. I was aghast. I didn't really know what the term 'symbolised' meant and so I mumbled some nonsensical reply.

He looked gravely at me and informed me that my response indicated that I wasn't yet fit to go home. Dr Wolfman looked dismayed, but as a GP he was subordinate to the consultant and so I imagine he had no choice but to agree. I left the consulting room and stood in the corridor, crying silently, whereupon I was approached by a West Indian nurse who gently asked me why I was upset.

I told him about the roses and the question that had left me baffled and then, for the first time in my life, my rage reached deep inside me and I found my voice. Still sobbing, and within hearing distance of the consultant, I roared, "He wouldn't have asked what it symbolised if I'd been looking at a fucking machine gun!"

Thirty minutes later the West Indian nurse approached me and with a beaming smile informed me that I could go home after all.

34. He Ain't Heavy, He's My Brother

Back in the seventies, when pool was king, I used to drink in the boozy triangle of Ye Olde Cracke, the Philharmonic and O'Connor's Tavern. The appeal of the latter revolved around its pool table, and the chance of playing against some of the most accomplished players of the game I'd ever seen. These included Phil Lewis and Terry 'The Hat'. Terry was a window cleaner, with a wit as dry as his chamois leather. I recall one afternoon when I was playing against Phil Lewis, a Liverpudlian of African descent who was possessed of an implacable calm and quiet authority. Terry was leaning against the bar doing the *Daily Mirror* crossword, when he looked up and mused aloud, "Three letter word meaning, to complete."

He had barely completed the sentence when a chorus of pedants, me included, shouted, "End!"

Like the true artist that he was, 'The Hat' waited for the sound of the eager helpers to die down, and, with a look of unadulterated triumph, said, "Thanks fellers."

Our faces were as red as the balls on the table.

One of the would-be code-crackers was Arthur Ballard, a man of such stature that even though he was in his late seventies he could deter the attention of aggressively-inclined younger men by his sheer physical presence. He had, prior to his becoming an artist, been a successful heavyweight boxer in the army. I knew none of this when he invited me to partner him against two of the pool-playing elite. All I was aware of was that he wasn't playing for fun. He enjoyed winning, which made it all the more surprising that he struck up a friendship with me, because on that day I was responsible for a series of resounding defeats.

The fact is, that when I encountered him, Arthur was deeply depressed and, probably for the first time in his eventful life, learning to accept losing. The problem was that his younger second wife had left him for another man. At the time Arthur was struggling to come to terms with the fact that the days when such a problem might have been solved by the discarding of jackets and an invitation to 'go outside' were long gone. By the seventies such behaviour was considered un-cool and Arthur, bless him, came from an age when Liverpool was so un-cool that people would make day trips from Hell to bask in the heat.

I don't know why, but over the course of the next year or so he confided in me. Perhaps he saw me as somehow vulnerable and wanted to 'wise me up'. Whatever the reason I am glad he befriended me, because when he wasn't in one of his dark moods of morose reflection he was a source of some of the funniest stories I've ever had the pleasure of hearing.

He had a friend called Kit Wright, a poet of some renown, who because he was kindly giant of a man used to tolerate having to listen to my own efforts at poetry. I still remember, with a twinge of embarrassment, trying to interest him in one of my verses while we – Arthur, Kit and myself – were in the Gladray club. This mithering took place where a particularly beautiful stripper was being *paid* to be the centre of attraction!

One night I met Arthur in 'Streets', which was one of the more salubrious bars that had sprung up during the renaissance of the Hardman Street area. He was with his young daughter, who looked about 17. As we sat at the stripped-pine tables sipping lager, Arthur bestowed a story on me that until now has been a private treasure.

In 1947 Arthur and his young bride, who later died of cancer, leaving the great bear of a man bereft, were touring South Wales in the company of an army captain. I can still see the look of distaste on Arthur's face as he recounted how the captain was later discharged from the army because he would eat nothing at all except chipped potatoes!

It was fairly obvious from Arthur's tone that the captain was some kind of khaki-clad albatross who had tagged on to the couple without any encouragement. So it is easy to imagine Arthur's mortification when, on entering a pub in Larne, the captain spotted Dylan Thomas and his wife Caitlin sitting in a side bar and insisted on dragging

Arthur over to meet the legendary poet, introducing him as 'a well known Liverpool artist'.

Now in 1947, as Arthur ruefully remarked to me, he was "less recognizable than Whistler's mother" and he stumbled back to the main bar through a haze of embarrassment. Later, when he had sampled a goodly share of Welsh ale, he went to the toilet. As he was relieving himself Arthur was startled by what he described as "a shrill voice" pipe up behind him.

"Alright boy? I was in Liverpool during the war. Loved it."

Arthur told me that when he turned to see who was addressing him and recognized the diminutive Welsh genius, he almost pissed on his own legs. Thomas, ignoring Arthur's poor aim, went on.

"Listen son… if you can get rid of that army pillock, me and Caitlin will be in here tomorrow. Alright?"

It *was* all right, and the following day Arthur and his wife shared a great time with Dylan and Caitlin, presumably while the captain was looking for a chip shop.

I last saw Arthur just before he went live in Chelsea. I was worried about his diet of pub sandwiches and so invited him to Sunday lunch. Now you would think that as the son of a butcher and a sometime navy cook that I would have managed to get the lamb right. Not so. I can still hear the click of his dentures as Arthur struggled manfully to overcome what was probably the toughest opponent of his life. He made no complaint, but all of a sudden told me that he had to go and see a friend about something. In all probability he was, like the long departed captain, looking for a chippie. Sorry Arthur.

Arthur was singled out for praise by John Lennon because the ex-boxer had put his considerable weight behind the Beatle when art college administrators sought to have Lennon thrown out. He also prevented the expulsion of Bill Harry, who later founded the *Merseybeat* newspaper. All in all, Arthur made a massive contribution to the Liverpool scene. He was a real knockout.

35. Li'l Old Wine Drinker Me

"Das Leben ist viel zu kurz, um schlechten Wein zu trinken!"
(Life is much too short to drink bad wines!)
Bernulf Bruckner

I have something in common with Dean Martin; neither of us was born in Italy. However, apart from that shared circumstance, we were complete opposites. He could sing, was devilishly good-looking and allegedly liked wine.

While not exactly tone deaf, I am hard of hearing in a musical sense. In the past I have often misheard lyrics and been embarrassed when someone has pointed out, between snorts of laughter, that while I was singing, "You did the bumps of time in your prime didn't you…" Bob Dylan was singing, probably correctly, "You threw the bums a dime in your prime didn't you…"

The quality of some of those early pressings was garbage, that's all I can say!

Whereas Mr Martin's genetic inheritance meant that he looked like a Roman god, my DNA guaranteed that I was two horns short of resembling a depressed Triceratops – and to think they called *him* Dino!

It was, however, his alleged fondness for vino that distinguished me from Dino. You see my early experiences of wine were quite awful. My first vintners, Bent's Brewery, Yates's Wine and Doctor Penfold's, the cheap scourge of Australians in the 60s, aimed not so much for the palate as the pocket, and their cheap wines, which promoted a strange sense of wellbeing in others, was to me an instant emetic. Indeed, you could say that my relationship with the grape was not so much bacchanalian as bulimic.

Once, during a bout of post-prandial retching, I couldn't help re-calling one of the signs that festooned the walls of the Wine Lodges:

'Wine is a good servant but a bad master.'

There must have been kinder masters in the gladiator trade!

Who can forget Yates's Wine Lodges, the home of Australian White wine, 'Bismarck Leading Port' and migraine-strength hangovers? Who can remember, with any clarity, those distant days before the Australian wine industry eventually produced a wine that was light years from its beloved jungle-juice?

These modern wines bear such names as 'Jacob's Creek', but to me, delicate sixties flower-child that I was, 'Aussie White' tasted rather more like the contents of almost any creek, after a team of thirsty sheep shearers had drunk dry the local pub and then relieved themselves into said waterway. It was, no doubt, the fruity content of the wine that impelled people to drink it mixed with mineral water.

I recall the time aboard the *Empress of England*, when a diner, unsure of wine etiquette, asked a bedraggled and hungover steward,

"What is the best accompaniment to white wine?"

"Lemonade!" was the snarled reply.

All in all, I was a novice in the world of wine bibbing, and my naiveté led to one of my most embarrassing experiences.

It was in the late seventies, when wine bars were springing up all over Liverpool and Beaujolais was the new Bitter. I had been invited to a meal by one of my tutors. He was a Canadian, but exuded an air of culture more in tune with Paris than Liverpool. He liked Jacques Lacan's poetry, which was often interspersed with algebraic symbols rather than words. Talk about impenetrable!

Anyway, I decided that I had to buy a decent bottle of wine if I wasn't to look like a complete galoot, so I paid a visit to real wine merchant, somewhere in Lord Street. I selected an expensive German white wine; guided by an article I had read averring that the best wines did not carry labels with pictures on them – you know the type, nuns, towers and Portuguese sailing ships – and so I was quite taken by the simple Gothic lettering that read 'Niersteiner'.

My girlfriend and I arrived in good time for the meal and I handed my host the bottle. He glanced at the label and smiled encouragingly.

Forget the exams I thought, I'm halfway to passing the wine test. That was the high point of the evening.

The main course, lovingly prepared, was Pork in an anchovy-based sauce. Now there are certain periods when women are, well… *off* fishy things. As I caught sight of my girl's face, which by then was paler than the napkins, I realised that it was one of those days.

She struggled through the meal and we were both relieved when mein host suggested we retire to the living room and have a drink. He brought gin and tonics for the women and then went to the kitchen to bring some wine for him and me to sample. I was a little anxious in case I had bought a duff wine, although, on reflection, even if I'd bought a bottle of Aussie White, sixties vintage, it would not have been as big a *faux pas* as his *Porc la Mer*. That said, I was a bundle of nerves as he returned with two glasses of the diamond-clear wine.

He sat down and sipped delicately from his glass while I took a large gulp from mine. I instantly experienced stabbing pains in the region of my right eye and simultaneously my incipient ulcer kicked in like a wild thing when the vinegar, cunningly disguised as wine, hit my stomach. Enveloped in shame at my gauche purchase I blurted,

"Jesus Christ! Sorry about this German crap! It's bloody awful!"

My tutor looked at me, over his glasses, and said, "Actually, it's a Muscadet".

He hadn't opened mine.

The rest of the evening passed slowly, amid a blur of shame and boredom. I was even relieved when my tutor's wife, who wasn't listening unless you were talking Shakespeare, fell asleep.

Perhaps anchovies have a soporific effect, or it might simply have been a case of *in vino veritas,* as she had grown bored with the company of a graceless Scouser who didn't know how to drink neat acid and maintain a smile on his stinging lips.

To this day I don't know how my Niersteiner tasted, but I am sure of one thing, and that is I'll never touch Muscadet again!

36. So this is Christmas

I have often wondered how so many paradoxical ideas manage to insinuate their contradictory presence into our minds. Offhand, for instance, I can think of the notion that justice is blind and impartial – this in spite of the fact that in the last quarter of a century at least two American presidents have openly flouted the law and got away with it, while murderous tyrants such as Stalin and Mao died peacefully in their beds. I suppose that at some stage in our past someone must have been powerful enough to have Justice brutally blinded, before whispering in the lady's ear, "Any more nonsense about fair play and I'll have your throat cut too!"

The figure most responsible for our general gullibility is also the most loved myth on the planet. This icon of generosity was the first to gain entry into the virgin territory of our infant minds, while driving a sleigh pulled by a team of improbably named reindeers called Rudolph, Dasher, Donner and Blitzen. Uttering a hearty, "Ho! Ho! Ho!" St Nicholas smashed through the crystal gates that guarded our green innocence, and in so doing created a permanent thoroughfare for all of the subsequent conveyors of nonsensical ideas.

As each nonsense-filled juggernaut rolled unimpeded into our consciousness, the warehouses of our minds were inexorably filled with equally paradoxical ideas. The misinformation highway was wide open and there were already tailbacks a million miles long. By the time I was five, the idea of a virgin birth was as easy to accept as the Holy Trinity. Nonetheless, this is hindsight and I never questioned Santa's existence. Nor did I question the fact that his enforced lay off for three hundred and sixty four days of the year meant that he was probably so broke that he couldn't afford to have his beard trimmed, much less purchase toys for every kid on the planet!

Of course the modern Santa is a myth within a myth. The original was always depicted as a lean forester clad in green boots and fur pelts, but in 1931 Coca-Cola introduce their version of Santa, a fat man togged out in the red and white house colours of the fizzy drink brigade. Within a decade the older, leaner, Santa had been replaced by a man with a figure that modern Americans would instantly recognise, given the level of obesity that prevails in the land of the fried chicken.

I was in thrall to the myth. On Christmas Eve my mother only had to tell me that Santa was in the house next door and for one night of the year I would instantly fall asleep for fear that he might by-pass the bedroom of a child who was still awake. Given that I am a lifelong insomniac perhaps his greatest gift to me was that annual night of easy slumber.

It is said that it is better to give than to receive and my mother epitomised that sentiment because her excitement was if anything greater than mine. I distinctly remember one year being woken by a gentle poke in the ribs. I stared around in the pre-dawn gloom and followed my mother's gaze to the corner of the room where stood my heart's desire, a gleaming Hercules bicycle. She hadn't been able to contain herself. I learned to ride it that very day with the help of two friends who simply pushed me at speed up the road before letting me go.

Now in those days the only vehicles that made regular visits to our road were Mr Critchley's Ice Cream Van and various horse drawn carts carrying either coal, rags and bones or domestic refuse. My mother's fears for me, however, ensured that she perceived things otherwise. To her, the roads were little more than extensions to Brand's Hatch and within weeks had persuaded me to let her return the gleaming bicycle to the shop whence it came.

Ten moths later she was so depressed I was sent to live at my Aunt Alice's. As she lived on a farm the loss of my bike was not as noticeable, and even that was nowhere near as noticeable as the temporary loss of my mother. I spent that Christmas day with my father's family, but he was on yet another voyage, and I was all at sea.

"I saw four ships a sailing..."

37. Nick Nack Paddy Whack

I can remember when English pubs used to smell of old-fashioned beer. That was when the mere act of passing a saloon bar on a hot day was to find oneself assailed by the reek of stale ale. Depending on the state of one's stomach, that warm fruity blast of alcohol could be either titillating or debilitating. Nowadays many pubs are furnished with electric fans that simply swallow the boozy bouquet in one gulp, leaving the air as sanitised of aroma as a pint of chilled lager.

Drinkers in post-war Liverpool had the choice of imbibing beers produced by a handful of breweries: Higsons, Walkers, Bents and Threlfals, who between them exercised a virtual monopoly. Not that it mattered much to the beery brotherhood, who rarely exercised their limited choice. Instead, they usually chose to engage a particular beer, and often stayed married to it for life. Taking up beer drinking in England is a rite of passage on a par with marriage, the difference being that while men often leave their wives for the delights of the bar, very few ever make the reverse trip.

I can still recall that the fierce parochial arguments concerning the relative merits of Bent's bitter over, say, Walkers – conducted with the same fervour that Parisian café society debated existentialism – left me cold, as bitter simply gave me heartburn. I never really got into drinking until the eighties, when the lager revolution dispatched the enfeebled aristocrats of English beer to the guillotine.

As late as 1970 there were bars in Liverpool that barred entry to women and there were many more which hosted 'men-only' rooms. I don't think the ladies were missing too much, as the landlords made hardly any concessions to the women. For instance, all of the glasses in the pubs were designed for men. If a woman wanted a gin and tonic she usually received it in whisky glass so small that after the tonic had been added the liquid level was such that the addition of ice, had such a decadent item even existed, would have been impossible.

By the seventies improvements were being made, and although the spirit glasses were still only designed to hold a double whisky, paper cocktail umbrellas were being unfurled even in the driest of pubs. Almost surreptitiously the French and Germans achieved, in the shape of wine and lager, the first successful invasion of England in a thousand years. The most successful of the early wine bar/bistros in Liverpool was a huge place called Kirkland's, which had once been a bakery by appointment to Her Majesty Queen Mary.

In a thrice, English cottage loaves had been usurped by baguettes and, overnight, women drinkers were *de rigeur*. The bar of Kirkland's was always strewn with gorgeous wine-bibbing women. The ambience of the place was a cocktail of Gallic flair and Scouse humour. Unlike the Norman Conquest, the continental dominance of England's watering holes was not to endure, as the remnants of alcohol's *ancien regime* were planning a counter assault on the alien viticulture.

Although created by promotional consultants catering to the needs of the English market, the next wave of invaders arrived bearing the insignia of the Emerald Isle as 'theme pubs' whose motifs consisted of Shamrock and Guinness, burgeoned almost overnight. The speed of the assault was such that it felt as if old Liverpool had never been. Pubs that had once borne mundane English names were now called 'Durty Nellie's' or 'Scruffy Murphy's' as, despite the English breweries' propagation of all things Irish, the old racial hatreds relentlessly insinuated themselves into the mock and mocking nomenclature.

I mean, in Ireland, who would dream of trying to entice patrons into a pub which sounded like it might well be playing *mein host* to the bubonic plague?

The truth of the idea that ideology creates its own history was never made more clear than in the creation of these sham shrines to shamrock, which were transformed so hastily that some of the three-legged cooking pots, those signifiers of 'Irishness' which festooned the mock beams, still bore the labels, 'Made in Taiwan'. I was recently drinking in an Irish theme pub called 'The Flute and Firkin' in Hardman Street; it is a huge barn of a place and as I listened to the newly-arrived students extolling the authenticity of their surroundings I wanted to scream at them, "Ten years ago this was a Ford dealer's!" Instead I allowed my mind to drift back to the eighties and the four wonderful summers I spent in the company of my wife on the West Coast of Ireland.

She was born in Ireland but at the age of two had moved with her family to Southern England and so speaks with a pure home-counties accent, which serves to underline my belief that the geographical location of one's birth is immaterial – it is the language we inherit which bestows on us our cultural identity. I mention this because the only adverse encounter I ever had in a real Irish pub occurred in County Sligo when, on our entry into the bar, a local Yahoo burst into rendition of "These are my mountains", with the obvious intent of putting two British interlopers in their place. He was sorry he did, because my wife, her beautifully modulated voice dripping with venom, looked him straight in his eyes and spat, "They used to be mine too, but I wanted to see what life was like without the smell of pigs!" The one-man-choir blinked and spent the rest of the time we were there staring at the bland head of his Guinness.

That incident apart, I have only the fondest memories of Irish pubs. I loved the casual utility of those small pubs that doubled as grocers or post offices, where the genial host would serve you beer and then bacon rashers lovingly wrapped in brown paper and string parcels. I remember too the pub where we bought butter and the lady behind the bar wrapped it in a cabbage leaf to keep it cool.

Of course, not all Irish watering holes are small and folksy. One of the best times I ever had was when my wife's cousins took us to a country club in Tralee. I suppose it was the Irish love of dancing that helped determine the design of the place, because there was a huge dance floor and a stage where the band played. I was in good fettle, having had a fair amount of whisky.

The combination of Bushmills and Guinness was enough to keep me dancing all night. Then came the moment I will never forget.

The band struck up with a lively tune and I immediately went into my Saturday Night Fever routine and just as I was emerging from a Travolta-esque twirl I noticed that everybody was standing stock-still and singing. It was the national anthem! Everybody laughed at my choreography for clowns and simply put it down to the fact that I was a Brit. Imagine boogying to the Stars and Stripes in Texas! I can hear the cocking of hammers from here.

Quite the most amazing experience we shared was when we were camping near the town of Newcastle West. We had been drawn to the town because of the beautiful river that flowed alongside the main road. At that point the river was very shallow and a mass of shimmering ripples as it bored and bounced over the numerous rocks. Many species of ducks abounded. When we went into the local pub we were made to feel thoroughly welcome by the landlord and landlady. They had only moved back to Ireland that very year, after having spent thirty years in London. They invited us to attend what they called 'the Duck Dance'.

At first I thought it was a gathering of Chuck Berry enthusiasts, as he was the only person I knew of who performed a dance by that name. However, it transpired that the Landlord and his wife were raising funds to ensure the safety and maintenance of the ducks we had seen thriving on the river. We agreed, went back to the tent to put on our best duds and before long were back in the pub that was by now a heaving throng of drinkers.

There was a darts competition and the entrance fee was fifty pence, with the winning pair taking all. Now I don't know whether it was the fact that we were camping in a country where it rains so often that it is the only place on earth where being born with webbed feet is not considered to be a disability, or that we simply looked needy, but the landlady did her best to help us win the cash prize by pairing us with the two best darts players in the pub. Needless to say we lost badly, as my skill with a dart is only surpassed by my expertise with a croquet mallet and my lady had never played in her life.

At about eleven o'clock everybody went to a local hall where there was laid out the most stupendous array of food I've ever seen. There was everything from chicken wings to beef sandwiches, and, ironically, confit of duck! I have never seen so much food and drink put away as that night. The party was still going on at two in the morning when the landlady asked us if we'd like to go back to the pub for a 'stay behind'! At five in the morning I was blowing for tugs to tow me back to the tent but mein hosts insisted that we stay in their spare bedroom. I was so grateful, as our tent was not only likely to be damp and wholly uninviting, but it was at least a mile away!

As I dragged myself back to the reality of the 'Flute and Firkin' I saw two Japanese tourists tucking into chicken Madras and rice. 'How very cosmopolitan,' I thought, and then wondered if it would be possible to find fish and chips in Tokyo. I don't think so, because the Japanese are more resistant to alien cultural forms than us. As I was observing the Japanese tourists, one of them placed on the table a wireless laptop computer and began to dial into the internet, no doubt checking his e-mails in Kyoto. 'Clever enough to do that,' I thought, 'but not smart enough to realise that you are being ripped off by an ad-man's version of England'. Or maybe that's what he was writing home about!

> *Dear Mamasan,*
> *Please buy up all the old Samurai gear you can get your hands on as I am opening a bar called 'The Mikado' in Liverpool. Brits love all that imitation stuff.*
> *Yours truly*
> *Yoki*

I suppose Marshal Mcluhan was right, the world is a global village but the problem is that so many of us are being treated as global village idiots.

38. Black Velvet

Until my mother re-married the joys of a holiday had been restricted to day trips to New Brighton and not much beyond. My stepfather's only aim in life was to make my mother happy and so it was that within a year of their meeting I found myself on board a ship called the *Mona's Isle* headed for Douglas on the Isle of Man.

It was May, and the silver grey of the Irish Sea mirrored the mercurial sheen of the leaden sky. My stepfather Jimmy always took his holidays in May to avoid the headlong rush to Britain's windswept beaches and to take advantage of lower accommodation prices. He was a generous man but only a butcher's shop manager and not exactly flush with money. Nonetheless, I was soon ensconced in a large boarding house by the sea; the first time I had ever experienced eating in a large dining room *and* having a choice of cereals.

Later that day we went for a walk along the promenade, where I played slot machines while my mum and dad had a drink in the pub next door. That would be the pattern of that and any subsequent holidays, because there is only one thing worse than a British seaside holiday, and that's a British seaside holiday out of season.

There were very few facilities for a grumpy thirteen-year-old and so I found myself eschewing coach trips around the island in favour of mooching about the arcades while my parents took in the awesome wonders of the water wheel at Laxey or made wishes crossing the famed Fairy Bridge. I have a photograph of Jimmy and myself in which my face is partially obscured by a large chewing gum bubble. I wouldn't even co-operate for a normal photo, so you could say that I was the Moaner of Mona's Isle.

My overriding memory of that holiday was of going fishing on a real boat. Actually, it wasn't really fishing because we simply baited lines of hooks with bits of herring and lobbed them over the side on the voyage out. On the return journey the lines were hauled on board by hand and any fish that had been lured by the bunches of feathers, which looked as if they had started life inside a pillow, were dragged aboard. The catch was invariably something called Pollack, a grey, uninteresting and largely unappetising fish that apparently liked to hang about feeding at the mouth of the sewage discharge pipes.

I took my share back to the hotel, thinking that the cats would welcome them, but the look on the face of the landlady gave to the world the first example of frozen Pollacks. I can still feel the chill.

The following year we went on another holiday, of which I have fonder memories. This time we had no need to develop sea legs or pack any of the sea-sickness pills we had ferried to and from the Isle of Man, as we were going to Wales.

The journey began at Edge Lane, which was the Liverpool depot of the Crosville bus company.[5] We piled our luggage where we could and set off, and it seemed very much like those Latin American buses which convey farmers and their produce to market. The only thing missing was a crate or two of live chickens. Perhaps they don't practice voodoo in Aberystwyth.

After about two hours of chugging along tortuous Welsh roads (this journey took place long before the building of the wide coastal roads) we reached our destination, Dyserth, a small place whose claim to fame lay in its proximity to a rather pretty, albeit small, waterfall. We had rented a house for a week but the owner was somewhat remiss in meeting us and so we had to wait an hour before she turned up.

I should reveal that by then our family had an addition, a baby boy called Stephen, and my mother was not best pleased at having to wait in the open with her precious cargo exposed to the cold air of the hills. When the woman did arrive she showed us around the house, opening cupboards and doors for us to inspect, but there was one room that she studiously ignored. My mother taxed her about it and she revealed that the room was off limits. Now my mother had just

---

[5] Crosville, with its delightful destinations, Prestatyn, Rhyl, Llandudno etc, has long gone, but in 1959 it was a thriving service connecting Merseyside to the rural charm of North Wales.

waited in the cold, fondly cradling her newborn, and had also paid to rent a complete house, not a selection of rooms. The woman's bizarre injunction only served to make my mother determined to find out what went on behind the green door. The landlady's head had hardly bobbed down the hill out of sight before the 'No trespassing' sign had been metaphorically torn down and we were inside the holy of holies.

The sight of a veritable mountain of cigarette coupons stunned us. Bundle on bundle of prize-redeemable coupons, all bound by rubber bands, tumbled about our feet. There were so many that they could have been used to exchange for a car if such a prize had existed!

Apparently the previous occupant had operated some kind of scam, quite what we never found out, but I do know that a few weeks after we got home to Liverpool the Royal Mail service delivered a baby tri-cycle for my baby brother, courtesy of W.D. and H.O. Wills. That was the only thing the tobacco giants ever gave us, apart from chronic coughs.

The next day I went into lone-wolf mode and prowled around the village, where I met a young lady who was, in fact, related to the guardian of the royal treasure. In the time it takes to say hello I managed to make a fool of myself. I asked the dark-eyed beauty how long she had lived in Dyserth, which I pronounced 'Dye-serth'. She collapsed laughing and informed me that it was pronounced 'Dizzerth'. Oh *cariad* how could you! Mortified, I fled, following the signpost for the waterfall.

Sadly, there's not a lot you can do with a small waterfall really, apart from avoid the spray, and so I soon found myself walking past the local pub. Now I was only fourteen, and I looked even younger, but I decided to try my hand... To my surprise, the landlord served me a pint of 'black velvet' – Guinness and cider mixed – a drink that I had heard was very much in vogue, and so I had my first ever drink in a pub.

I went home bathed in a mild alcoholic haze and, finding nobody there, switched on the radio. The sombre tones of a newsreader informed the world and me that comrade Kruschev had boasted that the Soviet's H-bombs would, if necessary, sink Britain as if it were an aircraft carrier. Now, to a leftward-leaning boy, this was not only a horrific prospect but also a betrayal. As my eyes alighted on my baby brother's clothes, which were hanging from a wooden airer, I wondered what his chances were of reaching his teens in that crazy world, and I experienced the most intense feeling of melancholy I had ever known. I suppose it was in Dyserth that I adopted my anti-nuclear views, which I have held ever since, and so despite being gently ridiculed by a Celtic princess I came away from that holiday older and wiser.

The following day I was back in the warm confines of the pub, where mein Welsh host cheerfully handed me another glass of foaming Black Velvet. I noticed a young couple playing darts and sidled up to them, hoping that the man would ask me to play, as it was obvious that he could throw a mean arrow, whereas his lady was a near lethal liability – every dart she threw bounced back from the board with the snarling unpredictability of a Blue Streak, that singularly useless British guided missile. Sure enough the young Irishman, who was on honeymoon, invited me to play. I wasn't that much better than his bride, but at least my darts took root in the board and the only eye I endangered belonged to the bull!

Later that afternoon I blithely accompanied the couple on a walk along the river that was the source of the falls. To this day I don't why they didn't ask me to find some other, less involved companions. I mean, they were on their honeymoon and being Irish would hardly have been blasé about their love life! Instead, every day for the rest of the week they would share a drink and the dartboard with me, before embarking on another walk.

Horst Jankowski once wrote a song called 'A Walk in the Black Forest'. I think I should have written one called 'A Walk in the Gooseberry Bushes'! I can only hope that the lovely couple had a long and fruitful relationship.

Quite the most hilarious consequence occurred on the day of our departure. As the taxi passed the pub, in which my parents had never set foot, the Landlord, who was taking the air, spotted me and gave me a genial wave. My parents looked at each other bemusedly while I just 'copped a deaf un' and stared into the distance.

The following year I was working and missed the annual holiday; in any case I was soon to be embarking on a career in the Merchant Navy. You can take the word 'career' in this case in its alternative meaning – 'out of control and heading downhill'.

39. Tweedle-Dee & Tweedle-Dum

My maternal uncles were non-identical twins. In fact they shared hardly any discernible characteristics. One was taller than the other and altogether bulkier. Even their personalities were at odds, as one was probably the role model for Grumpy, the irascible dwarf who shared a house with Snow White, while the other was altogether happy. Having only known this type of twinning, it came as a complete surprise to me that there were also identical siblings.

My introduction to the phenomenon of zygotic twins happened one summer during one of our periodical returns to our own home, an event that sometimes occurred when my mother couldn't find an alternative place to escape from her unhappy bonds of matrimony. The twins in question lived just around the corner from our house. They were identical in all respects. Both shared the same compact muscularity and even their quiet smiling personalities were mirrors of their good nature.

It goes without saying that their easy-going ways were ruthlessly exploited. I particularly remember a game we used to play in my front garden that was loosely based on the exploits of Robert Taylor's incarnation of the Saxon hero, Ivanhoe. Our version of a medieval jousting tournament was to ride at full tilt on somebody's shoulders and attempt to wrestle our opponent to the grass. The prime mounts for this game of rough and tumble were the muscular and ever willing twins, who galloped themselves silly all day long while we knights served King Richard from the comfort of their shoulders.

As that summer, and its incipient rains, wore on, so the grass in our garden wore ever more thin until even the indefatigable twins were finding the heavy going something of a handicap, yet not once did they achieve the status of knighthood. The only spurs they acquired were the energetic heels of their Saxon overlords and the occasional sticky aniseed ball. The reason for their permanent roles as urban steeds was twofold. On the one hand they were by far the finest warhorses in the street, while on the other hand they were notoriously averse to the demands of personal hygiene, and, of course, their equestrian exertions greatly exacerbated their seasonal ripeness. The latter circumstance ensured that only those of our knightly retinue who suffered from chronic sinusitis would willingly allow the twins to straddle their shoulders, and even then the nasally challenged only ever tried it once.

My next encounter with twins came when my mother decided it was time to flit the castle and take up residence with my Great Aunt Alice, who lived in Kirkdale. So once more I had to attend another strange school, St John's Primary.

The school stands out in my memory because, of all the educational establishments I have known, its architecture summed up the Victorians' attitude to working-class children to a tee. You see, the playground was on the bloody roof! Now I don't want you to imagine that we infants were all roped together and supplied with crampons along with our free milk. It was a flat roof, with a wrought iron railing around the perimeter.

Now, as you will readily acknowledge, our recreational options were somewhat limited. Skipping, for instance, was a potentially fatal activity as an over-enthusiastic jump into the whirring rope could have resulted in tragedy. Again, all ball games were naturally out of bounds, and so we used to play 'football' with a small block of wood. Now, whenever I begin to reminisce about post-war shortages my children assume bored expressions and exclaim, "We know Dad... You had nothing to play with except a block of wood!" Callous swine!

In between peering fearfully through the railings I read endlessly about twins. Now please don't run away with the idea that St John's was a hotbed of genetic research; it was just that while I was a pupil of the gentle Miss Pope I came across a series of books that depicted the lives of twins from almost every culture. There were 'The Dutch Twins', 'The Irish Twins', 'The Eskimo Twins' etc. The adventures of multi cultural twins fascinated me and the hours I spent devouring their stories were among the happiest I've ever known. However, my education with regard to ethnicity was incomplete, as many major ethnic groups were ignored entirely. For instance, as far as I know there was no 'Twins' idyll set in the antipodes. The Aborigine twins must have been on permanent walkabout because I never came across them on the bookshelves. Similarly, the Maori, Indian and African twins never made it into Lucy Fitch-Perkins' canon (which is a great shame when one thinks of the forests that have perished due to the plethora of later publications concerning the sociopathic Kray twins). In fact, the only representatives of the African races appeared in the volume bearing the appalling title, 'The Pickaninny Twins'. There was no mention of Jews or Arabs although the Roma got a mention in 'The Irish Twins', where the identical Gaelic siblings encountered 'dangerous Gypsies' [sic]. One wonders if there was ever a German translation of 'The Irish Twins' and whether perhaps Doktor Mengele, the murderer of both Jew and Roma, ever read it.

What *was* my infant mind absorbing?!

40. Just Another Day

Christmas day used to be the focal point of the dark winter months; its mixture of colour and warmth mingled with the smell of fir trees, sage and onion stuffing and tangerines, which pervaded the crisp winter air long before the day. Nowadays – to employ the words of Paul McCartney's song – It's Just Another Day'.

People talked about the magic of Christmas as if it somehow derived from the supernatural activities of elves and fairies, but for many people the magical quality lay in the fact that for one day, at least, they could enjoy a decent meal while nestling in the warm bosom of the family.

People in those days took little for granted. Whether it was food, warmth or shelter, they were genuinely thankful for what they had, much like young Mary and her child amid the donkeys and oxen.

For me, much of the pleasure of Christmas in Liverpool stemmed from the siege-mentality that accompanied the festivities. For weeks before the 25th of December my mother would be in a state of near panic as she contemplated the logistics of providing food and drink for the family while the shops were closed for a minimum of *three whole days*. The adequate provision of milk and bread were the things that occupied her most. Would there be enough to feed the four of us through the 'famine' that we called a feast or would we be reduced to eating left-over turkey on crackers?

Nowadays some supermarkets are open on Christmas day, so if you have forgotten the silver polish for your caviar spoons you can be easily spared the embarrassment of having your guests tuck into their Beluga with dull silverware. Such a blessed relief!

Of course, for many people the big worry was the availability of a capon, a turkey or a joint of pork. Butchers were gods in those days and had total control over the quality of meat that would grace the dinner table. People would place their order months in advance and then pick up their chosen centrepiece without even being allowed to examine it. If it was a turkey or a capon they would boast about its size as if it were a baby and neighbours would come into the house to admire it, saying things like, "What a beauty! What weight is it?" To which question the proud owner of the mound of pale and purple-pimpled flesh would reply, "Just over seventeen pounds! They had a terrible time delivering it." Never, outside of the death of a royal personage, was a carcass so well attended as that bird.

I distinctly remember one Christmas Eve when we had just taken possession of a house with some of the most primitive facilities this side of the stable at Bethlehem. There hadn't been time to have a gas cooker installed so my mother was cooking a capon in the oven at the side of the fireplace. The smell of cooking hung in the air as tangibly as the crepe paper decorations on the ceiling and every breath I took created a hunger I have never experienced before or since.

I begged my mother for some of the meat but she refused, offering by way of compromise a sandwich of sage and onion stuffing fresh from the oven. I accepted gratefully and was rewarded with a culinary experience that has never since been matched. When I see all the celebrity cooks on television wittering on about all kinds of bizarre stuffing like 'chestnut and coriander' or 'apple and macadamia' I just think … nuts!

Even the television in those days was conducive to a sense of well-being, in contrast to recent years. Not long ago 'Titanic' was chosen as BBC's film for Christmas Day and after watching it I re-lived the sense of loss and anguish I had first experienced many years previously while watching 'A Night to Remember', a black and white depiction of the same tragedy. I first noticed this trend towards the depressing Christmas movie several years ago when my wife and I watched a film called 'Terms of Endearment'. We had no idea what it was about, but the title seemed to indicate something romantic. It was, in fact, a dreadfully sad story about a young woman who died of cancer while being ministered to by a man who had once been an astronaut. The sadness of her struggle, combined with the knowledge that incredible amounts of money had been spent lobbing Jack

Nicholson into orbit while cancer research relied mainly on charity, completely and utterly finished us off.

Some things never change, though… This Christmas our youngest son confirmed all the rumours we had heard concerning his 'pre-natal' examination of his presents, which we had naively left in our wardrobe, as usual. As he opened his presents he struggled manfully to appear surprised and delighted. At one stage he unwrapped a watch and, with a theatrical attempt at enthusiasm, said, "Oh… a Bart Simpson watch!" It was the flattest exclamation I've ever heard. Next year Santa won't have very far to go after he enters our chimney, because all the other toys will be in the flaming attic!

One thing that has changed beyond hope is the complexity of the modern toy. When I was young, the worst thing that could happen was that the percussion caps for my cowboy revolver would be forgotten, but even then the gun was operable as we always created the sound effects anyway.

A decade later, the necessity for batteries invaded our quietude. How many Christmases in Liverpool and elsewhere have reverberated to the sounds of hymns mingled with cries of children trying to resurrect battery-less toys? Currently I am the subject of recriminations because I bought a Playstation game for an NTSC (American) operating system rather than PAL (European). Next Christmas I'm asking for a subscription to *New Scientist*!

41. Hot Legs

Nylon stockings have been a part of my consciousness as far back as I can remember. No, I am not a fetishist, it's just that I can recall my father bringing back nylons from New York and distributing them among his relatives. Judging by the ecstatic reception he got, my father appeared to be a sort of Santa for grown-ups.

I can remember the fabulous patterns woven into the gossamer fabric. Either butterflies fluttered on calves, or severe geometric shapes spanned ankles that were set on stiletto heels, creating impressions of a New York skyline at pavement level. I remember too the all-important question. Were they 10, 15 or 30 denier? Oddly enough, the varying thicknesses of nylon almost seemed to approximate the ages of the recipients. The low numbers went to the young women, while the 30 denier found their way into my Gran's top drawer.

My mother told me tales of young women, who had no access to either a sailor husband nor a friendly GI, resorting to dyeing their legs with tea or coffee to create the impression that they were wearing nylons, while others went to the extraordinary extent of having someone draw pencil lines down the back of their legs to simulate seams. Imagine if that someone had suffered from the shakes... her friend's legs would look as if they were a pair of cobras emerging from a snake charmer's basket!

I once had an unfortunate experience with a pair of nylons and a trio of parrots. I was about eight at the time and my father had brought home three valuable African Grey parrots and, in order to keep out the chill air, had placed them inside a suitcase overnight. Anxious to help, and quite unbeknown to my father, I laid a pair of nylons inside the case, with the idea of keeping the avian collateral warm. The next morning I carefully inched open the lid so as not to allow the parrots a clear flight path. I needn't have bothered; they were all quite dead, strangled by my 15 denier duvet. My apoplectic father's curses and oaths out-thundered any of Wagner's epics.

It's just as well the birds were dead I suppose, otherwise they might have picked up a really bad swearing habit.

My most meaningful encounter with ladies' stockings occurred when I was twenty-two. And no... it wasn't the obvious situation. I had just moved to Skelmersdale, which was on the verge of becoming a massive overspill town some thirteen miles from Liverpool, and found myself working for a hosiery company. It was the most bizarre job I've ever had. The routine, morning, noon and night was depressingly familiar. I, and another unfortunate, stood opposite each other at the side of a moving track that was sited at the front of two chambers: one for dyeing and one for drying. Upright, with the thigh part lying on the track, stood the flat outlines of polished aluminium legs, 24 at each side, feet uppermost. It looked as if a gaggle of anorexic divers had been frozen just as their torsos hit the water.

Our job was to take the white, un-dyed, stockings, flip them over the toes of the legs and then stretch them out to eliminate any wrinkles. The track would then contract, concertina fashion, and the legs smoothly closed ranks before being shunted into the dyeing chamber. At the same time the previously dyed batch was shunted from the drying oven toward me and my 'oppo', giving us about two minutes to unload the dyed stockings and replace them with the white variety. We worked at lightning speed to keep abreast of the legs. This monotonous routine lasted for eight hours with a half hour break. I vividly remember suffering a recurring nightmare in which marching ranks of aluminium legs strode relentlessly over the end of my bed, crushing me beneath their trunkless procession. Throughout the whole of the shift, and indeed for the two years I fondled a million legs, I hardly ever spoke to my opposite number. This was mainly because there was just not enough breathing space, as we raced frantically to achieve our piecework targets, but also because he was an absolute plant pot. His name was Ashley Piers Smythe and he had a Pomeranian toy dog ... 'nuff said.

The only good thing to come out of all of that mindless activity was the fact that we were allowed to buy stockings at a price that enabled us to hawk them around the mushrooming estates and so make a small profit. I made enough to put down a deposit on a small house in Liverpool, which I had yearned for with the earnestness of a child lost to its mother.

Just before I returned to Liverpool in 1967 the arrival of the mini-skirt gave the stocking industry a kick in the groin from which it never recovered, because pantyhose soon became *de rigeur* and those old-fashioned stockings, which would have revealed bare and pallid thighs, went the way of all flesh.

In fact, I was to develop a severe a whiplash injury from the constant twisting and turning of my neck as the micro-skirt superseded the mini. In the end I was almost glad when fashion turned its usual cartwheel and ushered in the 'maxi'.

42. Disco Inferno

Like most of the great Liverpool clubs I ever knew, the Somali in Parliament Street was a cellar. It was a small place, little more than the servant quarters of a large Georgian house, but its underground reputation was huge. The dancing area was about the size of a snooker table, but its spirit was as big as Anfield stadium, and, like footballers, everyone was trying to score.

Some clubs are like convents; choc full of women, all of whom have someone infinitely better than you in mind, but the Somali was my lucky place. The music, which was relayed through an old-fashioned jukebox, was a mixture of pop, and other, little known, songs. The more obscure songs became synonymous with the Somali. They were usually songs whose sheer sensuality impelled people to the dance floor, that rapidly became a critical mass of overheated cores, all heading for voluntary meltdown in a nightly Chernobyl of desire. I only have to think of George Macrae, singing 'Rock Your Baby' on a hot summer night and I become slightly unstable. I sometimes wonder if it is merely a coincidence that Somalia is located on the Horn of Africa.

Now don't run away with the idea that the club was in any way salubrious. On the contrary, it was decidedly run down and dingy when the lights went on at the end of the evening. One night I was delayed by something and the lights – or rather light – was switched on. The contrast between the velvet embrace of the smoke-filled gloom and the searing glare of the single light bulb was as unlovely as it was stark. I never again dallied after last orders were called.

One night I took a young lady there. She was a fellow student and had led a sheltered life in a small Yorkshire town. For some reason which escapes me now, we arrived much earlier than I normally would have. I used to make my entrance about midnight, when the ambience had started a chain reaction, fusing the dancers into a swaying mass of radiant joy. When Joanna and I arrived this particular evening there was nobody there except the bar staff – a pleasant woman who was also from Yorkshire. Joanna stood aghast, staring at the place in horror, and I suddenly saw it through her eyes. The walls, normally hidden from sight, were bare except for a thin covering of lime-wash or emulsion, which only poorly disguised the bricks, and the floor still bore the damp swirls of a mop that carried the pungent whiff of disinfectant. Joanna made her excuses and left.

Years later I met her there. She had overcome her natural fastidiousness and become an aficionado of warm beer, disinfectant and the Somali smooch, which for me is still the only dance in town.

Like the man said:

> "The mind is its own place
> It can make a heaven of hell
> Or a hell of heaven."

One night, that has since become legendary, there was a murder, a stabbing, and the Somali's patrons were all herded into police cells. As a result St Anne Street Police Station became, that night, the site of the most intense cannabis dealing this side of Katmandu. Happily, I had left early, taking my partner with me, which was just as well as she was notoriously straight-laced … straight, but laced with devilry.

The Somali held other, even hotter charms, in the shape of some of the best curries I've ever tasted, made by a genial man call Ali. There were only a few curries on the menu but they were so addictive that they formed my staple diet for four or five years. They were served with an optional side-dish called *kishimbush* – an irresistible mixture of cucumber, onion and tomatoes which was so drenched in chilli that people sweated profusely while eating it and, despite having eaten enormous mounds of food, were visibly thinner on leaving.

The Somali gave hard currency to the expression *"There's a hot time in the old town tonight."*

It's long gone now … but boy do I miss it!

43. Homeward Bound

My last voyage as a sailor was taken aboard the *MV Phrygia*, a Cunard 'Meddi-boat'. At the time I didn't realise that my marriage to the sea was about to be dissolved, but if my previous experiences aboard the likes of the *Cape York* had caused me to subconsciously petition for a *decree nisi* then my trip on the *Phrygia* signalled the arrival of my *decree absolute*. Not that the ship or the crew were anything but admirable. It was another, more elemental aspect that would rent asunder my brief and bitter liaison with *La Mer*.

We left Liverpool in late November, bound for Genoa, before going on to Naples, Torre Annunziata, Salerno, Valetta, Gibraltar, Casablanca and finally Tangier. The *Phrygia* was regarded by sailors as a good ship because it was only at sea for about six weeks at a time, and its ports of call were all pleasant places to be, especially in the spring and summer months.

In Genoa I was introduced to an Egyptian peddler who specialised in the sale of high-class wristwatches at very reasonable prices. In the early sixties the notion of counterfeit merchandise was restricted to the whores who offered love for sale, but stipulated 'no kissy'. I bought a Waltham wristwatch for five pounds and spent the rest of the voyage wondering how I could best conceal it from the Customs and Excise men. I eventually settled for wrapping it in cellophane and hiding it in a tin of shoe polish, carefully brushed over to make it appear normal. God knows what I would have done if it had been a kilo of Moroccan hashish. Knowing me I'd probably have bought a gross of shoe polish! Oddly enough, in spite of its immersion in Kiwi Black and its dodgy provenance, the watch is still keeping perfect time on my stepfather's wrist.

In Naples, which was the base of the American sixth fleet, I met a young marine who, despite speaking English, tested my understanding of my native tongue to the limit. I was having a drink in a dockside bar (where else?) when he introduced himself as 'Tom' ...

but it would be a while before I found anything else he said as easy to understand. I asked him which state he was from.

"Marrlin," he drawled.

Perplexed, I asked him to repeat himself.

"Marrlin," he murmured again.

Now I wasn't too bad with geography, but for the life of me I couldn't remember any such state. It wasn't until he said something about the Mason-Dixon Line that I realised what he meant. Maryland! He smiled and nodded and I smiled before deciding to take a walk, fearing we might get into a conversation about ... well, almost anything where mutual understanding was a prerequisite.

Above the cliffs of Salerno is a monument to the American dead of the Italian campaign, and to this day I can still see the dramatic outline of the huge illuminated cross which dominated the night sky. I wonder how many young men like Tom were asked where they were from as they lay dying? If they'd been from Maryland and found themselves being interrogated by an Englishman they might well have ended up with a question mark on their gravestone. Perhaps the war dead should have had one chiselled on theirs anyway.

We left Salerno for Valetta and I soon found myself in yet another dockside bar, where I encountered a young German sailor who was trying to be friendly. In response to his comradely overtures I was quite simply obnoxious. Looking back, my behaviour puzzles me, because my normal reaction to alcohol is to subside into silence. I can't be sure, but perhaps it was the memory of Salerno's dead that prompted me to tell him to 'Fuck off!"

With a wistful smile the young man shrugged off my churlishness and I staggered from my stool into the toilet. As I was leaving the toilet he was entering and I deliberately jostled him. One thing led to another and I suddenly found myself flat on my back with a bleeding nose and a concerned German youth kneeling over me. I repaid his care by throwing a feeble right hook in his direction while declaring him to be a "fucking Nazi!"

He promptly chinned me and stalked off. Quite right too!

The rest of the voyage was uneventful until we reached Casablanca. I was down in the hold, generally getting in the way, as the bosun, perched on the ribs of the ship, supervised the dispatch of a huge, flat, wooden crate of glass, which must have weighed in the region of five tons. Without warning, the crate shifted and trapped the bosun, crushing him with his hips side-on to the bulkhead. He screamed loudly, and then, with superhuman control, began shouting instructions as to how best to free him.

"Get the Wogs! Get the fucking Wogs!" he bellowed, and nobody questioned his lack of political correctness as they all, Muslim and Christian alike, struggled to rescue him. He had suffered a massive fracture of his pelvis and yet remained calm enough to ensure his own delivery.

Later that morning as I was recovering from the shock of the bosun's accident I was approached by one of the Moroccan stevedores, who indicated that he and his mates wanted to break open a crate of oranges which were part of the cargo. As he looked at me hesitantly I was appalled that they should have to ask whether or not they could steal something that must have been so abundant in their own country, and, furthermore, that they were so obviously hungry. I agreed and shortly afterwards one of them offered me a long pipe that he had clipped together from a series of smaller lengths before filling it with a greenish-looking mixture. I took a few puffs and gave it back to him. Later, as I climbed laboriously up the ladder to the deck I was wholly ignorant of the fact that I had partaken of *kif* and had inadvertently become an early pioneer of the sixties drug culture.

When I had sufficiently recovered from my unwitting flirtation with hashish I remembered how cold and miserable-looking my Arabic Timothy Leary had been. It was, after all, December and even in Casablanca it gets cold. I decided to try and remedy the stevedore's discomfort and found several pairs of thick socks and a pullover, not stopping to think how the socks would fit inside his sandals. When I offered them to him he accepted with good grace and gratitude creased his weathered Capo Dimonte face. A few minutes later he knocked on my door and offered me an old square tobacco tin. When

I opened it I saw his pipe, in its constituent pieces, and a heap of *kif*. I indicated that I didn't want to take it from him and he reluctantly withdrew. Years later, at the peak of the hippy era and during a trough in my marijuana supply I would ruefully reflect on my casual rejection of such an offering.

The voyage home was to take about a week and would prove to be a hell of a time. As we crossed the notoriously stormy Bay of Biscay a gale force nine blew up. For days we had to walk the decks clinging to hastily-rigged lifelines as waves pounded the decks and white foam raged around alleyways that seemed permanently submerged. One day, as the ship lumbered through some of the fiercest seas I've ever seen, I took my turn at the wheel. The ship was difficult to handle as it lurched from one wave to the next. Suddenly, seemingly out of nowhere, a huge freak wave, almost vertical, obscured the feeble sun behind its green and terrifying majesty. I watched, fascinated, as it rose higher in the water, towering above its companions with watery hauteur, until the startled cry of the second mate penetrated my trance. "Turn your head into the wave! Now!"

I did as he bid and after what seemed an age the prow of the ship sluggishly veered to meet the gigantic threat. In an instant the power of the rogue wave created a sickening shudder from stem to stern and I honestly thought we were going to founder. The captain must have thought so too because he burst into the wheelhouse and thundered:

"Do you want me to put a *man* on the wheel!"

I just looked at him dumfounded as I had only done as I'd been instructed. The second mate opened his mouth to protest but his furious superior simply bellowed the same question.

"Do you want me to put a man on the wheel!"

I was as frightened as I've ever been, but with a rising sense of indignation I screamed back "No I don't!"

As if taken aback by my vehemence the captain simply shrugged and retreated back into the chartroom. Later, when I voiced my fears that we might have sunk to the second mate he said, presciently, "If you don't like this kind of sea you'd be better off on the buses."

As we arrived in the Mersey a young deck boy, a red haired kid, began to speak with mounting excitement about going to see some band called 'the Beatles', who were performing in some place called 'the Cavern'. I didn't take much notice at the time, but I have often wondered since then if the youngster ever got to know any of the Fab Four. Who knows, I might have sailed with a Beatles' roadie or something.

My last morning in the Merchant Navy was memorable for the fact that, while addressing a fellow sailor of African descent I stupidly invoked his wrath because I used a commonplace but nonetheless racist expression. He wagged his finger at me admonishingly and then invited me to his home, where his wife cooked for us the tastiest meal I have ever had. I have tried many, many, times since to re-create what was essentially a simple meal of fried cod, onions, tomatoes and rice sprinkled with Cayenne pepper, but have never yet succeeded.

Some years afterwards, at the time when African/American athletes competing in the Mexico Olympics were demonstrating their anger at white supremacy by raising black-gloved fists in salute to Black Pride, I saw Lou in the Globe pub in Casey Street. He was a tall man to begin with, but dressed as he was in black leather from head to toe he looked extremely imposing. I waved to him, but he just gave me a stony stare. I can't say I blame Lou. After all, I, and my stupid mouth, had been part of his problem. Years later I would see a lot of Lou's brother Chris, a genial man who, whenever he met me and my baby son, would always fish from his pocket a handful of coins, which he would gently deposit in the child's hand.

44. Ticket to Ride

One of the most enjoyable jobs I ever had was when I worked as a bus conductor for Liverpool Corporation Passenger Transport. I had previously been working for three weeks on the railways, as an assistant brake changer. This task involved lugging coffin-shaped slabs of cast iron up and down a siding while some other lucky so-and-so checked the brakes for wear. I would then come into my own, by handing my burden to him, whereupon he would whack it into place with a sledgehammer. Three weeks was enough. I punched my ticket and headed for the offices of the Bus Company.

Three days later I was taking a simple maths test before being despatched to Edge Lane bus shed for training. Within a week I was boarding my first bus, horribly self-conscious in my dark navy uniform, the trousers of which I'd taken in to give a tighter fit.

My first run, like every new boy to the job, was on the Dock Road, at evening peak hour. My employers reasoned that if we could withstand the onslaught of the legendary wit of the stevedores we could cope with anything. In reality, the dockers were just tired men going home, with little energy left for baiting rookie conductors. What strength they did have in reserve was spent in trying to avoid paying their fare. Their method was as funny as it was commonplace. One of them would come down the stairs and say, "Feller behind's payin' lad." The phrase would be repeated until about ten men had skipped off, then the last man, theatrically furtive, would deposit a heap of copper in my hand and whisper, "Ee-are lad… get yerself a bevvy." The heap of coins, all halfpennies, amounted to the full fare of just one man.

The next day I was working on the notorious 'belt', a circular route running from the city centre and back which linked with all the other routes that radiated like wheel spokes from the hub of the Pier Head. For the next year the 26 bus was to prove my ride and joy.

Route 26 was the busiest and most frequent service in the city. At peak hour they ran at two-minute intervals. Imagine it, a bus every two minutes, thirty in an hour! Of course, due to the vagaries of the traffic many buses got stuck very early in their journey. Then the next bus would pile up behind it and another and so on. This inevitably led to the bitter refrain, "They always come in bloody threes!"

On one notable occasion, when the Beatles returned home in triumph from their first conquest of America – resulting in hundreds of thousands of Liverpudlians taking to the streets – no less than ten 26s, nose to tail and empty, stood stranded in Sheil Road like the abandoned green skin of a gigantic caterpillar.

Prior to my becoming a bus conductor my dating opportunities had been restricted to dancehalls and the like. But the buses, to my stunned surprise, provided the most fertile source of female companionship I'd ever encountered. It stands to reason really; during peak hour an average of 300 young women an hour passed by my low-slung ticket machine. If a young conductor could not attract at least one of them he must be either disinterested or have a face like the rear end of his vehicle.

One young woman, called Maria, rang my bell with such force that I still start when I think of her. I first noticed her one morning as she went to her job in the Ministry of Defence. She had thick dark hair tied up in a bun and wore horn-rimmed glasses so severe that they clung to her ivory skin like facial manacles. Even so, her beauty could not be held captive; her smile would set it free in an instant.

I had refrained from my usual approach and instead made joking remarks about her obvious shyness. One day I casually asked her out. To my surprise she not only agreed, but also made a remark to the effect that she had thought I would never ask. After about three months I blew it. To this day I bear faint traces of the powder burns.

Of course the job had its bad moments. On Saturday nights we trawled drunks with the ease of cod fishermen off the Dogger Bank. One night as we were making our way up Scotland Road we stopped outside of an ancient tavern known as the 'Honky Tonk'. Two men were plastered to the wall of the pub and, just as I rang the bell, one of them lurched free and stumbled aboard the already moving bus, leaving his companion still glued to the tavern. The rest of the journey descended into a farcical slanging match as the drunk rumbled away, fulminating about the loss of his mate. Suddenly, as I momentarily turned my back on him, he went for me.

I had pinned him to a seat, where all he could do to utter dire threats against my person, when out of the corner of my eye I noticed Frank, my driver, peering anxiously at the commotion from the safety of his cab. Observing that the situation was under control Frank, all of five-feet-four and about as aggressively inclined as Mother Teresa, sprang out of his cab and in no uncertain terms threatened to decapitate the drunken offender, or words to that effect. To this day we still laugh at his timely 'rescue'.

Fiddling (the larcenous non-musical variety) was endemic among conductors, but on 'the belt' it was *de rigeur*. You didn't really have to try very hard. Quite often we were so overwhelmed with passengers that the platform was a maelstrom of honest people jumping on and off, all hurling money but rarely waiting for their tickets. The result was a net profit, because at the end of the day you would have an excess of cash. Everybody fiddled, including the office staff, and they would always ensure that their calculations *never* coincided with ours, which then enabled them to deduct X amounts from our wages. They knew we were 'at it', so they were 'at it' too.

I remember once when, just out of interest, I enlisted the help of Arthur, a medical student who worked his vacation on the belt, to see if the cashiers really were cheating us. He was aided by Stan Ball, an inveterate gambler who could compute odds faster than the tote and another man known as 'Click-Click' because of his amazing ability to imitate the sound of a ticket machine in full flow, and who was so meticulous about his embezzlement that he kept double entry waybills. We totalled my cash against tickets and paid in the exact amount of money. The next day I got a 'short' note for sixteen shillings!

The year was 1964 and I was, alas, fiddling while my Rome burned. In a world of opportunity and broadening horizons I was careering along the route to personal disaster ... but that's another story.

45. Confessin' the Blues

Most internecine struggles revolve around religious or territorial disputes. For instance, the Israeli/Arab conflict is even now being waged between two groups who are essentially half brothers, since both groups share descent from Abraham through his legal wife, Sarah and his concubine, Hagar.

In Liverpool there has been a fraternal war smouldering since the day Liverpool Football Club defected from its parent club, Everton FC. This division, while perpetually characterised by the brutal cut and thrust of wit and bloodcurdling repartee, has, by and large, remained good humoured. Considering that our localised conflict is now of a longer endurance than the *actual* Hundred Years War, it speaks volumes about Scouse humour.

While other cities exhibit similar rivalries, such as that which exists between Glasgow's two famous clubs Rangers and Celtic, those contests usually engender almost unwavering loyalty of solid blocks of supporters, drawn from families who stand shoulder-to-shoulder behind their chosen team. In Liverpool, however, even close-knit families are often riven by rivalry. Mothers, fathers, sons and daughters, uncles and aunts are often locked in life-long division. It is the existence of this family matrix that probably explains the non-violent nature of the antagonism far more easily than the presence of a veritable host of comedians.

Given that my mother supported Everton, along with most of her siblings, it would be natural to expect me to have spent my life like a medieval knight in search of the 'Golden Vision'; natural perhaps, but hardly typical in this town. I am, in essence, an apostate, an infidel, a lost sheep togged out in a black fleece. On that unhappy note I might add that my conversion to LFC required no revelation on the road to Damascus. It was, I suspect, due solely to my teenage hormonal imbalances.

To this day I can still remember the very first match I ever saw. My father, a dyed-in-the-wool Liverpudlian, had taken me to see Everton thrash Vasco Da Gama 5-3. To this day I don't know why he did that, but perhaps it had something to with the fact that after the match he and I were given a guided tour of the ground by a member of the ground staff, who apparently knew my old man and who gave me a sheet of paper bearing the signatures of the Everton team. Sadly, like so much of my important memorabilia it has disappeared into the lost and never found repository of keepsakes.

That episode has, however, given me occasion to experience totally the underlying closeness of Scousers despite their footballing predilections. One night in the late 70's I was ensconced in the Albert public house in Lark Lane, sharing a pint with an Evertonian friend of mine. Raising my voice above the noise of the bar and the shrill voice of the divine Kate Bush wailing about her lost love, Heathcliffe, I happened to mention that I'd attended the Everton v Vasco Da Gama Match. I had barely begun to name that day's winning team when my mate took over and proceeded to mention every player.

"T.G. Jones..." (pause for a reverential sigh) "The great Tee Gee!"

Peter Farrell..." (pause for a smile of remembrance)...

Feeling both wicked and lucky, I allowed him to continue his litany of love and then, just as he was taking a sip of his pint, I said innocently, "Yes, but don't you think it's about time the youngsters were given a chance?"

I thought he'd die laughing, or choking, as he spluttered his lager down the front of his immaculately-pressed shirt. His response, while printable, was simply libellous and so I won't repeat it. In any case, I've seen my mother's marriage certificate!

In the intervening years between seeing the mighty Brazilians humbled and the humbling of my mate, I had been to Goodison Park on many occasions and it wasn't always as an away supporter. I can still see the diminutive figure of Bobby Collins as he danced a jig around the Arsenal defence three times in the act of scoring a super hat-trick. Looking back on it now it was as if somebody had put a Rolls-Royce through a car-crusher and then put footy boots on the block of steel that came out at the other end before unleashing the resulting Chieftain tank on opposing defences.

You see, on Saturdays my mate Puddy Ashford was responsible for the crowd's intake of Everton Mints and I used to accompany him. No. He wasn't a transvestite and no, he didn't don a blue dress and bonnet and dole out toffees![6] He sold sweets from a tray. He used to have the same job of hawking Barker & Dobson sweets at Anfield, where I also accompanied him, as we somehow got complimentary tickets.

For the record, I hardly knew any men who dressed as women in those days, apart from 'Denise', who lived in Coltart Road and who was the talk of the town because of his dress sense. His role model was Alma Cogan. Enough said.

It was at Goodison Park that I saw the Golden Vision himself, Alex Young, chip a goalkeeper from the edge of the penalty area, an incredibly beautiful sight that I'd never previously witnessed.

A few years later I was in a club, 'The Beachcomber', where I was short of a light for my cigarette. I looked around and saw someone sitting at the bar about to light up. I approached him, tapped him on the shoulder, and casually asked him for a light. I can still see the look of vague shock that crossed Alex's face as he dumbly offered me his lighter. Had I been an Evertonian I would probably have packed up smoking rather than disturb the blonde demigod at his play. The truth is I didn't recognise him or I'd have bought a book of matches!

It was due to the influence of my friend, the sweet seller, that I was present at Anfield when the whole Beatles/Kop/Shankly thing took off and converted me forever to being a red nose. Nowadays, on those more frequent occasions when I've seen an Evertonian ecstatically celebrating a goal scored *against* Liverpool *by* Man Utd I think, "There but for a bag of toffees go I."

The saddest event I ever witnessed at Goodison Park (also known as 'the school of science') was during the infamous 1966 World Cup

---

[6] [1]Everton's mascot was a lady toffee seller and so on matchdays young ladies would dress in period costume and distribute free toffees to the crowd.

game when Portugal's cart-horses kicked Pele out of the competition. It was in the same year that I almost electrocuted myself while I was dancing around after Everton's Derek Temple had added to Mike Trebilcock's two goals to win the thriller against Sheffield Wednesday in the FA cup final and discovered that ale and cathode ray tubes don't mix.

Incidentally, my Evertonian friend was so religious in his worship of his beloved Everton that when they really went on the slide and successive seasons became a dog-fight to avoid the unthinkable, as his is the club that has remained in top flight football for almost all of its existence, he couldn't take it any more, and, so rumour had it, occasionally visited Old Trafford to watch Man United. That might sound like a joke but it's true. Sometimes pain makes us do crazy things...

I recently watched Vasco Da Gama thrashing Manchester United in the recent world club championships and couldn't help but think, "the Brazilians weren't even in the game that day at Goodison..."

46. Where Have All the Flowers Gone?

I first saw Liverpool football team in 1959, when they were languishing in the old second division and as far from the domination of Europe as Tom was from catching Jerry. I used to oscillate between Anfield stadium and Goodison Park, the home of Everton, Liverpool's great rivals.

Then the sixties happened, like no other decade ever happened, and I found myself caught up in Liverpool's rise from obscure provinciality to the most vibrant and recognisable city on the planet. The local accent was mimicked the world over, bearing out the adage that imitation is the sincerest form of flattery. The Beatles' domination of the world of music was matched by the Mighty Reds' irresistible conquest of Europe and by the mid-eighties I had grown rather accustomed, not to say blasé, about the success of the latter. I stopped going to the games, contenting myself with the occasional television match.

Then one day in April 1989, during the Saturday afternoon football roundup, news began to filter through that incompetent policing had precipitated a murderous crush that would leave a 96 fans dying behind the fences at Sheffield's Hillsborough stadium.

The editor of the *Sun*, a certain Kelvin Mackenzie, whose appetite for the dingo droppings of his master Rupert Murdoch was prodigious, created a story that the victims were drunk (in spite of one of them being a ten-year-old boy, eight years from being of a legal age to drink). That story put about by Mackenzie has a long and undistinguished lineage of lies and deceit, originating in fascist Rome and Nazi Germany, because whilst democratic politicians certainly do lie, it is usually incidental to their purpose, but to Fascists deception is integral to their aims. Without deceit there is no Fascism. Think about it. The Nazis built 'Q-ships' – battle cruisers disguised as merchantmen – and told Jewish people that they were going to new lands in the east for re-settlement … where they were offered showers, given imitation bars of soap, and then gassed to death. Their malevolent deception was endless.

Goebbels put it succinctly when he declared, "The bigger the lie, the bigger the chance it will be believed".

Mackenzie, you no doubt think you are descended from some proud Scottish clan. Perhaps, but in my opinion your spiritual antecedents are closer to the Bavarian Alps than the Scottish Highlands.

I will never forget the week following Hillsborough as long as I live. To this day I can recall the image of the greatest floral tribute I had ever seen. On the following Sunday my wife and I, accompanied by our three-year-old son, joined the thousands of people from all over the planet who had gone to Anfield to mark their respect and grief. Our son wandered onto a part of the ground that was cordoned off by tapes. A young and officious policeman reprimanded me, saying, "Keep him away from the fence!" I will never forget the shock that registered on his youthful features when my son's normally reserved mother, who is not from Liverpool, retorted venomously, "You'd know a lot about fences wouldn't you!"

Just as the waves of the Mersey Sound reached the corners of the earth, so the shockwaves of Hillsborough touched many a soul.

Murdoch and Mackenzie – a curse on both your houses.

47. Barefootin'

Yesterday my son went to town to check out some football boots. He later told me that the boots he intended to buy – copies of those worn by Luis Figo – were no longer in stock. The originals apparently cost £110 while the 'cheap' copies were going for the knockdown price of £35! Now, for that kind of outlay I'd want Señor Figo to schlep over to Liverpool on a weekly basis and apply dubbing to the bloody things!

Not that anybody uses dubbing any more; modern boots are so lightweight that anything heavier than breathing on them would probably destroy them. In fact, there is so little to the modern footy boot that you could probably find more leather in a Vegan salad.

Profound changes in soccer footwear have taken place during the past fifty years, and I am old enough, or unfortunate enough, to have witnessed the transition at close quarters. The first football boots I ever owned were so uncomfortable that I am convinced they were designed by sadists. Whereas modern boots are made of leather so soft they could double as ballet shoes, the old style 'togger' boots were so stiff and unyielding that when in need of repair it would have been logical to ignore the local cobblers and drop them off instead at the nearest blacksmith's forge. Only a sadist could have designed boots ostensibly to protect one's ankles which, in fact, cut into one's legs like gin traps. They also had toecaps which were so hard they must have provided the inspiration for the protective footwear worn by construction workers to prevent their toes being crushed by stray bricks.

The first signs of design change emanated from the continent and it was no coincidence that when the previously invincible English national team was thrashed six goals to three by the Hungarians, the galloping Magyars wore low-cut scraps of leather while the English were shod in state-of-the-ark clogs. In truth it wouldn't have mattered what I wore, because I was to the beautiful game what Harold Shipman was to the Hippocratic Oath. I did, however, make the school team … twice.

My favourite male teacher at St Dominic's primary school was Mr Swift, a genial man who was light on punishment and heavy on praise. He once drew attention to one of my essays after, echoing my mother, I had written that Oliver Twist was 'reared' in an orphanage.

One fine July morning I met my uncle John at Finch Lane shops and persuaded him to give me enough money to buy a pen for Mr Swift, whose class I was leaving. Mr Swift was more than pleased and, I suppose, not a little appreciative, because the next year, when I was in a different class and he was the acting soccer team coach, he picked me to play for the school team.

'The pen is mightier than the sword' they say, but for all the use I was to that team, I would have been better taking up fencing.

It is a truism that footballing skills are best acquired in the streets, and therein lay my problem. You see, I had moved house so often that I rarely got to know anybody well enough to join in the street-football games. One of the few times I stayed long enough to make friends was in Kirkdale, where some lads invited me to join in their strange game, which consisted of making progress along an alleyway by dint of leaping from wall to wall and navigating obstacles in a specific order. My participation ended abruptly when I fell flat on my back and whacked all the wind out of my lungs.

Anyway, there I was in my very first football strip, playing for my school against a team from somewhere near Huyton village. Apart from a speculative shot, which hit the post, my contribution mainly consisted of doing a passable impersonation of a decapitated chicken. I was clueless and my sense of inferiority was heightened when I observed how talented our centre half was. His name was Eddie Dean and he played the beautiful game beautifully. I have sometimes wondered if he was related to Dixie Dean, who by all accounts was a half decent striker in the late Cambrian period.

My valedictory appearance was against Stockbridge Lane Primary School XI. I was given the role of goalkeeper, probably to keep me as far from the front line as possible. I had just had a crew-cut, which was popular at the time. The problem was that my hair was so limp my crew-cut looked like a facsimile of Van Gogh's cornfield. Anyway, every time I took a drop kick someone would shout, "use your area!" meaning that I should kick the ball from the edge of the 18 yard box rather than the goal line and thus get greater distance on the kick. This was a reasonable instruction, but I misheard and thought he was making an insulting remark about using my hair and so persisted in taking every kick from inside the six-yard box. Looking back, it might have been better to use my hair, as most of my 'clearances' presented the opposition with the softest goals ever scored. I retired from school, league and international football at the age of 10.

Of course, it wasn't just football boots that inflicted pain on their youthful owners. I can still feel the pain from Wellingtons that rubbed against my bare legs, tattooing them with a burning ring of fire. Then there were the ordinary school shoes that must have been made by the same sadists who invented footy boots because they were clearly advocates of the 'one size fits all' mentality. A size five was a size five, regardless of the varying widths or other dimensions the feet of the general populace might display and our vulnerable feet were jammed into the same regulation-sized shoe.

My mother's generation even took to slitting the sides of ill-fitting shoes in order to make them fit their broad feet. She would buy a pair of court shoes on Monday and by Friday they would be razored into something resembling high-heeled sandals. Those were the days when a visit to a shoe shop was immediately followed by a trip to the chemist to buy some sticking plaster to cushion sore heels against the backs of slipping shoes.

My own children have been cosseted since birth. Every pair of shoes they have worn was fitted by experts whose secret goal appears to be the worldwide elimination of chiropodists. My eldest son shot up rapidly after puberty and now measures six-foot-one. I mention this only because the shoes I'm wearing are those he passed through briefly when he was fourteen and took a size eight, as opposed to his present size eleven.

When my youngest child reaches the age of fourteen I am determined that the little chap should have at least four pairs of really decent shoes. It's the least I can do…

48. We Don't Need Another Hero

A friend recently asked me what books had the greatest influence in my life. My attempt to answer her led me to the realisation that my whole world-view had been largely determined by the exploits of a legendary figure from the Middle Ages. This man was a firm believer in the re-distribution of wealth and, in company with Spartacus, was also one of the earliest practitioners of organised resistance to oppression. I am, of course, referring to Robin of Locksley, a.k.a Robin Hood.

As a child I would haunt any cinema in Liverpool where any representation of my hero happened to be showing. In my lifetime I must have seen every film version of Robin Hood that was ever made, as well as every television series. However, my first introduction to the peerless Prince of Thieves was via the written word...

I can still picture the interior of the library in Dovecote. It was located above a crescent shaped shopping arcade and always seemed to be bathed in sunlight that sprayed liquid clarity onto the massed ranks of books. I can see as well the particle storms when the dust from a thousand volumes whirled, dancing and darting among the stabbing sunbeams. I would go there every week, select a leather-bound volume about my hero and then, after fingering with awe the gold embossed title, would rush home to exult in the achievements of the greatest humanist of the second millennium.

Perhaps it was the simplicity of the Robin Hood legend that appealed to me because, after all, there is nothing intellectually challenging about the concept of taking from the greedy to give to the needy, unless you are a politician and then the whole idea becomes fraught with ideological pitfalls. The characters were easy to identify, as the Norman villains all wore exquisitely cut clothes and sported highly manicured beards which screamed of vanity and a latent propensity for cruelty, whereas the Saxon villeins were invariably tousle-headed scruff-bags in dire need of a dental hygienist.

Similarly, the eating habits of the opposing camps revealed their differing status. The Normans always employed ornately wrought and bejewelled daggers to carve neat morsels of chicken or lamb from their gold plates, which they then washed down with goblets of fine wine. In stark contrast the Saxon ruffians simply wolfed ferociously at huge joints of venison held in one hand, to counterbalance the foaming mug of ale in the other. The varied modes of eating revealed the gnawing hunger of the Saxons and the burgeoning avarice of their Norman overlords.

One thing did occur to me many years later. You see, their Lincoln green togs afforded the outlaws wonderful camouflage in the summer when the trees were blanketed with leaves, but the question has to be asked, what did they wear in the winter when the trees were bare and snow lay on the ground? Nottingham nut-brown perhaps? Did they have an official date for donning the green?

My adolescence held many diversions, but the television series, 'The Adventures of Robin Hood' still grabbed my attention and to this day I can sing the song with which every programme began…

'Robin Hood, Robin Hood, riding through the glen
Robin Hood, Robin Hood, with his band of men
Feared by the bad, loved by the good
Robin Hood, Robin Hood, Robin Hood…

One consequence of my sojourn in the leafy retreat of Sherwood Forest was that my politics and sense of ethics have always been skewed to the left of centre. Now that was normal in the 1960s, when millions of students, workers and hippies took to the streets protesting about Vietnam and shook both our fists and our Locksley locks at the Americans in their Grosvenor Square Embassy. It was still acceptable in the early 70s, although the truth about Stalin, Mao and Ho Chi Minh was unfolding before our eyes. However, by 1985 the Thatcher/Reagan axis had rendered protest not only unfashionable but also downright dangerous. I still remember seeing pictures of the manacled flight controllers in America, whose only crime was to assert their rights as trade unionists.

After the Falklands war, when Britain defeated one fascist regime with the aid of another, in the shape of Auguste Pinochet, holding left or even vaguely liberal views was decidedly passé. Especially when the main protagonist of the movie 'Wall Street', Gordon Gecko, asserted, "Greed is good!" and in the glades of Sherwood, a sigh shook the trees to their roots as Hollywood betrayed its earlier incarnation of Robin of Locksley, Errol Flynn.

A few years ago I was watching a chat show when an American writer was being interviewed. He was a Jewish American who had been blacklisted during the McCarthy era and had fled to Britain, where, under a pseudonym, he had penned many episodes of the television series, 'The Adventures of Robin Hood'.

Robin Hood, Jesus and John Lennon had more in common than long hair and facial adornment ... they all led us to believe that all you need is love, when just having a job would have helped.

Why didn't I just stick to reading the classics – illustrated comic books? I could have been Uncas, last of the Mohicans fighting against the odds ... or Ivanhoe, fighting against the odds ... no, I tried being a Saxon ... the Scarlet Pimpernel, fighting against ... Oh forget it!

49. Super Trouper

My first visit to a theatre was in the early fifties. The venue was the Shakespeare theatre, known affectionately as 'the Shakey'. I vaguely remember sitting with my mother in 'the gods' – the steeply banked seats in the upper tiers that made me feel as if any sudden movement would result in my being catapulted into the precipice of the stalls far below. Looking back I think that the term 'Shakey' had several layers of meaning, as just getting to one's seat was a drama in itself.

All that I recall about the show was that it was a pantomime starring the daughter of my one of mother's friends, and I felt extremely puzzled about the young lady, as she was dressed as a man. I eventually understood when I came across the notion of principal boys being girls. Like that made a lot of sense!

It was my return to full time education, in 1974, that really introduced me to the world this side of the footlights, as my English literature tutors went to great and unpaid efforts to persuade us to illuminate our understanding of the set texts with visits to the theatre. We visited many of theatres in the Northwest of England, such as the Octagon in Bolton or the Crucible in Sheffield, more famous now for hosting snooker championships, where the drama hangs on the tails of a tuxedoed sharpshooter intent on potting a winner. I would love to say that those visits made a lasting impression on me, but the sad fact is that I can barely remember the names of the plays I went to see. Instead, the dramas that lodge in my memory owe little, if anything, to the efforts of their authors and more to the circumstances surrounding the visit.

Sometime in the early eighties my girlfriend offered me the chance to visit Stratford on Avon to see *Hamlet* at the RSC. The trip was being organised by one of her fellow teachers, who apparently had an affinity with skylarks, because we had to board the coach at 6 a.m.

Our journey to Stratford was a deadbeat's nightmare, as almost every passenger held an opinion about *Hamlet* and they lost no opportunity to voice their pet theory. Hamlet was gay ... he fancied his mother ... he was on smack ... he was on day release from a psychiatric unit and was zonked on ye olde prozac ... whereas I was desperately trying to catch up on lost sleep after spending the previous evening in the Philharmonic pub, drinking copious amounts of Danish lager in order to get into the spirit of the theatre trip.

At last we arrived in Stratford, where the conversation suddenly changed, as my fellow travellers began stomach-churning discussions concerning the merits of quiche over lasagne. My too solid flesh wouldn't take any more and so I persuaded my girlfriend to go for a walk along the banks of the River Avon, which ran alongside the theatre, where people were feeding the river birds with pieces of locally baked baguette and exquisite herb-filled ciabatta. My face was as white as the serene and gluttonous swans.

The theatre was magnificent and the atmosphere was electric as the play began. Hamlet, portrayed by Roger Rees, appeared to be the smallest man on the stage. I had an idle thought that Hamlet cigars were also small and might have been named after Roger. I tried to pass on this precious tit bit of information to my girlfriend but she put her fingers to her lips and continued to gaze intently at the action. That was the last thing I remember as, without warning, I found my life suddenly rounded by a little sleep.

The journey home was infinitely worse than the earlier journey because the Shakespeare mob were by then in possession of a whole new set of theories *and* oodles of lasagne recipes, whereas I could barely remember the appearance of Hamlet's father, which was about the time I had given up the ghost.

My other memorable trip to a theatre was far more enjoyable, but for all the wrong reasons. As a student I had thoroughly enjoyed reading Arthur Miller's play *A View from a Bridge* and so when my girlfriend invited me to go with her and her class of seventeen-year-olds to see it performed at the tiny Neptune theatre I jumped at the chance. Miller's play is a mythic tale set in modern Brooklyn and deals with the deadly effects of jealousy and betrayal. Briefly, it concerns Eddie Carbone, a tough-looking forty-year-old longshoreman, and his wife, who are raising as their own the daughter of the wife's dead sister. The niece is a beautiful teenager who Eddie guards jealously. At one stage he accuses her of 'walking wavy' ... and thus the intimations of tragedy are writ large. Tragedy becomes inevitable when Eddie is persuaded to give shelter to two brothers, Marco and Rodolpho. They are illegal immigrants – known as 'torpedoes' – who hail from Italy. Naturally, the young girl falls for Rodolpho, which incenses Eddie, who is unaware of his own desires, and the older man betrays the 'torpedoes' to the immigration police. This departure from time-honoured codes of behaviour results in death and loss on a tragic scale... Heavy stuff, and not exactly a barrel of laughs, you would think. However, like me, you would be wrong, because that night at the Neptune I saw a great tragedy transformed into the most hilarious comedy I've ever witnessed.

Before I proceed, I should point out that my girlfriend and I had previously agreed to act as if we were not together, so as to deflect the interest of gossiping teenagers. You can imagine the kind of questions they would have asked...

"Whose that drop dead gorgeous feller miss?"

"Does he work out miss, 'cos he looks dead fit?"

"Will you be going to live with him in Beverly Hills miss?"

Okay, I am guilty of hyperbole, perhaps, but they would most certainly have asked questions!

As we settled down in our seats we barely looked at each other and I affected great interest in the programme. As I did so I reflected on the fact that I had always felt that Eddie Carbone would be best played by someone like Marlon Brando in a his role of Stanley Kowalski in *A Streetcar named Desire*. However, it transpired that on the day before opening night the actor who played Eddie Carbone had gone down with flu, thus creating a vacancy for the role of the smouldering Italian. You can imagine my sense of bewilderment when I saw the replacement take to the stage.

The new Eddie Carbone was about sixty-five and possessed of a silvery wig the likes of which I've never seen before or since. As it slid about on Eddie's head it looked for all the world like the love child of a drunken hedgehog and a used Brillo pad. I couldn't contain a snort of derision, but fortunately it was drowned in the general intake of breath that turned the small theatre into an eerie echo of a gale-swept shore.

I sneaked a glance at my girlfriend and noticed that she was furiously chewing her theatre ticket as if it were a stick of Wrigleys. Beyond her I could see the ranks of open-mouthed teenagers as they beheld Eddie 'Methusaleh' Carbone leering at his teenage niece, who was being played by a truly lovely young girl. Zen monks might be able to hear the sound of one hand clapping but believe me, that night I heard the sound of a hundred jaws dropping. I myself was in silent stitches and trying to make myself invisible.

Worse was to come when Marco, Rodolpho's gigantic older brother, made his appearance ... and what an appearance! He was wearing an old Arran sweater that had been washed so often that it had gone stiff and bellied out. Every time Marco turned around quickly the woolly belly of the sweater was always fractionally behind its wearer, so that with every pronounced movement it looked as if the brooding Italian giant was doing a tango with his own pullover. Marco's living pullover was a star turn indeed, and before long just about everybody in the place was helpless with laughter. The poor actors, amateurs all, gallantly played on. Why I'll never know. Had it been me I would have leapt from Miller's bridge!

When the illegals discover the extent of Eddie's treachery they are stunned. In the tense atmosphere that ensues Rodolpho wants immediate retribution, but his older sibling counsels caution. At one point Marco indicates that he understands why his brother is angry. Our Rodolpho, in a voice three octaves higher than Jimmy Somerville at his shrillest, retorted, "Angry? I'm furious!" That quite finished me off. Forgetting all my self-imposed rules I collapsed, choking, and buried my head in my girlfriend's lap, where I lay helpless for about two minutes. Luckily, nobody noticed my lapse, because the whole audience was similarly convulsed with hysterical laughter. And lest you think I exaggerate, let me offer you an example of how that cliché came to life in front of my weeping eyes. To the right of me a man slowly, but inexorably, fell to the floor, hugging his stomach with one hand while attempting to stuff the other into his mouth.

They might have been an amateur cast, but they really had 'em rolling in the aisles!

50. Can I Get a Witness?

Whenever I find myself in need of an inexpensive way to escape the daily routines of my home-life I usually rely on the sights and sounds that the city of Liverpool provides freely to its citizens. For example, if one tires of visiting the plentiful art galleries and museums then it's possible to take a stroll in one of the myriad parks or gardens which green the banks of the Mersey.

One day I became aware that the debatable charms of artists such as Jackson Pollock and Mark Rothko had begun to pall. The truth is, I had given up trying to work out just exactly why some people were prepared to pay a king's ransom for work that would embarrass an amateur interior decorator. That realization meant that the Tate modern was temporarily proscribed from my list of economy-class boltholes.

I had at the time become a little bit bored with the museums as well, and so, as the weather was less than clement on that June day in 1992, I found myself sitting in the public gallery of the magistrates' court in Dale Street. I suppose I wanted to see if the reality of the proceedings was anything like the scenes, which are common to television series such as *Perry Mason.*

There were certainly lawyers, defendants and judges present, but any resemblance to the popular image of a courtroom drama ended there. For one thing, the proceedings rarely lasted more than a few minutes, not even time enough for Raymond Burr to cough, give a wry smile and then cast a triumphant glance in the direction of the perennially hapless prosecutor. That said, Perry has never once managed to make me smile, much less force me to suppress a chuckle, which is exactly what happened during my sojourn at the magistrates' court.

Don't get me wrong; I didn't intend to find any cause for levity in the proceedings. In fact, my sympathies were with the defendants. It just happens that the two trials I observed that day might have been written for a situation comedy.

The first case concerned a young woman who was claiming breach of promise. This, in the latter half of the 20th century! The wronged damsel was about eighteen and quite arresting. It appeared to me that not only had she fallen from the top of the ugly tree, hitting every branch on the way down, but also she had courageously clambered back up, only to fall again, and, presumably, again and again. She certainly put the plain in plaintiff. As if her Gorgon-like features weren't enough to deter a potential suitor, her demeanour was a truly terrifying. Truthfully, she could have wrestled grizzlies for her a living, assuming anyone could find a regular supply of willing bears. I couldn't help feeling that it was a brave young man who had ever even looked at her, much less jilt her.

Her argument was that the youth in question had obtained her sexual favour by promising to marry her. Some favour! I couldn't help thinking that he must have been stoned off his face or else they had conducted their courtship in the middle of the night, blindfolded in an abandoned railway tunnel.

The defence counsel listened politely to her tale of injured innocence and then, after going through the routine, 'Are you so and so of such and such an address...' held up an envelope and asked, "Do you recognize this?" at which point the young woman blanched, before snarling "Where did yer get that from? It's private that!"

The defending counsel buckled slightly before the wrath of the Basilisk but he rallied, turned to the judge and, a la Perry Mason, purred, "Your honour ... this is an invitation to a sexual encounter sent by the plaintiff to my client ... if I may I would like to read it to the court..."

He was never allowed to finish his sentence or read the letter because the harridan from Hell stormed out of the witness stand barking furiously, "Yer not making a fuckin' show o' me!" and with a toss of her head she left the court, followed by her troupe of character witnesses, who seemed all terribly dismayed that they hadn't had their day in court.

My own thought was that she was a rotten sport for not letting us hear just what terms of endearment she had employed while wooing her erstwhile beau. The mind boggles.

Oddly enough, it was a character witness who was the star of the next case, which concerned shoplifting. The accused was a woman of about fifty, who had been apprehended by a security guard outside Marks and Spencer's allegedly in possession of stolen goods. As she stepped into the dock I noticed two young women in the benches below me rouse themselves from their depressed huddle and wave to her. She smiled back bravely and listened intently as the charges were read out. The case seemed to be cut and dried until a surprise witness entered the dock.

He was a shabbily dressed man aged about sixty and, with a pronounced Scottish accent, claimed to have seen the encounter between the defendant and the security man. His evidence, related to the sympathetic-looking defence counsellor, purported to demonstrate that there was a case of mistaken identity and that the real miscreant had escaped into the crowded street. At this point the two women below me, who were obviously the daughters of the accused, hugged each other with delight and their mother grew pink with joy at words of her saviour.

Their joy was short-lived, however, because just then the prosecutor received a note from a clerk and waved it ostentatiously in the direction of the magistrate, who allowed him to intervene. There was a hushed silence as the prosecutor theatrically perused the note.

Fixing his gaze on the character witness he asked smilingly, "Are you Hamish McCleish of … no fixed address?"

Hamish shuffled before cautiously agreeing, "Aye…"

There was another pause, and I noticed the daughters' shoulders sagging slightly. They had intuitively recognized that Hamish was not perhaps all he appeared. Sure enough, the prosecutor's next question, delivered in a tone of honey and vinegar, dispelled any doubts from their minds.

"And do you have fifty nine convictions for shoplifting?"

The daughters slumped in their seats at this, but then they brightened up again when Hamish replied confidently, "No. No me Sir!"

I was suddenly intrigued as it was possibly another case of mistaken identity. My own hopes were dashed when the prosecutor asked mildly, "Ahem...how many is it then?"

Hamish hesitated and then mumbled, "Fifty eight."

It was clear from the expression on the face of the accused that she had no prior knowledge of Hamish and it eventually transpired that he was something of a serial character witness in cases of shoplifting and often came forward to allege that the case was flawed because of mistaken identity or that the evidence had been planted.

I got the distinct impression that the shoplifter's daughters would happily have planted Hamish in the nearby St John's gardens.

51. Blowin' in the Wind

The other day I passed a beautiful old Georgian building, known as the Irish Centre. It lies abandoned at present, no doubt awaiting rescue in the heroic clutches of a developer. It used to be a thriving locus for the Liverpool Irish community, where, in typically Irish style, young children mixed with adults and discreetly bustling nuns amid the exhilarating sounds of fiddle bands and the rhythmic pounding of junior step dancers.

In 1972 I was sharing a flat, just up the road from the centre, with a bunch of students, all of whom were mad for music. One evening a guy called Allan asked me if I wanted to go with him to see a concert at the Irish Centre. I was doubtful, as I was in my Jim Morrison period and had a fair idea of what ranked as entertainment behind the doors of the Irish Centre. However, Allan assured me that the group were "meant to be good", so we ambled along to the centre and, after ordering the house wine (Guinness) we sauntered through into the large hall at the rear. I was bemused because the cream-painted walls were writhing with psychedelic images and cartoons, courtesy of a slide projector. As I sat down in the near-deserted hall I couldn't help wonder what the nuns thought of it all, but they never came anywhere near. It was just as well, because after a fair old wait, and two more pints, the group appeared on stage, dragging a naked body, which they deposited behind a battery of drums and cymbals.

For a while the drummer slumped behind his bass drum, clad only in a sticking plaster that clung to his upper arm like a half chevron. Then, before the stupefied gaze of the swelling audience, he awoke from his drug-induced sabbatical and tore into his 'skins' whilst playing out of his own ... and the roof nearly came off. It was only later I realised that the group I had seen would become something of a rock legend. They were called Hawkwind and that night the feathers really flew in the Irish Centre when they let rip with their chart hit 'Silver Machine'. Without doubt, the nuns that night must have been Sisters of Charity or Sisters of Mercy ... or maybe even the Sisters of the Poor, because by keeping out of sight they showed all three qualities in abundance.

Perhaps that was the night when The Irish Centre began to descend into its very own Celtic twilight, caught up in the winds of change and falling, dove-like, to the hawks of time.

52. Stuck in the Middle with You

One of the most bizarre things my mother ever said to me was at the height of Beatlemania, when it seemed that every kid in Liverpool was making a pilgrimage to Hessy's music store to buy, or simply worship, a guitar. I had just returned home from working on the buses when she uttered the immortal line:

"You won't try to be famous, will you John?"

I was dumbstruck, and to this day I haven't got an inkling what induced her to think I was about to clamber aboard the juggernaut that was the Mersey Band Wagon. I mean, it's not even as if I had any kind of singing voice...

I well remember one New Year's Eve when I was sixteen and too young to join the mass of revellers who were congregating at the junction of Lodge Lane and Smithdown Road, so 'I who had nothing' stayed at home with my face pressed up against the window pane. My Gran suggested I sing a song to entertain our solitary guest, a middle-aged man whose name I forget. I attempted a quavering rendition of 'Are you Lonesome Tonight' in a tone so flat you could have played pool on it. My Gran, ever eager to encourage me (or perhaps it was a sign that my tone deafness was genetically determined) asked me for an encore. I sang it again and the visitor kindly nodded approval, but I got the distinct impression he was secretly wishing he'd stayed at home in his own parlour and taken a chance on being lonesome!

The only comparison I can make with the sound of my singing that night is to ask you to imagine that there is in existence an album called 'Leonard Cohen sings Elvis Presley'!

By far the most embarrassing demonstration of my status of being melodiously challenged occurred after I was given a Dansette record player for my nineteenth birthday. The model I had was quite novel because it incorporated a microphone, which enabled me to sing along to any record – a sort of embryonic Karaoke machine. I used to stand in my bedroom and accompany my favourite singers, whilst gyrating à la Tom Jones. About a week after acquiring the means to destroy great pop songs I was standing outside my house when a young woman, whom I vaguely fancied, stopped and began to speak to me. 'Hello...' I thought, 'I'm on here...' but my vanity took a tumble when she asked plaintively, "What's that racket coming from your bedroom? I hear it every time I go past your house!"

I mumbled something about my baby brother messing about with the volume of the radio and fled.

When I recall my mother's fears that I might be tempted to exchange my ticket machine for a Fender Stratocaster it occurs to me that her concern may have had stemmed from a conversation she'd had with a local celebrity called Tony Jackson, who had just left the pop group 'The Searchers'. I'm not sure what reasons he gave for abandoning the band at the height of its fame, but I suspect she saw showbiz as a morass of danger.

Her attitude was more common among working class people than might be thought. It is as though the prospect of advancement brought with it the dangers of corruption and a loss of communal values. It was considered safer to keep one's head down and let the middle classes get on with whatever they were doing. This notion has its roots, not in Liverpool or any other modern city, but rather in ancient Athens, the home of democracy – a democracy where only free men had the vote, while all that slaves had was the odd day off.

Myths in all cultures transmit values and rules of behaviour and the Greek Myths are amongst the most widely known. Take these two myths, ostensibly unrelated, which transmit the same warning....

The first concerns Icarus, who was warned:

"Icarus, I advise you to take a middle course. If you fly too low, the sea will soak the wings; if you fly too high, the sun's heat will burn them. Fly between sea and sun! Take the course along which I shall lead you."

The second concerns King Procrustes, who used to make visitors sleep in a special bed. If they were too small for it he would have them stretched and if they were too tall, their feet would be severed.

Both Myths seem to be saying the same thing: be average ... don't get above yourself ... *conform*. It seems odd that legends my mother had barely heard of should influence her thinking, but there it is.

Phillip Larkin once wrote: "They fuck you up your mum and dad..." yet Icarus would have done well to heed his father.

So what do we do?

53. Just Walking in the Rain

Between the ages of four and ten I was as familiar with cinemas in Liverpool as I was with the interior of my parish church. They had much in common. The 'Granada' in Dovecote, for example, was as huge and as lavishly-decorated as St Dominic's, whose formal religious mosaics were matched by the cinema's strict outlines of giant art nouveau motifs which seemed to support the very roof of the picture palace. The church reeked of pungent, cloying, incense that curled heavenwards like flights of circling angels, shaken from their slumber by the swinging of the censor. The cinema, too, evoked sublime feelings as wraiths of cigarette smoke danced in the flickering light of the projectors until they formed an azure veil between this flawed world and Hollywood's perfect creations.

Each place of worship performed its own rituals, both of which involved receiving something that had to be queued for; whether it was the communion wafer delivered by a softly intoning priest or popcorn ministered by an usherette singing a litany of her wares. The respective blessings would then be taken to the privacy of a seat and masticated in sanctified silence. Neither came wholly free of charge; both church and cinema occasionally stripped me of all my worldly wealth.

But I remember one visit to the cinema that cost me absolutely nothing. It happened in the winter of 1954. An Irish family – the O'Neil's – had recently moved into our street and I had made friends with the eldest son, Martin. One night Martin's mother asked me if I wanted to go to the West Derby Plaza, my Saturday matinee venue, as she had obtained complimentary tickets – from Cadbury's, no less. I accepted with alacrity.

The rain was fairly lashing down as we walked towards the bus stop and so I was appalled when Martin's mother traipsed past it and headed cheerfully down the road towards West Derby. I quickly realised that bus fares for six would be quite a sum to her and so I buckled down to the two mile walk, even joining in the strolling choir led by Mrs O'Neil. The icy rain pelted us unmercifully and our spirits soon descended into our saturated socks. Eventually, even she could only manage a croaking version of 'Ave Maria'.

At last we arrived at the Plaza, all breezeblock and asbestos, as profane as the Granada was sacred. We joined the queue and spent ten or so minutes waiting to be relieved of the complimentary tickets. Then we went in and settled down in anticipation.

The film turned out to be a promotion depicting the gathering of cocoa beans in the heat of the tropics and lasted twenty minutes. My feet hadn't even begun to warm up as we started the long trek home, during which there was no further singing, only a muted chorus of uncomplimentary remarks concerning Cadbury's as we passed beneath the few newly-arrived television aerials, whose H-shapes seemed to whisper 'Hello'.

54. There's a Place

Ever present in the tourist guides for Liverpool, the 'Phil', as it is known locally, is probably the most ornate pub on Merseyside. From the opulence of its mosaic floors to the burnished copper engravings set into the horse-shoe shaped bar-front, the whole place is a monument to the pursuit of perfection. Even the magnificent wrought iron gates of the main entrance, set between the great slabs of polished granite, bear the Latin motto, 'Pacem amo'. Now I too love peace, and it is a strange thing, but during all the years I was a patron I never saw the slightest altercation, much less any conflict. Perhaps the natives had an innate understanding of the language of ancient Rome. After all, the imperial army was based in nearby Chester, and so who is to say that the odd cohort of Italian legionnaires didn't find its way to a Liverpool tavern, thus leaving Scousers a lingering linguistic legacy, by saying such things as, " I'll havva pinta dat beer and wonna doza porka pies over der. Over der, ya divvy! Next to dem pork scratchings!"

This could explain some of the idiosyncrasies of Liverpool speech, although the fact that there is no Theta, or 'th' in Gaelic is probably a better explanation of our predilection for saying 'dat' instead of 'that'. In the spirit of *quid pro quo*, the locals might well have introduced them to the joys of kicking a pig's bladder around the fields. How else can one begin to explain the Italians' proficiency at soccer?

The Phil's clientele was as mixed as the mosaics beneath their feet. Poets, hippies, students and all manner of civilians thronged the passageways that ran between the bar proper and the enormous back room that is so large that it could almost have hosted a five a side soccer tournament. I loved the sheer hurly-burly of it all, the seemingly endless ebb and flow of restless humanity bearing drinks as if was a festival dedicated to Aquarius, which was appropriate enough because in those days, before the introduction of strong lagers and real ales, British beer was something of a watery affair.

Of course, the Philharmonic was just one of several popular watering holes frequented by my friends and me. There was also the quaintly named 'Ye Old Cracke' and the 'Roscoe Head', but my personal favourite was and is the Phil. Perhaps the peace and harmony of the place appealed to me, or maybe it was because being bigger it could accommodate more ladies per square foot than the other two establishments put together. The fact remains that my solo performances in the Philharmonic led to many a moonlight sonata. As far as I am concerned the motto over the gate could have read, 'Be lucky'. After all, it was located in Hope Street.

I knew a man once, an artist and lecturer called Arthur Ballard, who was probably the only teacher John Lennon ever praised, as Arthur had prevented the expulsion from the local art college of Liverpool's most illustrious son. Arthur told me that his father had been involved in the Philharmonic's construction, which was apparently undertaken by the same person who built the staggeringly palatial 'Vines' in Lime Street. Arthur, an ex-army boxer turned artist and raconteur, who possessed a wealth of amazing stories, told me that the spectacular interiors of both pubs was the work of ship fitters who, when not engaged in the construction of floating palaces, turned their considerable skills to furbishing the pubs. Thus the Philharmonic is not only a monument to perfection it is also a museum to a long-lost craftsmanship that probably disappeared when the Titanic pitted cold steel against frozen water.

55. Banana Boat Song

As a child I was very familiar with the term 'skin boats', which was the name given to those vessels that plied their trade between Liverpool and the banana producing countries of Africa and the Caribbean. My father had often sailed for the biggest of the 'skin boat' companies, Elders and Ffyfes, and I have many memories of him carrying a suitcase in one hand and a huge stalk of green bananas in the other.

We had an airing cupboard next to the fireplace where the unripe fruit would be stored while it underwent the change from coolest green to the warmest of the primary colours. I don't know whether my mother thought that the cupboard possessed magical properties because she once tried to use it to mature a bottle of home-brewed beetroot wine. Now I don't want to convey the erroneous impression that my mother was a high-priestess of viticulture, because she was nothing of the sort. She had simply decided to try and make some wine from one of the few readily-available commodities of the post war austerity years. As I remember, somebody had given her the recipe for the 'wine', which lay in the cupboard for four years, long enough for real wine to be considered vintage, where it stubbornly refused to metamorphose into anything either drinkable or even mildly alcoholic as the notion of including yeast had been completely overlooked.

Nowadays, when I observe the sophisticated equipment available to amateur wine makers, I can't help but laugh at our periodic tasting of the vile juice that looked like wine and tasted like the dregs of a pickle jar. Her signal failure to produce an alcoholic beverage stemmed from the fact that she had 'adapted' the recipe to compensate for the fact that she had no equipment other than an aluminium pan, a supply of sugar, beetroot and an empty Tizer bottle. Looking back, I am thankful that the basics of wine making had eluded my mother because had she even remotely succeeded we could have had a ticking bomb in the airing cupboard!

Of course, bananas aren't the only fruit and I cannot forget the time my father decided to ripen a huge pineapple in the cupboard. By the time it had ripened he was long gone on another voyage and we were left with a pineapple the size of a small pig. Just up the road from us lived my great uncle John, who was chronically ill. I decided that a dose of pineapple would do him the world of good. Accordingly I sliced the pig in half and, clutching it to my infant bosom, made my way to Gainford Road, where I roused him from his sick-bed. I cannot forget the look of bewilderment that swept his ashen face as he silently accepted the fruity offering, the exposed flesh of which was liberally coated with fluff from my flannel jacket.

Years later I was given the opportunity to sail on a banana boat, the SS *Chirripo*, which belonged to Elders and Ffyfes, and I was intrigued by the prospect of following in my father's watery footsteps. I had sailed on several ships before the *Chirripo* and, apart from the *Empress of England*, with its icy white sheen, they had, in the main, epitomised Masefield's poetic vision – "Dirty British coaster with a salt-caked smokestack..." and so when I saw the *Chirripo* berthed in Garston dock, looking for all the world like a man-made iceberg as it glistened in the autumn sun, I felt vaguely cheered.

I don't know why I was surprised by the sparkling vessel, because, after all, bananas are not exactly dirty. True, the fruit is over-sprayed with chemicals, to the point where a stalk of bananas could be used to represent the periodic table, but dirty they are not. The boats that transport bananas are little more than gleaming maritime refrigerators, with flat bottoms to facilitate their navigation up the shallow rivers of Cameroon.

Of course, it was my job, as a rough-tough sailor boy, to keep the ship clean. Thus I spent seven weeks with a bucket of water at my feet and a lump of cotton waste in my hand as I washed the incessant salt spray from the varnished handrails or dragged a holy-stone over the pure white wood decks. That said, the crew were pleasant and the weather outward bound was fair.

Each evening, after the monotonous task of making an already ship-shape ship even more ship-shape, we were given an anti-malaria pill and a measure of rum to wash it down. Apart from that routine there is little I remember about the journey to the Cameroon port of Tiko. The ship had to navigate a long, winding river before it could be berthed and a French pilot came aboard. His assistant was a native of Cameroon, which at the time was in the process of throwing off the French colonial yoke. It so happened that the Frenchman miscalculated during a peculiar feat of manoeuvring, the likes of which I have never seen before or since.

The river we were sailing suddenly resembled a T-junction, formed by the confluence of another river at a perfect right angle to the one we were on. In order to steer the ship into a sharp right-hand bend, the starboard anchor had to be quickly dropped, so that our propelled stern would swing in a leftward arc while the bow was stationary, restrained by the anchor in the mud of the riverbed. That was the theory, but unfortunately the anchor didn't grip and the rapidly-moving ship ran aground. Before you could say 'monkey business' the ship was alive with small primates and glass-tailed lizards, so called because when they were captured by their tails they simply abandoned the appendage and grew new ones.

The French pilot was a picture of dismay, while his native assistant exuded unadulterated joy at the imperial failure.

On our arrival I was astonished at the visible signs of poverty that abounded in the drab jungle town. Everywhere there were wretched men dressed in torn and tattered shorts, carrying umbrellas! Tiko, you see, is directly in the path of the equatorial rain shadow and so every afternoon, as regular as clockwork, a deluge of monsoon proportions would ensue and the murky looking rivers would be permanently swollen.

A few of us decided to take an old man's offer of a boat ride. The payment for the trip was three quarters of a white loaf, which lay in the muddy bottom of the dug out while its owner steadily paddled up the brackish river, which was hemmed in by giant mangroves. I noticed that the dugout was riddled with tiny holes made by wood boring parasites, which our ferryman had plugged with clay. But every so often I was disconcerted to see a breach in the clay defences and water bubbling through the tiny hole. After about ten minutes the bottom of the canoe was awash and I was getting seriously worried, and not just for our safety, because the loaf was visibly sodden.

One of the men decided to relieve the old man of his onerous task and was paddling merrily when we found ourselves heading for the gnarled roots of the mangroves that were suspended in the water like the claws of a monstrous pre-historic bird. There must have been something deadly in among the trees because the old man panicked and began screaming for our oarsman to back paddle. Still shaking, the boat's owner took the paddle and got us back to the jetty *post haste*. To this day I don't know what danger existed in that part of the jungle, but one thing I cannot forget is the shame I felt when, on stepping out of the canoe, I squashed the old man's payment. His sad resigned eyes still haunt me. Worse still, I didn't even have any money with me to compensate the poor fellow.

Back at the ship young African boys were diving for coins tossed into the river by crewmembers. I don't suppose it was easy finding coins in that muddy gloom and I imagine it was even worse when they finally got their precious reward ashore only to find that the 'silver' coins were in fact pennies, wrapped in the foil from cigarette packets.

One day we were invited to play a game of football against the local administrators, only the Europeans though; the idea of officers playing against the 'lowly' natives was considered *infra dig*. I have since wondered if an infant Roger Miller (the Cameroon footballer, not the singer of 'King of the Road') was present and whether he decided there and then that he could almost defeat England on his own during the future world cup of Italia '90.

On the way to the train that conveyed both bananas and people to the urban areas I saw a man sitting next to a sign that read 'Avocado Pears'. Thinking they would come in handy at half time I bought a huge bag of them, which I immediately dumped because when I bit through the thick skin of the 'pear' I was almost ill.

The match was to be played in a clearing in the jungle and before the kick-off we had a kick about with the local lads. One of them, barefoot and aged about eleven, kicked the ball to me. It arrived about groin height and so I put out a hand to avoid the possibility of gaining a third testicle when I felt a most fearsome pain in my thumb, which had been pushed backwards by the force of the shot. I didn't enjoy the game and I think we were thrashed anyway.

We got back to the ship drunk and frustrated, as the local girls were of a chaste demeanour, in spite of our vigorous pursuit of a clothes-for-sex programme, which was *allegedly* the currency of love in that part of the world. I still have vague recollections of wandering around a village with my socks in my hand, reeling both from the rum and the open disdain of the local maidens.

However, worse things happen on big ships. One of our number, an old man called Jerry, who was a fireman, a harmless old man whose growl was far worse than his bite, had saved up his ration of rum and drunk it all in one sitting. I say 'sitting' because when I last saw him he was prone and quite dead. He was buried before I had even recovered from my hangover and before the tropical heat had rendered his memory stale. I can't help but think he would have been better off without the pills and the attendant rum, thus taking his chances with the mosquitoes.

The soil on his jungle grave had barely settled when we sailed for Oslo, via Senegal. The leafy debris from the ship's unscheduled trip into the jungle was still attached to our cross trees so that it resembled the fabled masthead of the 17th century Dutch Admiral, Von Tromp, who lashed a broom to his mast as a symbol of his 'success' in ridding the seas of the British Navy. It was on this leg of the voyage that I had my only chance to employ an aspect of seamanship I'd learned at training school in Sharpness. It concerned the use of a contraption known as 'the bosun's chair'.

The chair was simply a plank of wood attached to a loop of rope, which passed through a pulley fixed to the top of the mast. The idea was that one sat on the plank and hoisted oneself up the mast by dint of pulling on one half of the loop. On reaching the desired height, in my case the top of the mast, there was a heart-stopping moment when all that prevented one from plummeting to one's death was the friction of the two parts of the rope which one held firmly in one's hand while lashing the slack to the dangling plank. It really was an ingenious way to get high into the rigging, but one false move of the hand and it would have been instant death.

I had been ordered (I nearly wrote 'asked') to apply black paint to the top half of the rear mast, so as to disguise its soot-caked surface, which was constantly in the path of the funnel's exhaust and marred the otherwise pristine appearance of the floating wedding cake. I had an accident when my foot collided with the tin of paint and, horror of horrors, the deck, so smoothly white from years of holy-stoning it could have graced the union of a couple of ice skaters, was instantly awash with thick, sticky, black paint.

The first mate went bananas and threatened me with a 'bad discharge', which was the maritime equivalent of a reference. So it was with deep anxiety that I found myself clambering on the cross trees of the after mast, faced with the problem of getting the new tin of black paint safely to the topmast. I decided that for safety's sake I would lash the handle of the tin to the bosun's chair. I then had to find a way of getting the chair over the open manhole that allowed access from the lower mast to the cross trees. Taking great care I hurled the chair across the gap and suddenly heard myself screaming when the attached paint tin followed the chair and dispersed its contents on the gleaming decks below, where the ever-present wind whipped it into a black and white mosaic.

That was in 1963 and I imagine that my successors, if that's an appropriate expression, have by now, through the application of a multitude of holy-stones, erased the last vestiges of my action painting on the high seas.

Worse was to follow in the wake of my incompetence when we entered the port of Dakar. It was late afternoon and I was at the helm and so had the simple task of steering the ship to its berth, which meant that I had to bring her to rest alongside the long harbour wall that lay parallel to the vessel's starboard side. It was normal practice in such circumstances to fix one's eyes on a reference point so that the ship didn't drift off course to either left or right. Accordingly, I strove to ensure that the bow was pointed constantly towards a large crane which was standing on the far dock wall that lay at a right angle to our berth. How was I to know that it was a mobile crane and that it was moving slowly to my right? Well, I didn't know, and as a consequence the ship, at my prompting, veered in the same direction. Before I could say 'Oh dearie me', the hull was on intimate terms with the concrete quay! The first mate, on hearing what must have sounded like a competition between every steel band in Senegal, raced to the bridge, looked at me, groaned, and cradled his head in his hands.

We sailed from Dakar with fading foliage in our foremast, a disfiguring scar on our hitherto gleaming hull and an indelible blemish on my reputation. I was really looking forward to going home.

Our route to Oslo meant that we had to pass through the Skageraak, the channel that separates Norway from Denmark, and we did so during an incredibly violent sea. At one point, when I was keeping lookout on the 'monkey island' (an open cage above the bridge) I could see a lighthouse directly ahead of us as I was talking to the second mate, who was also present. The ship was battered by a thundering wave and suddenly the lighthouse was shining somewhere to my immediate left. Flat bottomed, the vessel yawed alarmingly and the second mate, fearful that that he would soon be swimming for his life, was comically barefoot as he instantly kicked off his boots.

I was simply frozen to the spot.

I remember Oslo not only for the array of stunningly beautiful women thronging its streets, but also for the pretty gardens where I sat and drank Tuborg lager while listening to a group, ironically called 'The Deep River Boys', singing 'Where have all the flowers gone?'

Gone to Avocados and Bananas every bleeding one!

56. Food, Glorious Food

About sixteen years ago, after the birth of our eldest son, my spouse and I arrived at a fairly momentous decision. She would work full time and I would continue part time teaching in the evening and look after the baby by day. It made economic sense, as her career was well established while I was little more than a dilettante. We could have employed a baby-minder, but at the time the newspapers were constantly churning out horror stories about the mistreatment of infants at the hands of their carers. Furthermore, prior to my panic attack, I had often told friends a tale about a ship's steward I knew of who had his own idiosyncratic, not to say criminal, way of dealing with children. It was a blackly comic tale but it had come back to haunt me.

His job was to look after the children of post-war immigrants from Liverpool to Australia and New Zealand on a notorious vessel called 'The Captain Cook'. Apparently he had total control of the budget for the children's food throughout the four to six week voyage and every morning he would enter the crèche area and gather his flock around him saying, "Right kids, what do we all want for dinner today?"

The children would be rapt as, with his face a contorted mask of distaste, the steward slowly continued.

"Meat?"

"No ... Boo!"

"Cabbage?"

"No ... Boo!"

"Potatoes?"

"No ... Boo!"

"Or..."

At this juncture the timing of his pause would have rivalled a Shakespearean actor, "Jelly and Ice Cream!"

Needless to say, the low protein offering always won hands down.

After a month of a diet that would have been condemned even in austerity Britain the children looked woefully under-nourished and the latter-day privateer was eventually forced to walk the metaphorical plank, but not for his embezzlement. You see, he had a way of dealing with dissenting children that was, well, unusual… If any child was ever tempted to bemoan their lack of culinary choices in the presence of his or her parents, the buccaneer would gently chide the child and pretend to cuff it about the head with a linen napkin, which he carried at all times, and which concealed a large wooden spoon. It was only after he had raised too many lumps that the parents collectively raised Cain.

So, with all those precedents in mind, I stayed home and cooked for my babies (another followed) and although I've never regretted it one iota, it could be argued that it was a dubious career move. In employment terms I was out of the loop and in the soup.

The routine that the babies kept included bouts of sleeping and so I was able to find the time to prepare all our meals from freshly bought foodstuffs. I had maintained that regime for almost seventeen years and so you can imagine my anguish when my eldest son recently expressed a liking for Pot Noodles! Worse, he now takes great pride in the fact that his first foray into cooking involves emptying a packet of Batchelor's dehydrated pasta, which is, as far as I am concerned, chemically-anointed crap, into a pan of milk and bringing the contents to the boil before simmering for five minutes. The resulting gloop is then pronounced delicious!

You see, I had plans to carry on a tradition inherited from my mother, who had instructed me from the age of fourteen in the arcane mysteries of making our local delicacy. Now almost every person in Liverpool has a mother who can legitimately lay claim to creating the definitive version of the stew which we call 'Scouse' – and all those claims are legitimate, regardless of variations in recipes and the execution of those recipes, because, as someone once pointed out, 'Mother's food is best because it's made with love'.

Talking about execution reminds me of the time when I sat down to eat a plate of my mother's scouse, which I loved dearly, as it was always made with floury potatoes, which ensured that the meat and vegetable stew was of such a dry consistency that any leftover Scouse could be eaten cold, on bread, without any excess moisture dissolving the bread.

Anyway, that night I noticed that my Mam wasn't eating, but I was so hungry I didn't ask why, and instead began devouring my supper. After a few mouthfuls I noticed that my dad's complexion had begun to rival the beetroot that he liked to accompany his Scouse and my own mouth was on fire. We finished our meal in tortured silence and it was then that my mother came clean... It transpired that as she was seasoning the stew the lid of the pepper pot had fallen off, allowing the entire contents of a tub of Lion-brand white pepper to smother the surface of the pan of Scouse. She had managed to scrape most of it off, but it had been impossible to get it all. I can only thank the stars that she got most of it out, or we would have suffered third degree burns of the alimentary canal!

Talking about getting burned, I had a mate in Cammell Lairds who had been married for only a week when his bride proudly placed her first plate of Scouse on the table. It was their first night at home after the honeymoon, and he told me later that the portion was so large he wasn't sure whether he was meant to eat it or jump over it. However, under the intense scrutiny of his loving wife, my friend dug deep and steadily ate his way through the Scouse Mont Blanc.

His wife clasped her hands and asked if he'd enjoyed it. He replied in the affirmative but was horrified as she smiled delightedly and said, "You can have some more then, 'cos I've made loads!"

57. Video Killed the Radio Star

My first memory of 20th century technology is of a push-button radio, or as people used to refer to it, a 'wireless'. It was quite a handsome thing, with its light oak veneer and tiers of ivory looking buttons that were pre-set to certain stations. Oh the sheer wonderment of being able to press buttons designated Hilversum, Dusseldorf or Athlone and hearing foreign speakers in my Huyton living room!

I think it had previously belonged to my grandfather. He was a great radio buff and was inexplicably fond of opera. I say inexplicably because he had as much hope of attending a performance of 'Carmen' as I have of playing Don Giovanni at *La Scala*. He was studiously discerning in his choice of singers, Gigli was his idol, and he was utterly dismissive of the 'upstart' Mario Lanza. Before my mother 'won' it, my grandfather had in all probability heard Chamberlain's querulous declaration of war on that very wireless; given my grandfather's sojourn in a German POW camp in the great war, I have sometimes wondered if he had ever listened to, and possibly understood, the ravings of Herr Shicklegruber.

I recall with fondness those Sundays in our small council house when my mother and I would sit, amid the aroma of roast dinner and Mansion furniture polish, listening to 'Two-Way Family Favourites', a show designed to link the British army abroad with the folks back home in which servicemen in far-flung outposts around the world would request songs for their loved-one's birthdays and vice-versa. In today's cynical atmosphere the show would probably be more about confrontation than celebration. I can almost hear Jean Metcalfe's dulcet tones announcing, "This is the BBC overseas service and I have a request to be played for Regimental Sergeant Major Mike 'Bully-Beef' Smith. It's from your wife Elspeth … and it's Del Shannon singing 'Runaway' … which is highly appropriate as Elsie has just gone AWOL with a private!"

The joys of radio were superseded by the advent of television and, for reasons which escape me, my father bought one of the earliest sets. I mean, he was always at sea, so why he bought a television I don't know, unless, of course, he wanted me to enjoy the world he had encountered via the cathode ray tube. At that time the only show in town was the BBC, as Independent Television was still but a twinkle in the ad-man's eye. Strange that a television company so reliant on advertisers was said to be 'independent'. In the early years of television, when programmes were in short supply, I used to spend hours staring at a pre-recorded film of a pair of hands moulding clay on a potter's wheel. Little did I realise that I myself was also clay in the hands of the broadcasters, who helped shape my world view on a daily basis…

My early exposure to the ethereal Cyclops had given me an ability to solve those dreadful problems which plagued the early years of the medium – wavy lines, horizontal flickering etc – to the extent that I became something of a media consultant, and some of my neighbours sought my expertise in order to resolve their television sets' erratic behaviour. I remember one couple who thought I was a demi-god simply because my thumping the back of their set produced a picture. Sadly, nowadays, you'd need a degree in electronics to cut it with the neighbours.

The novelty of television was rapidly disappearing as we became more familiar with the medium. I had cousins, Sheila and Keith, who had an uncanny ability to predict exactly when a commercial break was about to occur. They used to compete to be the first to shout, "End of part one!" and every time, at that precise second, the scene faded and ushered in something along the lines of:

Omo washes, not only clean
Not only white, but bright!
Omo adds bright, bright, brightness!

I was always the last to guess.

Oddly enough, their father was also a seaman and had bought their television. Perhaps sailors saw some affinity between air-waves and those on the ocean...

By the late fifties almost everybody I knew had access to a television and I can remember sitting with my Gran in the semi-darkness of her pre-fab, ogling the box in the corner. My Gran used to love having her grandchildren brush her hair, which had, when she was a relatively young woman, turned quite grey and which, by the time she was seventy, had gone beyond white to Jean Harlow highlights. One night I was brushing her hair while we were watching a thriller when suddenly she shouted frantically to one of the endangered characters,

"Look behind you!"

As a media-savvy youth I was amazed at her naiveté. After all, the play was set on a train, so the noise of the engine would have...

My first colour set was bought by my wife in 1980, at Christmas, and I was able to enjoy one of my all-time favourite films as Robert Newton snarled and swaggered his way to Treasure Island. Now, you would expect that during all of those years between 1955 and 1980 I would have had a valid TV licence, but you would be wrong. In fact, the first time I ever saw a licence was when my wife brought hers, along with her television when she moved in.

Her foresight in buying a licence almost equalled my foresight in marrying her, because one day, shortly after she arrived, there was a knock on the door and I opened it to reveal two grinning officials who wanted to see my licence, as they had already established that I had a TV. Their smiles rapidly disappeared as I appealed to my wife, who before our first son was born could remember the location of everything from a shirt to a button, and asked her to find the licence. She produced hers, which was transferable! If only they had called a year earlier they could have laughed all the way to my bank!

When our eldest son was born in 1985 we didn't even need a phone because, as a child of the mind-expanding sixties, I was probably hoping for a breakthrough in mass telepathy. However, the prospect of my child falling ill, coupled with the fact that public telephones that worked were as rare as those which were free of teenagers calling their friends, prompted me to buy a phone. The installation of that simple arrangement of wires and magnets opened the floodgates of technology and drowned forever the Luddite in my bosom.

Since those primitive days I have acquired all manner of technologies from computers to juice-extractors. Many of those items have found their way into that part of the universe known as the Galaxy of Obsolescence, and I still can't believe my profligacy when I recall the expensive goods I have dumped, given away or replaced because they were outmoded.

I remember the first colour printer I ever bought, or rather received as a birthday present. It made such a racket that I had to escape into the garden until it had finished printing, and I only knew that the print run was over when the birds returned! I'm presently looking with yearning at a 'wireless' PC.

Plus ca change, plus c'est le meme chose!

58. Wash Day Blues

One of the modern technologies I have, until recently, strenuously avoided coming to terms with, has very simple controls consisting of knobs and dials. I am referring to the washing machine. To say I am ignorant of the workings of a Hotpoint is an understatement. Indeed, I have perfected launderial incompetence to an art form.

I can remember when I was living the bachelor life, taking my laundry to the local laundromat, where I would hover in front of a machine and do a passable imitation of an alien trying to operate a chocolate vending machine. I would stand there, coins in hand, looking hopelessly lost, until a kind housewife would come to my rescue, shoo me to a seat, and proceed to fill the maw of the machine with my smalls. The psychologist's term for such behaviour is 'learned helplessness'. In Liverpool we called it 'acting soft'.

In my defence I can only point out that, when I was a child, the only men who did the laundry without being dismissed as 'a big girl's blouse' were usually of Chinese origin and spent most of their lives operating some infernal contraption or other while bathed in enough steam to remove oil-based graffiti from a pebble-dashed wall. That said, I did hump the odd bag of washing to the 'Bendix' or the 'Bag-wash' – which were the generic terms for self-service laundries when I was a kid.

There was a Chinese laundry in Lodge lane and I have a singular reason for remembering it. One winter's night in the mid sixties I was waiting at the bus-stop with a girlfriend whom I was escorting back to her Huyton penthouse – well, her high-rise in Bluebell Lane. Anyway, as we stood there, watching the idle spiralling of discarded chip papers, a small car drew up and Mr Lau, the laundry wizard, drew up and offered us a lift. My response was to inform him that Huyton was quite a distance away, but he simply gestured to us to climb in.

It transpired that Mr Lau had just taken possession of his first car and wanted to give it a run. His pride in the little car, which model I can't remember, was obvious. As he drove his car with studied care, his hands constantly patted the steering wheel as if he were petting a purring cat. The shop that housed the laundry has long since gone up in smoke, not from the result of a carelessly-placed smoothing iron, but as a consequence of the 1981 riots. Not only has the laundry disappeared, but also the premises that once accommodated a small haberdashers on the corner of Vandyke Street, which sold many of the shirts that Mr Lau transformed from what were essentially limp rags into starched and shining perfection. He didn't get any of mine though. My mum owned an Indesit washing machine, which, when it wasn't dancing the cha-cha-cha across the kitchen floor, because it wasn't weighted down inside with a concrete block, used to turn white shirts pink. The fault lay not with the machine but with me.

As a teenager, my favourite night of the week was Friday. I had nothing against Saturday, but unless I was lucky enough to win on the horses on Saturday afternoon, I was usually spent up. So on Friday evening I would have supper, watch 'The Beverly Hillbillies' and get dolled up for a night on the town; one such night I was just about to iron my shirt, a technological feat I had mastered while in the Merchant Navy, when I was astounded to see that my white shirt was inexplicably a bright shade of pink. My mother was mortified and immediately dashed up to the haberdashers to purchase a new white shirt. That should have been the end of the matter, but the following week it happened again and once more I found myself brandishing a pink shirt in my mother's direction, demanding further reparation. My spoilt-brat routine resulted in another hundred-yard dash for my mother and a bill for thirty-nine shillings and eleven pence.

The pink scourge phenomenon continued for about six weeks and the mystery was only solved when my father saw me inserting matchsticks into the collar of my new white shirt, to lend it a stiffness it hadn't arrived with. Such practices were common, but most men decapitated the live heads of the matches first!

It's a strange fact of human life that a smell, a scent or an aroma can instantly transport us back to when we either first smelt it, or a time when we were particularly aware of that smell. This is because a smell, unique of all the categories of things in this world, cannot be given a name. We can only say that something smells *like* something else. For instance: that smells like 'rotten eggs', 'old clothes' or 'a rose'. This lack of a naming system means that there are no labels or language to clog up the journey down our sensory pathways. One sniff of freshly-mown grass and we are instantly walking barefoot in the park. "Er ... so what?" you might ask. Well, whenever I smell the steamy sweet smell of fresh ironing I immediately catch a glimpse of my Auntie Beryl. You see, my overriding memory of her is that she always seemed to be ironing for her five children and her husband John. In fact, I was in my late teens before I realised that, of the six legs I thought she had, four of them belonged to the ironing board!

Again, I only have to inhale the pungent scent of curry spices and I am walking into the living room of my Indian girlfriend, whose house was so rich in coriander, cumin and other exotics that it made my eyes water. My eyes were almost as moist when she went off with a car salesman from Hoylake.

My days as a dhobi dodger might well be numbered. Recently my wife was so ill that she couldn't even remove the cap from the fabric conditioner. Even my best method acting technique failed to save me and so last week I completed a full cycle of washing from gathering it in, to hanging it out on the line to dry. Do you know I'm damned glad I was able to dodge that particular column for some fifty odd years!

A woman's work is never done while there are men possessed of enough hand-eye co-ordination to throw socks into a basket.

59. Say a Little Prayer

I have been aware of that phenomenon known as prayer since I was a very small child. One of the earliest popular songs I can remember contained the lines:

> Answer me, Lord above,
> Just what sin have I been guilty of...

Thus, in a snatch of a lyric you have the essence of my Catholic upbringing, prayer, ignorance and guilt.

Of course it's not only Christians who pray. I once stood at Jerusalem's Wailing Wall, wearing my borrowed *yarmulke*, observing the piety of my Jewish hosts as they shoved pieces of paper containing their prayers into the chinks in the holy edifice. I was in the company of a Jewish kid from New York and was astounded when, as if divining my thoughts, he blithely informed me that he had once opened some of the prayers and discovered that they were pleadings for some of the more mundane aspects of existence, such as asking God to intercede on Eyal's behalf so that he might pass his exams, or for Zoah to do well in America. It was comforting to know that I'd come across another point of similarity between the old rival religions, because measurable stretches my own childhood had been spent on my knees, bothering God with banal requests for football boots, soccer balls and the red and white strip of Liverpool FC. My childish hopes for divine intervention were always dashed as my mother's choice of Christmas gifts never coincided with mine, in spite of my leaving enough hand-written notes lying about to transform our house into a facsimile of the remains of Solomon's temple.

Of course, people did pray for a more lofty purpose. For instance, if the subject of the prayers was seriously ill then Catholics in Liverpool would unveil the big guns, the Novenas. Novenas are a regular, typically monthly, commitment to pray for something or someone at a particular venue, which in our town was usually the Fox Street

Priory. Completing a Novena could take up to a year, which meant that the plenary had to make his or her way once a month to share mass with the Franciscan friars, whose gentle demeanour and brown habits somehow rendered our gritty city into a seaside Assisi.

Prayer to me then was as natural as breathing. I can remember climbing to the tops of trees and, feeling suddenly vulnerable, not to say terrified, I would clasp my hands together and offer God a deal.

"Get me down safely and I'll never climb another tree!" Although I have lost count of the times I reneged on that particular agreement.

In 1956 I was informed that I had passed the eleven-plus, by my teacher Mr Kellet, whose surly mien reflected his distaste for the fact that I had been in his class only a few months after a long absence attending at least three other schools as my mother engaged in her urban peregrinations, seeking refuge from my father (it was a condition of the contemporary divorce law was that they didn't co-habit or even meet). Mr Kellet, acting *in loco parentis*, was possibly annoyed, as I had probably usurped the place of one of his protégés. I will never forget the day he humiliated me in front of the class. We had been set a test in which we had to supply the animal to the animal's nickname: Leo is to Lion as Bruin is to Bear etc…

When I read 'Reynard is to Fox as Brock is to … I wrote 'Badger'. But according to Mr Kellet the correct answer was 'fireworks' as Brock's was a well-known brand of pyrotechnic! I protested on the grounds that we had been writing about animals. His face, white with anger, told me to be quiet, as I was wrong. Why he denied me I will never know, but I suspect that from that day onward I was perceived as a troublemaker.

Then I was told that I was to attend the most prestigious Catholic Grammar School in the area – St Edwards – for a 'recall'. I had no idea what that meant and neither did my mother, but I know now that it was some kind of evaluation to see if I was fit for 'The Eddies'.

On the morning of the recall, before she went to work, my mother constantly impressed upon me the need to pray at every opportunity when I got to the college. I have never understood her insistence on that, as she was only ever a sporadic churchgoer, but I always tried hard to please her. On my arrival at the school a Christian Brother ushered me into a small room where the smell of floor polish merged with the lingering aroma of beeswax candles. Wordlessly handing me a piece of paper to read, he left. Not knowing what the paper represented I cast a cursory glance over its contents and, taking advantage of my isolation, promptly fell to praying like a good 'un.

After about five minutes of my God-bothering the door opened and another Brother escorted me into the adjoining room, where I was questioned closely on the contents of the paper. For the first time in my life I was flummoxed, as I knew next to nothing about the text. When, weeks later, I was informed that I would be attending the Collegiate school in Shaw Street, neither my mother nor myself ever connected my time spent dialling the celestial network with my failure to be accepted by St Edwards.

True to form, my mother, not so much a lapsed as a decidedly relaxed Catholic, approached the education authority with a plea that I should attend a Catholic school. Thus it was that I found myself in my own personal hell of St John De La Salle Grammar School, courtesy of the confused piety of a sweet woman who, ironically, was soon to find herself *ex-communicado* after she divorced and re-married.

My subsequent years as a truant separated me from my pious environs and so, despite Christ's assertion that the open sky was his church, my dial-up account to God.com was always in the black. My heavenly modem packed up altogether on November 22nd 1963.

You see, my mother, in spite of being near blinded by an accident and having me for a son, still retained some vestiges of belief and had led me to believe that the church would always have its doors open should I feel the need to pray. The news of Kennedy's assassination sent me in search of solace and so that night, late on, I went to St Bernard's church in Kingsley Road, only to find that vandals had forced the priest to close its doors. I'm afraid I took it personally.

So does anybody want an unused mobile phone with a direct line to Heaven? At the risk of appearing at best cynical and at worst blasphemous, as far as I'm concerned, prayer is just another hook-up.

But you can say one for me, if you like...

60. Heart of Gold

For a working-class woman in the Liverpool of the fifties, divorce wasn't so much a removal of a barrier to freedom, but rather the erection of an obstacle course that only the fittest or the most desperate could survive. Possibly the greatest obstacle was the notion of collusion, whereby neither of the warring factions was ever allowed to meet, much less share the same abode. The law reasoned that if two litigants met face-to-face then they would naturally be tempted to connive at the grounds for their divorce.

Now, if you were a wealthy woman this stricture would be of little consequence. You simply upped sticks and lived in comfort somewhere else. My mother had to rely on the limited charity of relatives, interspersed with flats and rooming houses. This nomadic existence was not designed to foster home-making skills. All that was deemed important was food and shelter; *Home & Garden* was something you read in the doctor's waiting room.

By 1960 my mother had remarried and become pregnant with my half-brother Stephen. Her nest-building instincts, for so long dormant, returned like the first hesitant swallows that presage a long, hot summer. Her earliest adornments were fairly basic, as the house she and my stepfather rented had not seen any major modernisation since the advent of the Davy lamp. Indeed, even after they had installed electricity, at their own expense, the wall-mounted gas mantles remained operative for some time afterwards, shielding their delicate incandescence from the unblinking glare of the electric light bulb that suddenly dominated the room.

About two years later we moved to another street, not far away. The basics already existed, so my Mam decided to get a washing machine. It was a really flash-looking job from Italy, but when it was switched on it danced the cha-cha-cha all the way across the kitchen floor and back again. My old girl freaked out and sent it back, thereby rejecting engineering by Indesit and choreography by Verdi.

One day I was in the small side garden when I dug up a miniature coal scuttle. My mother discerned a glint beneath the blackened surface and declared it to be brass. At the time she was taking part in what can only be described as 'the great brass rush of 59'. Every week she would find another 'piece' and spend hours polishing it till it shone. So you can imagine that she was quite pleased at my find. Anyway, just as she was setting up the newspaper and Brasso the doorbell rang. It was my beloved Aunt Alice. She spotted the 'pay dirt' lying on the newspaper, and, like a Californian claim jumper, circled round, picked up the brass scuttle and immediately set to buffing and polishing. After about two hours the scuttle was shining and glittering in the light of the coal fire. Aunt Alice, with her dark eyes opened wide, looked appealingly at my mother, who, realising that she could no longer in all conscience lay any moral claim to the brass, indicated that Alice had 'won' it, whereupon Alice gave out a loud whoop of delight.

I accompanied her to the 26 bus-stop, where we chatted until the bus came. Her eyes never once left her trophy, not even when a cruel gust of wind hoisted it out of her shopping bag and wedged it tight under the wheels of the approaching bus, rendering it flatter than a gold mining pan.

All that glitters may not be gold, but the effort Alice made to bring a shine into her life was always 24-carat. Yet, as was usual in her case, the reward was pure dross by the scuttleful.

God rest her sweet and generous soul.

61. Catch a Falling Star

I was recently invited by a woman called Lyn Brown to visit Zoe's Baby Hospice in West Derby to have a coffee, meet the staff and see the babies. My first impulse was to find a way to maintain my near one hundred percent record of avoiding things I find difficult to cope with. However, after a few days of being conscious that I was somehow dodging the column, I asked Lyn if I could come over with a view to writing a piece.

In spite of once being so familiar with the area that I could have drawn a map of it in the dark with invisible ink, I had to ask the way to the hospice, because so much had changed. By the day's end more than mere geography had changed.

As I walked up the drive towards the health centre that housed the hospice I noticed a young couple extricating two young children from their car. One of the children, a baby of about twelve months old had a tube attached to his nostril, while the other end was located in a portable device which, as I later found out, was a feeding pump.

I couldn't help but notice that the young mother looked drawn and tired and so I assumed, correctly as it turned out, that we all had the same destination.

While I was sitting in the reception area, an arm's length from the young couple, waiting for Ann, the hospice manager, to collect me, I was acutely aware that I was dreading the prospect of being in the presence of distressed babies.

I asked myself what was I doing there and I was tempted to leave my small offering with the elderly receptionist, make an excuse and flee, but just then Ann came down the stairs and shook my hand.

We mounted some stairs and I soon found myself in a brightly decorated room, the ceilings of which were festooned with kites depicting such childhood favourites as Bob the Builder and the Tellytubbies.

I sought refuge on one of the bright blue couches that lined the walls of the homely looking room and watched a tiny girl in a powder blue jump suit energetically propelling herself along the floor. It wasn't until she turned to look at me that I realised she had Down's syndrome. She was so pretty and bubbly that it was almost impossible to believe that she was ill.

Just as Ann brought the coffee in the young couple entered the room and while the oldest child stared fascinated at the kites they settled down opposite me and adjusted their other baby's feeding tubes. It was then that I became aware of a young nurse hovering close by, whose demeanour betrayed her eagerness to hold the baby. The father, who had been cradling the baby, smilingly offered her to the nurse, who clasped the infant to her as if he were a prize.

Ann, who had been observing the scene, said, in mock reproach, "You could hardly wait to pick him up could you?"

The young nurse merely smiled. To have denied the charge would have been absurd.

As the couple, who were there to arrange respite care, left to be taken round the hospice, to see if it met with their approval, Ann asked me to accompany her on my own guided tour.

Within minutes, the dread I had felt was evaporating and by the time I left Zoe's Place I felt uplifted. This barely credible transformation was the result of listening intently to a woman who was so utterly besotted by her charges that the gloom which had enveloped me all day began to lift as I became more and more absorbed by both the ethos and the atmosphere of Zoe's Place. It is difficult to feel anything else in the presence of people who resolutely and joyfully celebrate life in defiance of death, even when the latter appears to have all the high cards.

Ann took me to the chapel where the babies are not mourned, but where their lives and tiny but nonetheless measurable achievements are celebrated. I caught sight of a photograph of a casket, the size of which confused me into thinking that there must have been a child older than five years old that had died in the hospice. I put this to her and she told me that when Zoe's babies are buried they take with them all of their favourite objects of love, such as cuddly toys, videos, cards etc, and so the caskets were built almost twice the size of the infants.

I was reminded of the feared and tyrannical Pharaohs who were buried with all the signs of their earthly might, and I couldn't help feeling that Zoe's babies were far more powerful because they were interred with the symbols of the love they had inspired.

In spite of Ann's strength of spirit the emotional strain was such that I was glad when she led me into the 'light room'. This was where babies were taken when they were overtired or in need of relaxation. There were bubbling water filled tubes of coloured beads, and a mirror ball splashed colours on the murals while curtains of brightly glowing fibre optics hung in the door openings. It was a glorious hybrid of Santa's Grotto and a Disco, which was a source of obvious delight to the baby who lay on the miniature waterbed following the random patterns, created by the slide projector. I almost shouted 'Bo Selector!'

It was during this interlude that Ann told me about the role of Mohamed Al Fayed in the maintenance of Zoe's Place. I was astounded to learn that the millionaire owner of Harrod's, who for years has been the object of vilification by certain members of press, was not only a benefactor to Zoe's but also a visitor. When she told me how she had seen the expensively-dressed Al Fayed down on his knees playing with the babies, his suit smeared with the chocolate he had given them, I couldn't help thinking that he ought to desist from trying to become a British citizen, because as far as Zoe's babies are concerned he already has a passport to a better place.

The most poignant yet elevating moment of my visit came when I was looking at the photo gallery of Zoe's Place children, most of whom were dead. Every child was smiling, happily displaying their milk teeth and I unsuccessfully attempted to console my myself with the thought that while no tooth fairy would ever redeem them for a bright coin, neither would they suffer the pain of toothache and its attendant terrors.

Then, as I looked at the smiling faces I recalled my uncle Stan telling me, as we stood in a frosted orchard all those years ago, that some of the stars we could see had died millions of years ago but the light they had emitted still shone across the universe. *Amen.*

In the confusion of emotions however, a thought struck me forcibly. These babies, the objects of so much love, reinforced my belief in the human spirit of compassion, a belief that had been kindled years ago when I read of an archaeologist who had unearthed a grave some six thousand years old.

The grave had contained two female bodies. One was a grown woman of some importance, which was signified by the fact that she was shrouded in a woven blanket. The other was a teenage girl, who had spent her life in pain because her body was so malformed that it couldn't have been otherwise. The beautiful thing was that the girl too was wrapped in an equally expensive blanket.

During the intervening millennia there have been many callous and crude attempts to deny such babies a place in life, but at Zoe's Place there is living proof that the essential impulse of humans is a loving one and it will survive.

When I listened to Ann's irrepressible fondness for her babies I found myself looking at the dark rings of fatigue around her eyes and I knew that just as we could date the age of a tree by its rings, so we could almost pinpoint the time when her beloved charges passed away. However, her attitude can be summed up by the lyrics of Graham Nash:

"Rejoice! Rejoice! We have no choice, but to carry on!"

Thank you Ann for the coffee, the optimism and the Teddy Bear... it is already much loved.

62. Do You Believe in Magic?

My mother's sister Alice was named after my grandmother's sister, and it was uncanny how the younger woman inherited the same madcap sense of fun from her own aunt. Great Aunt Alice was my mother's redoubt, confidante and friend. No stranger to sorrow, Alice was never afraid to open her door to it and offer it a cup of tea.

My earliest memory of her was some time in the early 1950s. I remember the fraught silence as we – my mother, Alice and myself, sat in the waiting area of Stanley Road hospital, where her eldest son, Pat, lay dying from kidney failure. The bright lights, multiplied by the reflections on the shiny linoleum and the palpable sense of helplessness in Alice's eyes as she wrung her hands in tortured prayer, are fixed in my mind still. Pat was the first of her crop, and as such was the apple of her eye. His death was an ill windfall that blew her no good at all. But whatever else died that night, Alice's humour remained as vital as ever. My mother, who can be convulsed with laughter at the drop of a hat, spent most of her time with her aunt in a constant state of hysterics.

One example of Alice's puckish humour can still reduce my mother to tears of laughter. It appears that one night Alice was taking my mother to a party at a house, which must have been moderately well off in the early fifties as it boasted a highly fashionable light fitting, in effect a mini chandelier, and a state-of-the-art record player. As they approached the house Alice looked sternly at my mother, and, with mock severity, said, "We have to behave ourselves here Rose Anne, they've got three lights and a radiogram!"

For the remainder of the evening my mother could only croak and cry with suppressed laughter while her mascara dissolved to mud. In seconds Alice had transformed my mother from being 'all dolled up' to being a rag doll.

Alice was always there when my mum needed support, whether it was to provide shelter, money or simply make a sandwich. I can't ever forget my ninth birthday. For one thing it was the first time I'd had a party. For another it introduced me to my great aunt's biblical bent. There were about ten guests, one cake, sandwiches and four bottles of Cream Soda. I remember the exact amount because I was with my mother when she asked the shopkeeper for 'four bottles of lemonade'. Now it was a peculiarity of Liverpool, prior to the Cola onslaught, that all carbonated drinks were called lemonade, regardless of flavour or colour, and so I was anticipating the proprietor's ritual response when he asked me, "What colour do you want?"

Pent up with excitement of my freedom of choice I blurted, "Dandelion and Burdock... No, Cream Soda." Then, as he reached for the bottles I stammered, "No... not the white one, the green one."

The proprietor didn't turn a hair as he decoded my request that he ignore the clear version of Cream Soda in favour of the virulent green concoction that must have contained enough chemicals to tan a rhino hide.

Anyway, as the party got into full swing (which, incidentally, was the proprietary brand of the lemonade) I noticed that as each successive round of drinks was brought to the table the hue of the lemonade had altered, none-too-subtly, from the colour of rain-rich grass to a sort of *Eau de Nil*. Curious, I went into the kitchen and saw my mother rocking with muted laughter as her aunt topped up the bottles with 'Adam's Ale'. Steeped as she was in the scriptures, my great aunt had truly imbibed the miracle of Cana.

Alice was a great organiser as well as being vaguely entrepreneurial. In her time she owned and let a caravan in Greasby, but I remember best the huge bell tent she and her husband, Bob, would erect in Moreton, which is probably the most windswept stretch of shoreline on Merseyside. The wind there rarely decreased in force to anything less than a stiff breeze and I can still see the billowing and rippling of the tents as they clung desperately to the grass in the lee of the great concrete sea wall that stretched to nearby New Brighton.

Oh happy days, when I would spend all the pennies bestowed on me by Alice's children, Tommy, Robert and Queenie, in the penny arcade. Yes, it was gambling, but at least one got some exercise jerking the handle which released a ball bearing that, after racing around like a demented thing, found repose in a tiny cup etched with the size of the prize, usually two pennies. The arcade owners offered worse odds than a casino. However, it was possible, with luck and a fair wind to make twelve pence last two or three minutes before it was all devoured.

In the mid-fifties, Alice and Bob, no doubt doing their bit to lend credence to Harold Macmillan's opinion that the British people had 'never had it so good', decided to open a chicken farm. Well, a sort of glorified allotment really, somewhere in Fazakerley. I am convinced that money was not the sole incentive, as it seemed to me that Alice was only truly happy 'roughing it', whether in a tent by a wind whipped beach, or in a wooden hut in the suburbs of Liverpool.

I was invited up the one day to help out with the gathering of the eggs, which involved accompanying Alice's sons Robert and Tommy as they gathered in the harvest. Neither of these men, each of whom shared the most biting wit I've ever encountered, was particularly serious about their participation in the egg ranching business.

As we prowled around the coops and surrounding mud patches I was astonished to see Tommy lift a chicken from its nesting box. Robert then snatched the egg from beneath the bird and, holding it aloft in both hands, like a priest at the offering of the host, exclaimed jubilantly, "Profit!" At which point both men collapsed with laughter.

Their irreverence to the growing popularity of the newest British working class deity, Mammon, didn't sit well with their father, for whom the word 'lugubrious' might have been invented. In fairness to great uncle Bob he was not a well man, and by the time I actually got to talk to him, when I was in my late teens, he was dying and bedridden, and any thoughts of being a poultry plutocrat had long since flown the coop.

Bob was the only man I ever met who truly embodied the notion of being a football club supporter. I say that because, quite apart from worshipping a felt effigy of the great Liverpool centre forward, Albert Stubbins, which Bob kept on his bedside cabinet, my great uncle held

two season tickets at a time in the club's fortunes when seats at Anfield stadium were easier to obtain than those on the average bus.

My last meeting with him before he died was some time in 1959, I think. At the time there was a great debate as to which man, Eddie Boot or Bill Shankly, should become the next manager of Liverpool football club. As he lay on his deathbed, struggling for breath, Bob said to me, "I hope to God they pick Shankly!"

They did, and he became a legend while making Liverpool FC a legendary force in world football. Great Uncle Bob died before Shanks was appointed.

Supporters? I met one!

When I was in my late twenties and in the company of a girlfriend, I paid a visit to my great aunt's. I didn't know it at the time but she would be dead within a few weeks. Perhaps she knew she was leaving and so decided to stop being my venerable relative and opted instead to regale us with some of the funniest stories from her past. She even had a funny name for her cat. She called it 'Get out!"

Only this morning as I wandered through the cornucopia of fizzy drinks at Sainsbury's I was reminded of great aunt Alice when my youngest son pestered me to buy him a bottle of something called 'Clear', which consists of carbonated water ever-so-slightly flavoured with peach. As I stared at what looked like opalescent tap-water I thought, 'Alice, when you spun out my four bottles of Cream Soda to refresh the multitude you were ahead of your time!'

63. Nobody Loves You When You're Down-and Out

Early in 1970 I was working for a firm in Edge Lane called Paton Calvert. I was allegedly part of the maintenance squad. I say 'squad' but the reality was that there was me, the foreman and an old man called Bob, who was 74 and as such was well beyond the age of retirement. Why he chose to work rather than potter about in his garden was made clear to me when one day he mentioned that although he lived in the same house as his wife they had been estranged for years and lived wholly separate lives inside their small council house.

One day Bob, who was a gentle old man with a ready smile, animatedly informed me that he had bought a record by Simon and Garfunkel that was, in his opinion, the finest song ever written. It was the first I had heard of the duo's opus, 'Bridge over Troubled Water' and the poignancy of Bob's enthusiasm for their hymn to reconciliation struck me forcibly.

Later that day I found myself in the Scala Cinema, or perhaps it was the Futurist, absorbed by the lives of two more of life's outsiders in what was to become one of my all-time favourite movies – *Midnight Cowboy*. The theme of alienation, *vide* Bob, Joe-Buck and Razzo Rizzo had thoroughly permeated that Friday and so on the way home and I found myself staring out of the windows of the bus recalling my own interactions with society's discards.

The first person I ever saw who could be described as a tramp or hobo used to turn up once year, usually in summertime, near my grandmother's pre-fab, which stood opposite the broad swathe of cinder-strewn wasteland that led eventually to Liverpool's Rugby League ground, or if one continued past the gates of that bastion of perennial losers, to the redoubt of perpetual chastity, the Carmelite monastery.

This particular 'gentleman of the road' was a sort of archetype who might well have been created by Richmal Crompton, a writer who introduced her character, William, to down-and-outs whose near outlaw status held a tantalising appeal for her schoolboy hero, and also for her readers. He was short, ruddy complexioned, round and, apart from a slight halo of reddish hair that lent him the appearance bloated blood orange, bald. He was possessed of a twinkling eye and a perpetual grin that entranced me and my mates as regaled us with tales his tramping. As he sat enthroned on the stumpy mile marker, it was easy to believe that he was indeed a king of the road, travelling incognito among his grateful subjects.

We boy courtiers competed to see who could bring the most gifts to the monarch of the back roads, which he graciously accepted as if they were his right. A pair of old socks, a tin mug, and even an abandoned army haversack competed for his approval. In retrospect it is difficult to imagine that he would have rejected anything he was offered.

The socks were my contribution and I was inordinately pleased when he promptly began to remove his boots, which were entirely made of rubber, in order to replace the socks he was wearing. However, my pleasure was swiftly curtailed because when he removed his old socks the thousand-mile smell of his feet was overpowering. I swear that even the summer flies cut short their already brief existence as, like miniscule Kamikazes, they dived to their death, splashing into the cinder sea.

It would be many years before I ever again allowed myself to get that close to a roadside aristocrat.

In the time since I have seen many beggars and outcasts, who in some cases were only marginally worse off than their countrymen. I saw poverty in Africa so severe that some unfortunates allowed heavy weights to be hooked to their tortured bodies in the hope of eliciting sympathy in the shape of a coin. I have also observed beggars in the Middle East who, rather than seek medical attention, allowed ulcers the size of a child's arm to fester on their bodies as they reasoned that the sight of their raw and oozing flesh would compel passers by to give them alms. For my squeamish part I couldn't get away from them quickly enough and so, shamefully, gave them nothing.

One encounter with a down-and-out haunts me to this day. It took place on Christmas Day 1972. I was sitting in my living room sharing a joint with some girls students who had descended on me because they had nowhere else to stay during the vacation period and I was in a kind of urban paradise, until one of the three girls, who had been preparing the Christmas dinner, ran into the living room and, trembling violently, begged me to go into the kitchen.

I sluggishly made my way to the kitchen, idly wondering if perhaps she had found something inside the Turkey other than giblets, but when I got there I was staggered to behold a fully paid up member of Hobos Anonymous standing there, holding up an old fashioned kettle in one hand, the bottom of which was entirely burnt out, and a half empty whisky bottle in the other.

Stupefied, I realised that he had pushed open the door that led from the alley at the rear of the house and then proceeded merrily into the kitchen. Aware that my student friend was on the verge of collapse I took the festive intruder by the arm and guided him to the alley, where, without any sort of protestation he stood staring at me, kettle aloft and swaying like a wind-whipped Christmas tree.

It was only later, when I began to reflect on the intrusion, that I realised I had pushed a derelict man into the street, on, of all days, the one dedicated to goodwill to all men and I bitterly regretted not taking the opportunity to give him something better than rejection. In my defence I can only say that shock tactics rarely work where charity is concerned.

A few short months later it appeared to me that the Gods of unredeemed debts decided that I should pay for my sin. I had left a bar late one Saturday night and rather than go home to my empty house decided to pay a visit to the all night café at the Pier Head. As I queued for coffee I was suddenly aware of a loud chorus of aggressive remarks aimed at an old tramp who was perusing an array of sandwiches. I turned to his tormentors and mildly reproved them, pleading forbearance because of his age and circumstances. Before I could say anything else I was confronted by one of the hecklers, who immediately challenged me to a fight. In the event I was knocked down so quickly that I heard someone cry "It's a fix! The bastard took a dive!"

My last close encounter of the weird kind occurred one beautiful summer's day as I was walking along Castle Street towards the Queen's public house. Striding towards me was a man wearing a raincoat that was open and so exposing his naked chest. As he came within touching distance of me, I reached into my pocket and attempted to offer him some coins. The white-haired apparition – whose upright stance and distant gaze brought to mind a biblical prophet striding through a concrete wilderness – fixed me with clear, sky-blue eyes and said, "I don't want any money thank you very much, but there is perhaps something you could do for me..."

Warily I asked him what it was that I could do for him, whereupon he shocked the life out of me by saying, "You see, I have been so long outside of things that I don't know what is going on in the world. Could you perhaps tell me what is happening … generally, that is?"

Nonplussed, I mumbled some nonsense about this and that, all of it inconsequential, but he seemed satisfied and, thanking me, the Jeremiah of the streets strode off to who knows where.

To this day I regret that lost opportunity, oft dreamed of by pedants such as myself, to enlarge on the great themes and discourses of the day, to discuss the antics of the great and good, and to do what I enjoy most … talk.

64. Dig a Pony

When I was a child I did a lot of riding. Well, every summer I would make several visits from Liverpool to New Brighton and on at least one of those visits I would indulge in the delights of a donkey ride. Looking back, I don't know who I felt the most sympathy for; the poor donkey, which looked for all the world like a moth-eaten sheepskin rug trying to impersonate an Irish Wolfhound, the morose looking man who held the donkey's reins while traversing more sand than Moses ever saw in his forty years in the Sinai, or my mother walking behind trying to avoid the fresh droppings that glistened wetly in the sand like windfall dates.

Of course, New Brighton was also home to the 'Bobby horses', those poor beasts of the merry-go-round, condemned to whirl in dizzying circles for all eternity, their carved nostrils permanently flared in a frenzy of fright. My mother used to tease me by telling me that there were men actually employed to wipe the sweat from their glossy painted sides.

For the next twenty odd years the nearest I ever got to a horse was in a bookies in Lodge Lane, where I often donated my last few bob to the Sid Thomas retirement fund. I had the wrong temperament for gambling as I always backed the horse I desperately wanted to win rather than the horse I thought would win. Superstition always prevailed over logic and I made so many coincidence bets I could have had a career in the emerging field of synchronicity. I once lost my last ten bob on a horse called Royal Doulton because it was running in a selling plate!

My introduction to real live horses occurred during a holiday in 1984 to Ireland, a country where horses are almost deified by the equine worshiping natives. My wife and I had seen a sign advertising horse riding lessons at what appeared to be a reasonable rate. Had I known what was to ensue I would happily have paid twice the price!

We made enquiries and a charming young woman of about twenty-one took our money told us that our horses, or rather ponies, were around the back. Adopting my best John Wayne stagger I walked to the stables where there were some really pretty piebald ponies. Just then the young cashier came through a door and showed us both how to mount our steeds. For once I didn't make a mess of things and I sat tall, well, upright, in the saddle awaiting instructions. The first instruction almost caused me to fall out of the saddle because, you see, the trick about horse riding is that you never actually sit in the saddle but rather you bounce up and down while standing in the stirrups. So, turning her pretty head, and looking directly at me with a wicked gleam in her eyes, our instructor said, "Just keep your eyes on my bottom and watch how it goes up and down".

Jesus Christ! Like I needed an invitation!

For the next two hours we rode up and down one of the most magnificent beaches I've ever seen, and, much to my wife's amusement, my eyes rarely left that equally magnificent derriere.

Our next encounter with a maned beauty was nowhere near as satisfactory, although my good lady thought it was hilarious. A few days later, inspired by our enjoyment on the beach, we decided to go riding again. As we had moved on from the area where the young siren resided we had to resort to a stable that was much bigger and seemed much more commercial in its outlook – which is to say, it cost twice as much as the previous establishment. From what I could see it was run entirely by men, two of whom, in my opinion at least, were fully paid up members of the tripe-hound club.

My wife and I waited in the large yard, eagerly anticipating our ride and wondering what our horse would be like. We didn't have to wait long before tripe-hound number one led out a magnificently towering black stallion. He was closely followed by tripe-hound number two, who had held the reins of a mount that looked as if it was the offspring of a union between a grossly stunted Shetland pony and a chronically sick donkey. Macho brute that I was I naturally gravitated toward the stallion. Imagine then my shock when tripe-hound number one led the horse away from me and attempted to hand the reins to my wife!

My response to this baiting was less than measured.

"What you playing at?" I roared.

Tripe hound number one gave me a blank stare, or more accurately a look of dumb insolence, and so, beside myself with fury and a burgeoning sense of humiliation, I thrust my face to within an inch of his and hissed, "Listen you divvy, either you give that horse to me or you won't just be kicking shit you'll be eating it!"

Fortunately for me his response was stillborn because my wife, trying desperately to stifle her giggles, simply strode over and took the dwarf horse from tripe-hound number two and that was that.

The *I Ching* says, "Don't run after your horse because if it is your horse it will return".

Yeah! Like I'm going to catch up with a horse!

65. A Nice Cup of Tea

'Char', as my Grandfather called it, has never been my cup of tea. In fact, I've disliked it since I was a very small child. I think it is yet more proof that despite the location of my birth, I am not truly English. I mean, an Englishman who doesn't like tea is like a vampire who faints at the sight of blood.

My aversion to tea began when I was about four, when I was present at a social gathering that was a cross between a wake and a potlatch. I can't remember how we got there but my Grandmother and I had ended up in a house where the owner had died and where her lifetime friends were sifting through the worldly possessions that had been promised to them by the deceased. It was vaguely reminiscent of that scene from *The Christmas Carol* where the old crones are selling the booty they had looted from Scrooge's deathbed.

Tomb raiding is notoriously thirsty work and before long the inevitable kettle had been boiled and the tea was stewing in a brown glazed teapot. An incredibly old lady, the sister of the departed hostess, handed me a pretty china cup, the type with handles so small that even as a child I found it a tight fit for my finger. Since nobody had thought to bring milk, and we were in a house that had been empty since the funeral, we had to settle for milk-less tea.

When mine had cooled sufficiently to drink I noticed something pinky-white gleaming just beneath the surface of the amber liquid. I gingerly fished it out and, with a shrill yelp, promptly hurled it to the floor. It was the top set of a pair of false teeth! What's more they had once graced the mouth of the dead woman.

Talk about a drink with a bite!

After that episode I steered clear of tea, and, truthfully, nobody tried to force me to drink the damned stuff again. It wasn't out of any consideration for my finer feelings you understand. It was, quite simply, that tea was rationed, and so the less I consumed the more there was for everybody else. Apart from Horlicks and Cocoa I never drank hot drinks on a regular basis until I was about thirteen.

It was my Gran's next-door neighbour, a genteel old lady who first introduced me to coffee. The coffee was my reward for doing her shopping. On Saturday morning's she would hand me a shopping list and a wicker basket. Imagine, if you can, Little Red Riding Hood's awkward adolescent brother and there you have me, toddling off to the row of shops just beyond the Greyhound public house. I still recoil in shame when I think of the time I bumped into Nancy, my mate Joey's gorgeous sister, while I was daintily tripping along with my basket over my arm! She pretended not to notice the basket and so I eagerly engaged her in conversation. I remember telling her that I was going to the barber's later that day to get a fashionable crew cut. She looked at me sadly and said, "But it'll never work. You've got a head like a field of wild mint!" She wasn't being cruel, but her candour made me blush. She was right of course. My hair was so limp I was always torn between the merits of Silvikrin Hair Tonic and Colman's Rice Starch.

Of course, the scarcity of tea in the austerity years wasn't the only reason I hated tea. My mother, never flush with cash, used to buy a brand of tea called 'Golden Stream'. If ever a product was appropriately named it was that! It was composed, mostly, of inferior leaves and stalks, which used to swell and clog up the tea spout like a logjam. When the tea had been drunk the bottom of the cup looked like an aerial shot of a beaver dam. Worse, it used to catch in my throat and cause me to gag. The morass of wet leaves did have some purpose though, and not just as a compost agent. My great aunt Alice was one of those women who used to read the tea leaves, a method of divination that consisted of swirling the residue of leaves around the bottom of the cup and interpreting the 'pictures' therein. I can still see my mother and her cousins, male *and* female, hunched around the dinner table awaiting the verdict of the leaf-reading oracle.

Great Aunt Alice would look up with her bright bird-like eyes and deliver the verdict. It was usually something like, "You'll meet a dark stranger." All those assembled would look at the recipient of the fortune with a mixture of envy and fear. I couldn't understand how they could expect anything else. I mean, the leaves were dark brown so just who did the men think they were going to meet, Marilyn Monroe!

For years I used to find it something of a joke that people would attempt to read the future in the discarded remnants of a cup of tea. That was before I heard about the ancient Greek soothsayer, the Sybil, who also read the future in leaves. Funny thing though, my Great Aunt and all her fellow Tasseomancers never saw that they would all be made redundant by the advent of the tea bag!

66. Climb Every Mountain

Next time you see one of those wartime naval movies, depicting men escaping disaster, have a look at the ropes that the sailors clamber down to the safety of the lifeboats. Those fragile-looking ropes, the sailors' lifelines, are punctuated with figure of eight knots that ensure the escapees have something to hold on to. It is perhaps less than coincidence that the figure of eight symbol is used to by mathematicians to denote infinity. Throughout the course of my life the knots on my 'life-line' have consisted of the many people who grasped my hand when I was about to founder.

In 1973 I was reeling from a financial broadside. In short, I had to find enough money to keep my mortgage afloat or else re-locate and find a bed-sit on the road to nowhere. To this day I am convinced that I would have shrivelled in such an environment. If that sounds unduly dramatic you have to understand that I am most decidedly not an exemplar of self-sufficiency. A la Barbara Streisand, I am one of those people who need people, and bed-sits are notoriously lonely places.

Nobody I knew had anything like the sum I needed and it appeared that I was sunk. In desperation I turned to a man called Geoff whom I hardly knew and asked him if he could lend me the money. He didn't hesitate and within hours I had deposited the necessary amount with my building society. Without his intervention my life might have gone down the tubes faster than any torpedo.

Several years later I was staying with some really nice, but quiet living people in their cottage near Bangor. Geoff turned up and, after sharing a joint, asked me if I fancied a car trip. I readily agreed as I had been at the cottage for two days and was fast running out of walls to climb. I don't know whether it was intentional on Geoff's part, or that he succumbed to his known love of mountains but suddenly he suggested that we climb a mountain that was in the nearby Glyder range. Not wanting to spoil a day out by pointing out that my Wellingtons were hardly appropriate climbing gear I agreed.

We ascended via the Devil's Kitchen and eventually reached the summit, where I was left gasping, not so much with the effort as at the spectacular view. I was stunned by the silent vastness of the sea suspended beneath the marked curvature of the horizon and I was reminded of an earlier comment of my friend Dave; that it was only at such times that we knew we lived on a planet. Geoff and myself just sat and stared, silenced by the grandeur, and you have to believe that Geoff was not easily impressed.

Way back in the early sixties he and his friend Tony had hitch hiked from Liverpool to India, where he had met the Dalai Lama. Of the two men, one from Lhasa and the other from Liverpool, only one ever got back to his homeland. Such a peak experience notwithstanding Geoff was still capable of being awe-stricken, and for once in our lives he and I were on exactly the same wavelength. Atmospheric interference was, however, on the way.

We decided that it was time to descend the mountain but had somehow lost sight of the marker stones denoting the walker's path and without warning found ourselves scrambling inelegantly down what appeared to me to be a vertical rock face.

The terrifying truth was that we had missed the walker's path completely and were in fact descending the rear face of the *Cwm*, that is a cliff that resembles the steep and slippery impression left behind when one scoop ice cream from a tub. Worse, there was no way back.

My every extremity was frozen with fear because I could not see anything other than a permanent drop into the gathering mist and I began to curse my stupidity in agreeing to climb a mountain wearing gear more suited to a milking parlour.

If Geoff was afraid he didn't show it as for over an hour we frantically slid or tobogganed on loose scree down the precipitous rock face. Our manic stampede convinced me that should I survive I would never make a career out of mountaineering!

Abruptly, we found ourselves perched on a ledge. Unable to see what lay below and with retreat out of the question we had literally to make a leap of faith.

I hadn't uttered a prayer since the night John Kennedy was assassinated but as I dropped into the void beyond the ledge I mouthed a silent offering to the God I had long abandoned. He must have been still listening because we both landed on solid ground and before too long had made it to the meadow at the foot of the mountain.

My legs were shaking violently when Geoff, whose long stride was eating up the ground as if the tongues of his shoes had developed an insatiable appetite for the earth beneath them, turned to me and, in his gravelly voice, said simply...

"Sorry about that John."

If I hadn't already realised how close we had come to disaster then Geoff's apology confirmed it, for at the best of times he could be an abrasive man with an oftimes caustic tongue; for him to utter a statement of regret was a bit like hearing the Dalai Lama scream sexual obscenities.

67. Those Were the Days

I went to Anfield football ground a few weeks ago with my 14-year-old son and experienced a kind of culture shock, because I hadn't been to watch a live game since the early seventies and was staggered by the air of cleanliness that pervaded the place. Where there used to be blizzards of chip wrappings and cigarette ends drifting on the Kop there was now a McDonalds. The meat pie is dead! Long live apple pie! God bless America!

I couldn't help but reflect that my son had missed a cultural experience by not queuing for ages to obtain a pale and rubbery looking meat pie and cup of tea served in a real mug. The pie and cuppa was the fans' final ritual before joining that heaving mass of humanity known as the Kop. The Kop, so called because it was so high that it resembled the Spion Kop, the site of a famous battle in the Boer war, was one of the wonders of the modern world. On match days twenty six thousand people – the total number of spectators at some Premiership grounds nowadays or the population of a small town – would be packed onto one steeply-raked embankment, the top of which seemed to caress the sky.

The noise created by this mountain of fervent support was awesome and quite often terrified the opposing players into making elementary mistakes. Of course, there was always the possibility of tragedy. When play was taking place at the Kop end of the pitch then all of those supporters straining for a better view would surge forward and a human avalanche would cascade down the concrete steps forcing those below onto the strategically positioned crush bars. I was often caught on them myself and one of my great fears was of being emasculated by the angled stanchions that supported the crush bars.

It has often been pointed out that before the Hillsborough tragedy the general attitude of the powers-that-be toward football fans resembled the relationship between a cowboy and his cattle, in that they were there to be rounded up, herded into pens and left to wallow in their own waste. Inadequate toilet facilities at football grounds was the rule of the day, and Anfield was no exception. A minority of men, who had drunk two or three pints of beer before the match couldn't escape the crush to attend the toilets and so used to roll their newspapers into tight cylinders and relieve themselves into the tube of newsprint. Naturally, there were those untutored fans incapable of reading who had no newspaper. Their preferred technique was to wait until the crowd moved in a downward surging mass and then relieve themselves in the resulting gap.

Wearers of fashion shoes were a rarity on the Kop.

It might be wondered why anybody would want to visit such a *pissoir* in the first place and the answer to that is simple. The Kop was the most stimulating experience I have ever encountered outside of the 1970 Isle of Wight Festival. The comparison is fair because the same sound of singing amid primitive conditions could be found at both venues.

The Kop's reputation for biting wit was already well established long before the 60s, but the advent of the Mersey sound, which was relayed to the crowd via a tinny Tannoy amplification system, gave the Koppites a new weapon for their armoury. At the slightest provocation they would break into a spontaneous and cruelly humorous parody of a popular song, aimed at the opposition.

At other times they would simply sing along with current hit songs and I will never forget a magic moment when the Beatles' 'I Want to Hold Your Hand' bridged the generation gap as supporters old and young joined the chorus with gusto.

Not all of parodies were of secular songs. In 1965 Liverpool won the FA Cup on Saturday and by Tuesday they were playing in the semi-finals of the European cup against the great Inter Milan. When Liverpool slammed three goals past the bemused Italians the Kop, to the tune of Santa Lucia, sang, 'Go back to Italy!'

The manager of Inter was called Herrera, and when the third goal went in he was treated to a customised version of a children's skipping song, which went, 'One, two, three, Herrera.'

Spontaneity was an ever-present factor on the Kop, so you can imagine my surprise when on my last visit I encountered the sort of muted enthusiasm you might experience watching a raunchy movie while your mum was present. Where once chaos had reigned, families sat amid the debris of their happy meals and were generally content to cheer only when something of import happened.

I saw something that did startle me though, that was when a mother slapped her daughter's wrist for dribbling coke down her brother's neck.

In hundreds of visits to the Kop I had never once witnessed any violence – unless, of course, you include the robust behaviour of Tommy Smith, Liverpool's iron-clad defender.

Incidentally, Liverpool lost that day … to Watford.

Watford were later relegated and I wondered if they would ever have a crowd of 26,000 at Vicarage Road.

68. And All That Gas

Just prior to my parents moving into our house in Tiber Street we were forced to rely on the hospitality of my father's work-mate, Eddie Barlow. Eddie lived in a small terraced house near Linacre Lane, Bootle, in the pungent shadow of the gas-works. The front parlour, which was generously allocated to my parents, was permanently shrouded in gloom, as it was directly in front of an enormous gasometer, the height of which fluctuated according to how full it was of coal tar gas.

Even when empty it was still high enough to mask the morning sun. Moreover, as if being deprived of sunshine wasn't bad enough the smell was appalling, and it permeated our lives, lingering in our nostrils, clothes and hair to such an extent that whenever I encountered clear fresh air I used to cough. We only stayed there for three months or so but it was long enough to acquire some indelible memories.

Take, for example, Eddie's wife. She was a dark-haired woman who spent her daylight hours with her feet immersed in a bowl of hot water whilst steadily munching her way through seemingly endless boxes of Cadbury's Milk Tray chocolates and listening to the radio. There are Sloths with more rigorous exercise regimes.

As far as I could see, her only contribution to her family's welfare was to prepare, once a week, their favourite meal of Corned Beef Hash and baked beans, a culinary feat which involved peeling potatoes and opening two tins, from a seated position of course. What was so ironic and sad about this was that Eddie was a butcher. Somebody once said that Mother's cooking is always best because it is made with love. If that is true then Eddie's wife was only a can opener away from being Merseyside's answer to that other exemplar of family values and home cooking, Lucrezia Borgia.

As for Eddie himself, well, you couldn't have wished to meet a nicer man. His life revolved around his two sons, his wife and fishing.

Perhaps he was so keen on the latter activity because a lake was presumably the only place on earth that he could contemplate an expanse of water without seeing his wife's feet soaking in it.

Whatever the reason I was grateful for his hobby because on Sundays we would board a train at Oriel Road and make our way to Ainsdale where there was a lake famed for its huge roach and rudd. Eddie referred to those piscatorial heavyweights as 'Daddyos' and spent many hours plotting ways to entice them onto his hook. While Eddie played Ahab I simply walked around the lake or played in the sand dunes, which are famed as a habitat of rare, natterjack toads. The lake, which was located close to the seashore and a perennial breeze, dispelled the noxious scent of the gas-works with the ease of sunshine dispersing mist.

One night, as the pale moon disappeared behind the gasometer, I found myself sitting on the doorstep accompanied by my mother who was ministering to me because I was suffering from stomach cramps and gas induced nausea. Alarmed by the fact that I wasn't responding to my exposure to 'fresh' air she hurriedly took me to Alder Hey hospital. The physician prodded away at my stomach looking for signs of appendicitis before admitting to being baffled by my condition. Turning to my mother he asked, with a demeanour approaching suspicion, what I had eaten that day.

My mother, who cheerfully indulged me in even my most bizarre fancies, replied innocently, "Well, he had about a pound of green grapes..." at which revelation the doctor turned pale, and was just about to say something when my mother continued, "And half a pound of tripe..." The doctor's pallor disappeared to be replaced with something like purple as he snapped, "Take him home ... and don't waste my time again!" Well... it could have been serious. More to the point, my mother just didn't believe in taking chances and she had spent a small fortune on a cab from Bootle to Knotty Ash, so I think his response, while understandable, was misplaced as she had no intention of wasting his or anybody else's time.

Time wasting was an area of expertise that was the domain of Mrs Barlow. That said, her boys never suffered from tripe-related illnesses.

69. Drive My Car

I've been a pedestrian since I was nine months old, when apparently my precocious feet forced my mother into buying child reins to prevent me scampering into the busy roads. My time as lead husky must have left me with a profound yearning for the open road because several years later, while attending Page Moss nursery, I took advantage of its open-plan design by sprinting into the busy thoroughfare of Princess Drive. A perimeter fence was very quickly installed.

Thus my first bid for individual freedom ended up with the imprisonment of my infant comrades. Perhaps the moral of that tale is that we should reside in the bosom of the community or else wait until all of our friends are ready to join us in our dash for liberty, and the chance to do our own thing.

That early skirmish with death on the road may well be one reason why, until recently, I had never learned to drive. A more likely factor contributing to my preference for 'Shanks's pony' is the fact that the location of my house was such that for most of my life I could often walk into the city centre faster than car owners could find a parking space. Moreover, my innate sense of thrift (sometimes erroneously perceived as meanness!) was offended by the notion that a new vehicle bought on, say, a Monday morning, was diminishing in value by evening.

The truth is that one my earliest experiences of cars almost put me off for life. It was sometime in 1964, when working-class car owners were still something of a novelty. I was having a drink with a young lady, called Val, who was so gorgeous that she turned more heads than Mao's little Red Book. Naturally enough there were always young men anxious to catch her lovely eyes. One of these legions was a rat-faced pillock whose name, if I ever knew it, now escapes me. As we were leaving the pub, Ratty insisted on giving Val and me a lift, to the obvious dismay of his mousey-looking partner. Not wishing to appear churlish I accepted. The vehicle that was to convey us to her home was a Ford Thames Van, which reeked of sweat and Swarfega, as Ratty was a plumber by trade and entirely at home in u-bends and sewers. As Val struggled to navigate from the front seat into the back of the van I was conscious that Ratty's beady eyes were locked onto her lovely thighs and I had a feeling that this rodent was going to be a nuisance. And I was right…

We were racing down the dip into Childwall Valley Road and Ratty was tailgating the car in front; possibly because the exhaust pipe of the other car reminded him of the entrance to his home. Anyway, the leading vehicle suddenly signalled left to go into Score Lane, which name was ironic, because Ratty was trying so hard to score with the delectable Val that he didn't notice the other driver's manoeuvre until the last second. As he swerved frantically, the van collided with the right hand side of the turning vehicle and suddenly we were spinning out of control on the wrong side of the road, heading straight into the oncoming traffic. As luck would have it we careered onto the grass verge and came to a timely halt.

Val's beautiful face was leaking blood as we all stood shaking on the grass. Then Ratty stunned us both by saying, "You'll have to go before the police come, 'cos I'm not insured…"

The Jack Russell in me rose to the surface and I was about to take the verminous bastard by his greasy neck when Val implored me to take her to hospital. I never saw Ratty again. Perhaps at a later date, while investigating a drain, he mistook Warfarin for Weetabix.

By 1978 I had sufficiently recovered from the shock to buy a motorbike. One day I was walking towards my bike – which was in its usual position, on the ground and on its side, as one of my neighbours, a female wrestler manqué, was in the habit of knocking it off its stand – when I collided head on with a lamp post. As I reeled in pain, all the while pretending that nothing had occurred, the way you do when you make a complete arse of yourself, I had a sudden and horrifying thought. 'What if I had hit that lamp-post while travelling at seventy miles an hour!'

I decided there and then to get rid of the bike, but I couldn't in all conscience sell it to someone, so I advertised in the Echo for someone to take it away for free. I can still see the haunted look on the faces of the two guys who turned up with a trailer as they wrestled frantically to get the machine onto the trailer before I had a change of heart. Such an eventuality was as unlikely as my suddenly developing a profound affection for plague-bearing rats.

So you would be entitled to wonder what it was that, some twenty years on, compelled me to take driving lessons. Quite simply my wife pointed out to me that if I couldn't overcome my phobic response to vehicles then within a year my sixteen-year-old son would be driving me around! Thus it was that in the twenty first century I attempted to acquire a skill that I had managed to avoid throughout the twilight years of the last millennium.

My choice of instructors was, initially, largely determined by financial considerations as my talent for fiscal husbandry, not to be mistaken for parsimony you understand, came to the fore. My first instructor was an elderly man whom I suspect supplemented his Boer war army pension by teaching people like me to master the art of the horse-less carriage.

My first lesson was largely spent watching him draw complicated drawings of engines and gears. I think his main consideration was that the more time I spent in scrutinising his etchings the less his petrol was being used. I mean, if I were go for horse riding lessons I wouldn't want to see anatomical sketches of its innards! The second lesson was a reprise of the first as my old mate Gottlieb Benz seemed to have more ink than petrol, and so I began the search for a new instructor.

Suffice to say that my second instructor was ... well ... strange. One day as I was driving along he slammed on the dual brakes. My propensity for guilt, fused with panic, manifested itself as perspiration and I frantically wondered what I'd done wrong. Turning to me he said, "There was a sparrow in the road." Then, in response to my expression of gaping disbelief, he further explained, with that infuriatingly smug tone of the soon-to-be beatified, "They are almost an endangered species." I couldn't help thinking that if that plant-pot ever pulled that stroke with someone who wasn't as easy-going as me he would find *himself* on the endangered species list!

I'd had enough of Merseyside's Saint Francis of Assisi and so the hunt for a new instructor was on once more…

My final instructor was as calm as the bird lover was twitchy. Dave, who was my mentor for what seemed so long that had I not eventually passed my driving test he would have been on my Christmas list, was coolness personified. His mode of instruction was almost akin to horse whispering, because he never once raised his voice to me, not even when I deliberately and maliciously aimed the windscreen at a passing wasp.

Unfortunately, the first test I undertook was conducted by a man who was quite simply an old-fashioned bully. He was semi-retired and would fill in whenever a regular instructor was ill. The test centre was in Southport, a town unique in that the poor are almost outnumbered by the affluent. His first instruction was to ask me to read a licence plate. The cars he pointed to were side on to me so I had to tell him that not only could I not read the number, I couldn't even see the plates. Grudgingly, he told me that I could move into a better position, adding ungraciously "… if you must."

I felt I was somehow inadequate and from then on I drove like a blind Rickshaw driver on LSD. The snide wasn't content with getting me into state of mind where even normally simple things, like making formal apologies to run-down pedestrians, became problematic. He couldn't refrain from putting the boot in when I messed up my reversing round the corner routine and casually informed me that people of my age were just no good at driving as it was a young man's game. For once, I bit my tongue and even refrained from answering him as he made provocative and politically-inspired comments.

One of his barbs invoked Maggie Thatcher, when, alluding to a tenuous point about reverse parking, he declared she had once said 'The lady is not for turning'. I can still feel his intense gaze and the pregnant silence as he waited, in vain, for me to rise to the bait. Worse, at every turn I would find myself squinting like a fighter pilot who'd been caught out by a bandit coming out of the sun as my tormentor relentlessly pursued the fiery orb with all the fervour of a demented druid at the spring equinox. My confidence was shot down in flames.

I finally passed the test at the Norris Green centre in Liverpool, where the examiner was considerate and wholly encouraging. My anxiety on that day was so obvious that an instructor going toward someone *else's* car encouraged me to try and relax! When, eventually, I was informed that I had passed I shook the instructor's hand with such abandon that it was only the fact that he was a man that prevented me from kissing it.

The gloom of three months feeling depressed and inadequate had been dispersed by Scouse sunshine.

"Beep beep! Beep beep! Yeah!"

70. Gone Fishin'

In the fifties, few people had any experience of tropical fish or aquariums. The most exotic species we were likely to encounter was that rare visitor to our shores, tinned salmon. Cod, robed in a thick yellow batter and anointed with salt and vinegar, was still king of all it surveyed.

I first chanced upon tropical fish when I was about fourteen. I had accompanied a mate to a large house, in Beaconsfield Street I think it was, where we were led into a large cellar containing bubbling tanks that teemed with multi-various species of marine exotica. I was left quite unmoved by the sight, but my mate Eddie appeared to be suffering from a terrestrial version of 'raptures of the deep', a disease caused by oxygen deprivation to which divers are prone and which causes them to go mad, often fatally so. I can still see Eddie, with his face pressed up against the glass, his eyes glowing and flashing like the iridescent *Neon Tetras* he beheld.

My next episode concerning marine life was when my stepfather caught the aquarist's bug and bought a tank full of exotics from one of his customers. It wasn't that Jimmy had discovered a latent propensity for zoology, but rather he had fallen in with the prevailing notion that a well stocked fish tank lent a certain decorative cache to a house. No doubt this is the rationale for the rapid growth of glass tanks containing snakes, spiders or scorpions. Frankly I preferred Woodchip wallpaper.

My tastes notwithstanding, Jimmy located his aquarium directly beneath the television, and so on any given night it was possible to see various beady eyed predators constantly opening and closing their mouths without saying very much. It was 1963 and David Frost was as much in evidence as the Guppies, Neons and Catfish.

On New Year's Eve of that year I brought home a young lady and as we acted out the hit song, 'Getting to Know You', it became apparent that she was shy of the glaring spotlight provided by a combination of the aquarium, the flickering of the coal effect fire and the television, which was topped by an illuminated, snow-covered plastic church that played a tinkling version of 'Ave Maria'.

The latter intrusion was so hideous and impiously commercial that it would have been far more appropriate had it belted out a version of the Dixie Cups' 'Going to the Chapel'.

But I digress... Recognising the romance-murdering properties of our domestic *son et lumiere,* and being a gentleman, I promptly yanked out the three-way plug from its socket. Thus it was that 1964 was ushered in by the breathless dark.

When I awoke the following morning I stumbled downstairs to find my dad had positioned about twenty small glasses in front of the electric fire, and in each receptacle was a tiny fish, a finny martyr to my nocturnal rite of passage. Miraculously many of the piscatorial victims of hypothermia, brought about by the abrupt cessation of the aquarium's heating, recovered. My long-suffering dad never once complained, he simply put it down to celebratory inebriation.

You might think that I'd learned my lesson *vis-à-vis* aquatic welfare, but you would be wrong. In the late seventies, whilst living the bachelor life, I succumbed to that peculiar syndrome whereby human beings find the young of almost any species awfully cute. It is a strange condition, which compels us to 'ooh' and 'aah' over a delightful puppy, only to find ourselves running like rabbits when confronted by its adult incarnation as a slavering Rottweiller. Anyway, I found myself entranced by some baby Terrapins and purchased two of them, whom I named Antony and Cleopatra.

One winter's evening I became anxious that they would be too cold to survive; this, in spite of the clear fact that they were cold water amphibians. Propelled by stupidity I boiled a kettle of water and, while the Egyptian lovers were basking obliviously on a flat stone, carefully poured a measured amount of hot water into their tank. Disturbed by the noise, Tony and his paramour slid into the water. Within seconds they were doing a turtillian version of the backstroke. Minutes later, as I fished their inert bodies from the tank, and felt how their once-hard shells had become soft and rubbery, I was stunned by the realisation that, good intentions notwithstanding, I had created a substantial portion of turtle soup.

The years rolled by ... so many, in fact, that the once heavily polluted river Mersey was once again yielding up catches of edible fish. I had taken to accompanying my children to the city centre pet store, which has now, sadly, closed after 129 years of continuous existence. Aquariums have become so sophisticated that they appear to be nothing more than liquid televisions. The backgrounds available ranged from depictions of Atlantis to underwater pirate caves. I was mesmerised. Marian, recognising the first intimations of my impulsive bent, persuaded me that they would prove too much work.

The implications of that awful word held me in check for at least a fortnight, but one day, while un-chaperoned, I found a small ad offering the whole nine yards – fish, tanks, gravel etc, and I was on the phone with the speed of an electric eel.

It was a bright Sunday morning when the tank arrived and I spent almost the whole of God's day of rest filling it with water, impatient for the time when I could release my myriad small fish into its depths and savour that moment when the *Neon Tetras* would mouth 'Let there be light' and thus illuminate my creation.

By two o'clock the fish were darting about the tank, no doubt wondering why I hadn't followed the previous owner's instructions to allow twenty-four hours for the chlorine to evaporate.

It so happened that Marian's childhood friend and her husband Ashley were visiting from Australia. Ashley had a fondness for curry and so I set about preparing one. It must have been the only time in culinary history when the pungency of a curry in preparation was overwhelmed ... by the distinctly musty smell emanating from the fish tank. Ashley and his bride were too polite too mention it, but my wife, much to my annoyance, kept asking me why I had brought home 'Swamp thang'.

I consoled myself with the thought that when the tank was fully operational it would enhance the bay window where it was located and I would be in receipt of many plaudits. Now, given that I had a passing knowledge of engineering it would be reasonable to ask why I had placed the metal-framed tank in the hottest spot in the house. The short answer is that I'm impatient and short-sighted to a degree that would shame a two-year-old in a toyshop.

When we had eaten the curry we decided to have our drinks in the lounge and talk more about the desert that Ashley and Sandra lived in. As we entered the lounge the smell of algae-encrusted gravel assailed our nostrils, but what was worse was that the tank had buckled in the heat of the summer sun and the carpet was sodden with gallons of escaping water.

Fortunately, the fish had not escaped. Instead, they were stranded on the bed of gravel, performing back flips and other complicated feats of gymnastics.

It took a week to dry out and clean the carpet, during which time I repaired the crack in the silicon adhesive, which held the frame to the glass. Unbelievably I hadn't connected the debacle to the distorting heat of the sun and within a week we had a repeat of Noah's nightmare, and this when my wife's students were arriving for a 'wine and cheese' do.

I leave it to you to decide which smelled worse, the Camembert or the algae and slime coated carpet. I placed my own ad soon after.

'Fish for sale - need some mollycoddling'.

71. Watching the River Flow

The ordnance survey map designated the 'Alt' as a Liverpool river, but it was little more than a reed-choked stream that skirted the local housing estate, dividing the inhabitants from the glories of the nearby forests that formed part of the estates of Lord Derby, a knight of the crown. But to us, unversed in the niceties of rural beauty, its sandy course was a break from the drab tributaries of tarmac and gravel that wound around our lives like a jungle watercourse going nowhere.

Nothing lived in that river, apart from the occasional water rat or disoriented frog. Its brackish flow did not derive from peat, mineral or leaf infusion, but from rusting prams, bicycle frames and a hint of effluent.

The Alt was a threshold to the mysterious, green-canopied wonderland of oak, beech, sycamore and ash that rose, giant-like, with outstretched arms from the vast mottled quilt of rhododendron, lying rumpled in the permanent ice-green twilight. We crossed that water rat infested river thousands of times in our young lives, and yet, astoundingly, nobody ever contracted any deadly diseases or the dreaded 'fever' – a folk memory from the time when our city lost legions to the scourge of cholera and typhus, which lurks still in the gutters, grids and legends of despair.

One hot summer's day, when the infinite freedom of the school holidays had settled down into a sediment of boredom, we decided to build a dam and have a cool swim. We did not lack helpers, as, like Han dynasty Chinese engaged in a great flood prevention enterprise, we beavered away piling up sods, branches, logs and anything else to hand. After about two hours the dam had risen to head height and the near moribund flow of the Alt was eventually as deep and inviting as a coral-fringed lagoon.

Like young otters we slid down glistening clay slides and splashed happily into the gently frothing lake, and, with two or three strokes, pulled ourselves to the other bank. Once there, and clear of the unsympathetic thistles, we shook ourselves dry, like pot-bellied puppies, and released a fine, dun coloured spray among the dandelions and cowpats.

That river was our Amazon, Rubicon and Nile. Alas, now vast housing estates of unbelievable ugliness squat on our Arcadian retreat, but in those days the only man-made structures for miles around were our forest dens, Teddy Kelly's patched linen tent and our version of the Great Grand Coulee Dam.

Characteristically, we eventually grew bored with our creation, and Paul Johnson, the scientifically orientated member of our tribe, whose status was signified by a strip of elastoplast that permanently obscured the right lens of his post-war, pre-Lennon, wire-framed spectacles, appointed himself chief sapper.

With studious care, he selected the pivotal sod, wrenched it free, and the brown sand of the river-bed was obliterated as a lacy spume of amber plunged between the banks of thistledown, mother-die and nettle, ahead of the disintegrating dam like youth fleeing from age, before settling into the sluggish rhythm of its serpentine meander to the open sea, and oblivion.

72. Me and My Monkey

I have a distinctly 'iffy' attitude toward pets and it is probably hereditary. There is a family legend concerning my mother's brother, Tommy, who as an infant was apparently terrified of the reclining stone lions that guard the approaches to St George's Hall, one of Liverpool's most imposing landmarks.

He later grew up to be a hard-case sailor who survived the rigours of his majesty's destroyer *Gypsy* as it protected the Russian convoys. But as a baby, the sight of those granite predators, which do indeed look as if they are about to spring from their pedestals, would set him to screaming with fear.

My own introduction to pets sounds like a bit of a shaggy dog story, but it's true. My seafaring father would often bring home animals, which, after his departure to sea, became the responsibility of my creature-phobic mother. One time he brought a dog home. I honestly can't remember its name, but it was a lovely liver and cream spaniel. I think my father must have been training it to be a cormorant, because everyday he would hurl it into the nearby pond and seemed to derive great satisfaction from the dog's aptitude for swimming. When my father departed on yet another voyage my mother was left with nothing to guide her except for her own inadequate dog handling skills. The truth is she was absolutely terrified of the poor beast and would do almost anything to avoid it. At night, when we were going to bed, she would leave a scone or biscuit at the foot of the stairs, and in the morning she would gingerly open the living room door before hurling the cake toward the far wall. Then grasping my hand she would run hell for leather to the safety of the kitchen.

The dog would hang its head to one side and stare bemusedly at this mother-and-son five-metre dash before tucking into its manna. Consequently I have a pronounced castration complex, which has dogged me for most of my life.

I remember one dreadful manifestation of my fear, which happened when I was about eighteen. I had just said goodbye to a girlfriend of less than two days standing. She was standing on the doorstep with her mother waving to me as I walked jauntily down the road. Suddenly, from inside the gate of a house I was passing, there was a hideous yelping.

All cool forgotten, I immediately went into a crutch-clutching crouch, much too the amusement of all those who witnessed it. What made it a total humiliation was that the 'brute' that had exposed my frailty was so small it could well have been a barking bath-brush.

Over the years my father would bring home a succession of parrots, monkeys and canaries, which he would produce from the inside pocket of his jacket like an off-duty magician. They always looked mildly stupefied, the result of drinking over proof rum I suppose. My father would deposit his animals in the house and then forget about them. It was like living with an absent minded Doctor Doolittle.

One day he asked my Uncle Teddy, who was about fourteen at the time, to take a suitcase full of Amazonian green parrots to a pet shop in Smithdown Road. I accompanied him and all was well as we boarded the bus from Hillside, but misfortune had also purchased a ticket... Now as you all know, when you carry a suitcase you can either have the lid lying hard against your leg or facing outwards to the world. As we walked along Smithdown Road at the busy junction with Lodge Lane it became apparent that Teddy had opted for the second option, because when the insecure fastener flew open the parrots baled out of the suitcase *en masse*, squawking what sounded suspiciously like, 'Libero!' The traffic screamed to a standstill as the parrots, whose wings must have been clipped, ran up and down the road. Pedestrians joined in the hunt and before long the road looked like an animal rights demonstration as people caught the absconders and put them back into the suitcase, only for the feathered Houdinis to escape again! Eventually we managed to get them all back and take them safely to the pet shop.

My favourite illegal immigrant was a Marmoset. Now I confess I have an affinity with monkeys, perhaps there is a family resemblance, and I loved that wide-eyed baby passionately. My father made a sort of canvas webbing with a leash on it so I could take it out when the weather permitted. One-day, as I walked proudly along with my monkey, I suddenly became aware that I was holding a piece of washing line and nothing else. The knot had failed and when I turned around I had really expected to see the monkey clambering on a roof, but it hadn't noticed and was simply squatting on the pavement. I was so relieved that as I retrieved it I gave it a big kiss. Had I been aware of its eventual fate I would have let it go free.

You see, unknown to me, the monkey already had a buyer – a fruit and vegetable salesman (that is, barrow boy) with a stall outside T.J. Hughes's and a sick child in a local hospital. The monkey was sold for thirty shillings and the next time I saw it was on the front page of the *Echo*, being cuddled by a little girl and dressed in a dungaree suit and a fez. Every time I pull on my jeans I think of that poor creature stuck in that hospital and forced to wear a monkey suit!

Quite the most tragic member of our menagerie was a budgerigar that was left in our care. As usual my father had left strict instructions that it be amply fed and watered. At the time my mother worked in Waterworths, the greengrocers, and, terrified of failing in her unwanted task, would bring home all kinds of fruit and salad greens which she liberally attached to the bars of the cage, which by the end of the first week resembled a very large Pimms. What nobody had told us was that budgies are the gluttons of the avian kingdom and will eat incessantly if food is available. The reverse of a cycle of deprivation was inadvertently set in place. The budgie would pig out on lettuce, tomatoes, cucumber and apples which Mam would replenish daily. On Saturday I noticed that the budgie appeared to be sleeping, at the bottom of its cage. It had, of course, snuffed it, but by then it looked like a small Parakeet!

My Dad never left any pets at home again, which was just as well, as my Mam soon afterwards flew the coop herself and found an animal-free environment for both of us.

73. Paint it Black

My introduction to the art of painting occurred when my mother bought a gallon of Dulux gloss and a bucket of emulsion, or 'distemper' as it was called then. I was fifteen at the time, about the same age as the wallpaper we had inherited from the previous owner of our recently acquired house in Vandyke Street.

Now my mother had brothers who were professional painters, but for some reason decided to enlist *my* services as an interior decorator. But I'd seen my uncles in action so many times that I was quite confident I could do it. The ceiling was easy to paint and after I had finished the woodwork I was ready to apply the paper.

My first piece of paper must have been suffering from a kind of vertigo, because every time I let go of it, in the belief that it was adhering to the wall, it arched its back and fell on top of me. After three or four attempts to get the paper to stick there was more paste on my head than on the brush and my mother was becoming more and more agitated. I was beginning to think that the bloody thing was alive! I did eventually get paper on the wall; two whole scraps, which had been beneath my thumbs when the rest of the length split and slithered to the floor like a drunken limbo dancer.

My mother's response to the emergency was typical. In a voice streaked with panic she pleaded, "Oh for Jesus sake leave it lad! I'll get your uncle John to do it!"

Affronted by her lack of faith in me I curtly told her to go shopping and to take her time. She reluctantly agreed and when she returned two hours later the job was done. Her praise of my efforts was lavish. However, there was a hint of discord when she mentioned that it didn't really matter that the match was wrong.

Looking back, the pattern was so out of true I have to conclude that my effort was to decorating what Muhammad Ali versus Brian London was to an equal contest. Nonetheless my mother still refers with pride to that day when I successfully navigated the rites of passage from the colouring books of childhood to the adult mysteries of Anaglypta, Woodchip and silk-finish emulsion.

I have done my own decorating ever since, studiously avoiding matching paper, and I have improved to the point where visitors no longer huddle in the middle of a room lest they be precipitously enveloped by wallpaper on walkabout. Over the years I have lost count of the gallons of paint and wallpaper paste I have got through, much less the number of sinks I have destroyed with a mixture of turpentine substitute and paint. I could write volumes about the clothing I have ruined and I am still haunted by images of paint encrusted jeans, shoes and shirts lying stiff in repose, like the mummies of the men who decorated the tomb of Tutankhamen.

I was about sixteen when my uncles, Frank and John, both ardent socialists, introduced me to what must rank as the most seminal single book I've ever read; Robert Tressel's masterpiece of working class travails, *The Ragged-Trousered Philanthropists*. I suppose that after reading about the dreadful drudgery of painters and decorator's in the bad old days, nothing I ever undertook in that field seemed arduous or daunting. I have never painted a room while suffering from hunger pains, or lain awake wondering if my stray brushstrokes would render my family homeless.

Uncle John asked me one day to help him remove some ice that was causing the gutter above the butcher's shop where my stepfather worked to drip incessantly. I helped him carry the three stage wooden ladders, which were so old and heavy they might have been previously employed to scale the walls of Troy before the Greeks hit on the wooden horse routine, and stared aghast at the mountainous height of the gutter, from which hung an icicle so large that it was a veritable sword of Damocles, waiting to impale anybody who got within ten rungs of it. My heart failed me and I had to admit my cowardice to my uncle. He didn't cast so much as an untoward glance in my direction but simply said, "It's alright lad, you just hold the ladder steady."

He then mounted the ladder and removed the offending blockage. He later gave me five shillings, which was not only a lot of money in those days but far exceeded what my contribution was worth.

I have an indelible memory of one day's painting, which no amount of paint remover could dispel; it was about thirty years ago, when I was painting the outside of my terraced abode in Liverpool. There was no garden to the house and so my ladder was mounted on the pavement, which left it exposed to prams and children on bikes etc... I was hanging from the top of the ladder, in my usual haste to get the difficult bits done so that I could get back to *terra firma* as quickly as possible, when I noticed a man walking towards me. He was about fifty yards away and so, after noting his approach, I continued slobbering on paint. I had quite forgotten about the man when suddenly I felt the ladder shake violently and while I was hanging on for life I saw him kneeling at the foot of the ladder.

Quivering with rage and fear I screamed, "Are you fucking blind!"

The reply, delivered in a small apologetic voice haunts me still.

"Actually I am. I'm sorry..."

I slid down that ladder without touching the rungs as if it were a fireman's pole and helped him to his feet all the while trying to persuade him to have a cup of tea, an offer he courteously declined.

Nowadays I have a front garden that has enough space to accommodate my ladders, my paint spattered rags and my incipient panic.

One rung at a time...

74. Walking on Sunshine

A bucket and spade holiday in the sun was what my family wanted and since that naturally ruled out Britain we trundled off to our local travel agents. I had tried to book a holiday online but it took so long that we were looking at a beach break somewhere in cyberspace in 2023!

The holiday rep, Joanne, was helpfulness personified. Taking into account our limited resources and preference for a quiet resort, she painstakingly found us a nice-looking apartment in Elounda on the island of Crete. She then arranged for us to be picked up at our door and taken to Manchester airport by cab as well as arranging our currency needs. She even checked the weather prospects and informed us that the sun would be shining all week. All that remained for me to do was to decide on which strength suntan lotion I needed. As a veteran of Pacific sunshine I opted for the lowest factor.

The ancient Greek warning, "Those whom the gods wish to destroy they first make mad," would return to haunt me with a vengeance.

A jammed door delayed our take off from Manchester and I was uncomfortably reminded that I had all my eggs in one basket. Eventually we took off and after two hours I had a stiff neck from trying to peer out of the window from a middle aisle seat. The boys were too involved with their headsets to notice that the Alps looked like a foreshortened wedding cake, albeit rather more challenging than the bland chicken dinner I was eating, courtesy of Air Tours. After about two hours my youngest boy offered me the headset, informing me that channel 8 was for 'oldies'. I tuned in to hear Steve Miller singing 'Fly like an eagle'. Loved it!

The heat, when we arrived at 3 pm, was overwhelming, as it was 43 degrees centigrade. Of course it was *our* baggage that failed to turn up and as the coach took off without us I had visions of spending the night inside the airport, but the holiday rep had booked an air-conditioned taxi to take us to Elounda, which normally involved a two-hour coach journey. I have often heard passengers cursing baggage handlers, but I never suspected that I would soon swell their numbers as the cab driver headed for Elounda. His brand new Mercedes was air-conditioned, but I was soon bathed in sweat as the driver began driving with one hand while talking into a mobile phone with the other. The twisting road was alive with vehicles, all of which were perceived by our personal charioteer as an affront to his dignity.

Stavros Ben Hur's favoured mode of driving was to nuzzle up to the rear of the car in front and then slide into a gap in the traffic which was narrower than the slit in a drunkard's eyes. My skin was leaking with perspiration and the deliquescence of fear as he eventually decided that driving with one hand was simply effeminate and cheerfully overtook a mobile cement mixer … sans hands! In an instant I was the personification of the Greek national drink, Ouzo.

The road suddenly turned inland and began to climb into the dun-coloured mountains. While my wife and boys commented on the beauty of the churches and olive groves that limpeted the hillsides I could only focus on the missing or twisted crash-barriers marking the spot where previous chariots had winged their way over the precipitous drop. I was never so happy as when we pulled up outside our apartment in Elounda. What is more, I now have a rough idea about who put the 'hell' in Hellenic.

The apartment was in a shady street whose white-painted houses were splashed with crimson Bougainvillea. My complexion was soon to become the same colour, but without benefit of the fragrance. After struggling with the key, which we had obtained from the genial male concierge, it became apparent that what the brochure had described as a two-roomed apartment, was in fact a double oven with only one temperature setting … roasting!

That night the temperature 'fell' to 31 degrees and my spirits sank to zero as I lay on the bed while a feeble-looking fan tossed warm air about the room. At one stage I got so worried about the boys that I went to check that they were still breathing. Inexplicably, they were fast asleep! Oh for the innocence of youth! My wife and I ended up sitting on the doorstep, watching the icy moon glide behind the baking mountains.

Almost everything in the apartment was made of concrete. Even the beds were simply mattresses laid on concrete plinths, presumably to deter wood boring insects, but to me they felt like altars to human sacrifice. The whole town was like a clay oven that was never allowed to cool sufficiently before the next day's cooking began again in earnest.

The darkest hour is just before dawn, and it is also the coolest, so I was able to get an hour's sleep before rising and setting out for beach. The sea looked beautiful ... and it was. As I plunged into the warm yet cooling Mediterranean I felt like Ulysses returning home from the fires of Troy.

The temperatures never changed throughout the week we were there, but I suppose we must have made some vague adjustment to our body thermostats because I eventually managed three hour's sleep a night. Even after quaffing prodigious amounts of Mythos, the excellent local beer, and consuming a three-course meal, it was as difficult to enter the land of Nod as it had been for Adam and Eve after their expulsion from Eden.

The heat apart, our stay in Greece was quite wonderful. Crete has often been described as the cradle of civilisation and the hand that rocked it instilled some wonderful lessons in hospitality in its children. Oh, I know it is in their economic interests to be pleasant to tourists, but there again many tourists go to London don't they? Nuff said.

Our immediate neighbours, a Welsh couple, recommended a restaurant to us and so we decided to give it a try. I was disappointed to say the least. You see, I have grown up in Liverpool with Cypriot cooking – which tends to be roast or grilled lamb dishes – and so when my *kleftiko* was served up stewed I was a bit aggrieved. I felt it was a potato short of a bowl of scouse. Worse, my wife's *moussaka* was almost cold, despite her having seen it being taken from a microwave and my eldest son's *spaghetti carbonara* was inedible. Only the 'baby' enjoyed his helping of lukewarm Ambrosia, which was actually *spa-*

ghetti bolognese. Perhaps the food's journey from Italy to Crete was responsible for our disappointment!

We decided there and then to find another place to eat for the following night. However, we reckoned without the geography of Elounda, which has one main street, ensuring that you have to pass every restaurateur in the town, even if you are just going for bread and milk. After another glorious day on the beach we decided to slip past the Eskimo Café to partake of our evening meal, but we were arrested by the charm of the Inuit restaurateur, for surely he must have been a native of Alaska. He pointed us to the chalk-written menu and invited us to partake of his spit-roasted chicken. Despite our misgivings we were too shy to refuse, and I was glad for that because it was truly the finest grilled chicken I've ever tasted. We decided that the previous night had been a hiccup and after paying our very reasonably priced bill we headed for the centre of town.

We hit upon a café bar called 'The Garden of Eden', where we were immediately ushered to a table by the most charming front man/huckster I've ever encountered. Small, energetic, dark and incredibly charismatic, he bore such an uncanny resemblance to Ratso Rizzo – Dustin Hoffman's brilliant character study in 'The Midnight Cowboy' – that I felt compelled to tell him so. He just smiled, but he was visibly pleased. When I asked him where he got his energy from he shrugged and smilingly put it down to drinking the juice of four kilos of oranges every day. It sounded plausible but I couldn't help noting that he had to shout his replies so as to be heard above the deafening crescendos of the in-house techno music, which was so loud it ruffled the waters of the harbour, which was garishly illuminated by lasers from the café.

The Café Eden was certainly a paradise for my fifteen-year-old because, apart from the music, which was right up his teenage street, he was taken as old enough to drink, and, to his delight, was served a series of the most flamboyant cocktails this side of Manhattan, and no doubt the other side too. All in all, it was a wonderful evening, made possible by the various stars of the kitchen, cafe and even those inhabiting the indigo sky.

Later, as I fought my usual battle with wakefulness I reflected on how civilised it was to be able to have a family evening where the various age groups hadn't succumbed to centrifugal forces, which is the norm back home, where the young cling to the middle of society's spinning disc while the elderly are spun out to the periphery and ultimately off the edge. In fact, it was very like being in Ireland, where people of all ages socialise happily in the same bars and clubs.

The following morning found us at the beach, which, after the heat of the night, had become our health-giving spa. The beach was a mixture of shingle and gritty sand and when we weren't snorkelling or generally messing about in the sea we dozed on sun beds under umbrellas, which were provided at low cost by the local council. There were, however, other diversions ... and how!

As the sun reached its zenith I was walking along the shoreline carrying my youngest boy's fishing net, trying vainly to catch what must have been atomic-powered tiddlers, when I saw a woman flick her bikini top off and throw it to the floor. What followed can only be described as a staggered Mexican wave, as woman after woman followed suit. Suddenly I was sunbathing in an open-air burlesque! My mouth looked like an open amphora as I stood there, net in hand, like a prurient Poseidon.

Oddly enough, within hours of their spectacular unveiling I had grown accustomed to the sand-spattered strippers and had even begun to note the incredible variety of T&A that lived cheek by jowl on that beach, and I am including the men. There were boobs and bums which pointed up, down, sideways and in one case all three directions at once ... or perhaps it was the heat haze.

The bikini top and the bra are possibly the greatest forces of anti-gravity in the universe. When they are removed the natural laws, à la Newton, take over, or should I say under. Never have illusions been so swiftly shattered as when those boobs hit the beach, quite literally in some cases! I'm not talking just about elderly men and women here, but young active people who between them have accumulated enough lard to grease the keel of a ship during its launch.

At the age of 56 I felt smugly trim and I jokingly mentioned to my lady that the combination of my anticipated tan and my Schwarzenegger physique might get me an invitation to sit on Olympus. But hubris was being writ large all over my steadily reddening body. After three days I had failed to tan, unlike my boys who were rapidly acquiring a Grecian look. Instead, I was so pink that I looked like a candy floss on two sticks and before long the boys were affecting fear of my approach and shouting "Run! Run! It's Chernobyl Man!"

The truth is, I did acquire some of the powers of a comic-book super hero. For instance, if I walked into a café the fabric of time and space was momentarily ruptured and I would find myself faced by open-mouthed people who were temporarily frozen in the act of raising a drink to their lips as they beheld me. Ironically, it was only my fiercely reddened skin, which precluded people from seeing my blushes.

That night we failed to escape the clutches of our genial restaurateur and I was once more disappointed when the 'spit roasted lamb' turned up stewed again. The next night we decided to brazen it out and we walked right past him, which left him looking sad-eyed and forlorn and me feeling irrationally guilty. However, our warrior-like resolve paid off and we found a wonderful place called 'Il Sole'. Not only was the food excellent, but the maitre-D, a Spanish born Dutchman called Ramon, provided some of the finest entertainment of our holiday. However, on our entry to the seaside restaurant I was disconcerted to see that I had earlier encountered the owner, and it hadn't been in the most amicable of circumstances.

Earlier that day, as I purchased a *Gyros*, those wonderful Greek concoctions consisting of spit roasted lamb, potato chips, yoghurt and salad wrapped in pita bread, I had a misunderstanding about the price and my change. I was in the wrong and had apologised profusely, but he was obviously hurt. However, such is the mercurial nature of Greeks that within hours of our minor spat he was lavishing free drinks and ice creams on us!

Ramon was a tall, lean and energetic man who spoke many languages so well that he could make humorous asides in all of them. He was enamoured of the catering industry and his mission in life was to let diners enjoy everything about their experience. The first night we were there a nearby couple asked for beers. Ramon, who has to cross a busy main road in order to obtain drinks and meals from the kitchen, placed the bottles down and glided away.

He hadn't got far when the man gently said, "Excuse me, the bottle tops are still on.", whereupon Ramon retorted with a smile, "You almost had a very cheap night!"

Everybody laughed and I felt as if I were back home in Liverpool. On another occasion when I asked him for the bill he replied, "Of course sir. It will arrive eventually, but in the meantime if you get fed up waiting you can run away because I haven't got the energy to chase you."

Needless to say, we ate there for the remainder of our stay.

The final highlight of my stay in Crete was to sit, drinking ice cold lager, watching Manchester United getting whacked by Liverpool in the Charity Shield competition. Another myth bites the dust of Crete!

For the first time in my life I was looking forward a nice bit of English rain, but when we got back to Liverpool the sun was shining. The sadistic swine had followed us home!

75. Spinning Wheel

I doubt if there are many people who haven't thrilled to the sight and sound of a travelling fairground. My earliest memories of a fairground, however, are of New Brighton's permanent funfair. In those days there was a pier at New Brighton, which accommodated the Mersey ferries as they conveyed happy families from Liverpool to the 'Las Vegas of the Wirral'. That's what New Brighton was in those days, an all-singing all-dancing one-armed-bandit that stripped you of your worldly wealth without so much as a glimpse of a jackpot or a complimentary drink. Unlike Las Vegas, however, the girls were always fully dressed, while the croupiers who took your money wore knotted neckerchiefs, and their tousled hair glistened from a liberal application of crude oil, or perhaps it was Brylcreem.

I used to plague my mother to take me across the river at every opportunity. She was always desperately in need of sleep and I used to take unholy advantage of her tiredness. I can distinctly remember her on one Sunday morning pleading with me for 'five minutes more' and, like the little swine that I was, I carefully watched the fingers of the clock eat up the allotted time before I raised her heavy eyelids with deftly probing fingers. Stupefied, she stared at me, and pleaded, "John, if you give me another five minutes I'll take you to New Brighton."

I agreed, and again began watching the clock with the ardent attention of a man scanning a crowd for a sight of his first date. As the moving finger, having writ five minutes, moved on, so did my poor mother, from the land of Nod to Pandemonium in a twinkling of her grey-blue eyes.

I loved the ferry crossing because my mother always made a beeline for the grandly named 'saloon', where she would buy a cup of tea for herself, with crisps and 'Full Swing' lemonade for me. I can still see clearly the design on the bottle of a young girl sitting on a swing in an English garden, which could have been the inspiration for Jimmy Rogers' famous song. The potato crisps were invariably greasy and the optional salt, in its twist of blue paper, was often moist, but nothing could have dampened my spirits as our snub-nosed craft buffeted its way through the grey Mersey, where the crests of the rippling waves resembled the outspread wings of kamikaze seagulls.

Once in New Brighton we would follow an almost traditional route through the various attractions, but the one that lingers in my memory was called the 'Grand National', a game that required little skill but which was nonetheless thrilling for all that. One simply rolled wooden balls into a hole at the end of a kind of trough and the faster you rolled the returning balls back into the hole, the quicker went your horse. I once won a glass fruit bowl on a black plinth for being the youngest competitor in the race, but I suspect I was awarded the prize because the Brylcreem'd proprietor had recognised that my old lady was the prettiest competitor by a distance.

When not engrossed in the sport of kings I spent ages window-shopping for rock, the garish confection made of one hundred per-cent sugar, which came in all manner of shapes and sizes. There were bars shaped as bananas, apples and lemons, and also the more traditional rock, striped with hues so virulent that they anticipated day-glo colours by decades, and down the centre of each stick was engraved the words 'New Brighton'. They really ought to have included the telephone number of the local dental hospital.

After we, or rather I had depleted the family purse to such an extent that paying the following week's rent would become problematical, my mother would eventually throw caution to the winds and we would have a fish and chip supper. We would then gather up the remnants of the day by walking the sparse beaches and slipping into seaweed-smothered rock pools.

Yet for all its glamour New Brighton was somehow tame compared to the promise held by the sight of a travelling fairground. Oh the sight and sound of it all as I approached the fairground and beheld the evening gloom rent by multi-coloured flashing lights and shaken by the sounds of the hottest pop records of the day!

I was a daredevil on the Dodgems, but most people of my age preferred the Waltzer, a huge whirling dervish of a ride, which entailed being clamped into in a wildly spinning chariot-like seat for four, all the while screaming like Banshees who had been recently released from a high security institution. I hated it the Waltzer. Any ride that relies on speed and obeys a centrifugal force makes me nauseous. So you can imagine my dismay when, many years later, I took a lovely young lady called Glenys Morgan on a pilgrimage to the entertainment Mecca of my childhood, New Brighton, and she opted to go on the Waltzer. What could a young dude do? Betray his cowardice by suggesting the Dodgems? I reluctantly climbed into the mobile hell and watched gloomily as the Brylceem'd roustabout slotted the safety bar in place. A Motown hit was playing at full blast, taunting me with its lyrics: *"Nowhere to run baby ... nowhere to hide..."*

As the ride gathered momentum I tried to affect unconcern, but my stomach was churning as if was on the spin cycle of a warm wash. As if my discomfort wasn't enough, a brilliantined sadist leapt on to the wildly spinning ride and began to manually spin our chariot still more! 'Fucking show-off,' I thought, not realising that for most people this bonus spinning of their individual chariot was an additional thrill. Glenys, pretty and demure in her white knee socks, was smiling happily as I leaned towards the greasy demon and motioned him to come closer. He lowered his head toward mine, without once taking his eyes off Glenys, and I whispered, hoarsely.

"Can you lay off the spinning our kid, me girl doesn't like it."

To his eternal credit he desisted at once, doubtlessly not wanting to queer his pitch should he ever, at some future date, get within an oily comb's length of the lovely Glenys. The ride continued, with my stomach rapidly approaching the rinse cycle, but at least the tortuous gyrations were slower than they might have been. Puzzled by my seeming intimacy with the roustabout Glenys turned to me and asked, "What was all that about?"

"I asked him to crank it up a bit, but he didn't want to know," I shamelessly replied. She nodded, glumly satisfied, and I realised that with one lie I had not only dished the romantic chances of the randy roustabout but had spared myself the embarrassment of dyeing Glenys's knee socks an unfashionable shade of carotene.

76. What's New, Pussycat?

I once spent three years at Liverpool University in the company of younger people, studying the ways in which advertisers and propagandists insinuate their ideas into our minds. When I graduated I thought that my course of study had all been worthwhile because it had armed me with a defence mechanism to protect myself against the blandishments and trickery of the powerful persuaders who daily access our consciousness in order to alter it for their own benefit.

You can imagine my surprise when most of my fellows declined the chance to spread the word about the devious methodology of persuaders in general and advertising in particular, opting instead to leap headlong into the tangled jungle of the jingle.

One day, about two years after graduation, I met a former classmate, a lovely young woman, who was now working for one of the biggest advertising firms in the world and I found myself tempted to abandon my low-level anti-advertising 'crusade' and apply for a job at her firm. I was tired of the Mickey Mouse jobs, which were, it seemed, the only forms of employment available after Thatcher's voodoo economics had pinned our manufacturing base to the wall, before demolishing it brick by brick.

One such job had involved persuading people that the new way forward was for them to volunteer to do the jobs that nobody else wanted to do – for example, having young kids hump cooking stoves etc from DHSS-owned warehouses onto lorries, which would then convey these household items to the homes of deserving cases. As far as I was concerned it was a betrayal of youth and I wanted none of it.

I had arranged for an interview with the young woman's employers and as a result was given an advertising project to complete at home. The project consisted of creating a brand name and an advertising campaign for a new cat food, and was designed to test my creative skills as a copywriter. The following weekend saw me attempting to construct a cat food portfolio that would launch the next big tin.

In 1981 the only things I possessed by way of art materials were two paint brushes, set fast in a jar of congealed turpentine substitute, and a pair of rust-flecked wallpaper scissors, so my wife and I drew up a list of items that were imperative to possess if I was to conquer the world of fantasy and illusion known as advertising.

By the following midday we had assembled a collection of assorted glossy magazines, wallpaper paste, scissors, a sheaf of A4 typing paper, coloured pencils and a set of plastic letter stencils. The magazines were intended to supply images of cats, but in the event we found only a handful, which wasn't too surprising as most of the magazines were of the *Cosmopolitan* type and as such were more likely to contain glamourpusses rather than domestic pussies.

My advertising brief demanded that I create a brand name for the non-existent cat food and then write copy that would underpin the main characteristic of the product. Namely, to ensure that one's cat enjoyed a balanced diet of fish, meat, cereals, minerals and vitamins.

I didn't foresee any problems peddling a concoction that in essence would have fulfilled the gastronomic aspirations of a third world family. How wrong can you be!

I decided that the product would be called 'Choice', hoping to capitalise on the connotations of choice cuts of meat and fish as well as the freedom to choose the best cat food available. The biggest problem was presented by the need for an illustration that would convey the idea of balance. I had a vision of a cat dancing on a set of scales, but wouldn't you know that among all those magazines there wasn't a single picture of scales, not even in the luxurious bathroom scenes. Given that most models spend hours weighing themselves I found the omission of such essential technology inexplicable.

Eventually I ended up with a sheet of A4 on which was pasted a cut-out of a bored looking cat perched precariously on my poorly drawn sketch of a three-legged milking stool. It looked like a cinema poster promoting 'Carry on Witches'.

Believe it or not my mangy montage took six hours to create, which is ironic given that my lady could have enlisted the aid of one of her twelve-year-old pupils who would have done an infinitely better job in ten minutes.

At the end of our labours my nerves were as frayed as the edges of the cut-out cat and we were in a constant state of hysterics because Graham, a visiting friend of ours, who had been press-ganged into joining the enterprise, kept commenting on the 'Van Gogh like quality' of my milking stool. Within hours of embarking on the project our sense of frustration led Graham to rename it 'Pussy Slop'.

All that remained was to create the copy that would impel cat lovers to buy the damned stuff. As I remember there was lots of drivel about keeping one's cat young and balanced in both body and mind. Can you believe that? A cat food that doubled up as a subscription to the Maharishi's transcendental meditation classes?

Monday morning arrived and I set off to Brunning's agency with my sure-fire promotion nestling inside a red and white striped Kwik-Save shopping bag. That was a big mistake, because for one thing it was drizzling steadily and my dog-eared cat was visibly peeling off the A4. For another, I was asked to wait in a swish waiting room in the company of another candidate who had a portfolio so large that helicopters could have landed on its leather-bound surface. The red and white stripes of my Kwik-Save bag merged to my shade of blushing pink as we cringed in the shade of a potted palm.

I was interviewed by a Bunter-esque young man who was surrounded by so many racks of coloured pencils that his desk looked like Cape Canaveral on the 4th of July. He evinced polite interest in my exhibition of tripe and then asked me what I had planned as a television advertising campaign for Pussy Slop.

I was aghast. I'd spent hours creating a masterpiece of absurdist art and now he wanted moving pictures! I mean, can you imagine how I felt, given that even after my skilful exploitation of my meagre resources I had ended up with what looked like a school's entry for an RSPCA poster?

I didn't get the job, of course, and it served me right for backsliding in my beliefs. Later, in the warm confines of 'Ye Olde Cracke', in receipt of several pints, I remembered that the TV campaign had been part of the brief, but after hours of auditioning silly looking cats and having my photo-realistic milking stool castigated I had overlooked it. For the record, here's what I came up with…

Since my brush with the world of glamour had occurred during the onset of Thatcherism and a heightening of the cold war, the following scenario would no doubt have been enthusiastically accepted by any Ad agency worth its salt.

SCRIPT

[A CAT IS SITTING ON A DINGY EAST GERMAN MAT, GAZ-ING DISDAINFULY AT A FULL DISH OF 'KOMRADES'S KAT FOOD']

[CUT TO CONTENTED WEST GERMAN CAT DOZING CON-TENTEDLY NEXT TO AN EMPTY BOWL MARKED 'CHOICE']

[DISSOLVE TO COMMIE CAT LOOKING FURTIVE]

Commie cat sneaks out of the house and picks its way through a marked minefield. Its ears prick at the sound of a rifle bolt being pulled and it makes a mad dash to scramble over the wall, narrowly avoiding a hail of bullets, released by a Kalashnikov-wielding cat guard.

[CAPITALIST CAT EMBRACES COMMIE CAT.] (Don't ask me how!)

[VOICE OVER]

"Cats. Revolt against revolting food! Make sure you have your Choice!"

To think, that but for the want of a PC, a decent art programme and a printer I could have rivalled Snaachi and Snaachi!

77. The First Cut is the Deepest

This morning, as I was trying to clear some of the clutter from my desk, I found myself staring at one of my old passport photographs. In all modesty I must say I was the essence of seventies chic – long hair, beard and an oddly glazed look. I was also struck by the resemblance between the Taliban leader Mullah Omar and myself. The only difference between us, as far as I could discern, was that he has only one eye, whereas I was in possession of two, which is probably a happy consequence of my not playing with bazookas. I can only imagine that at that time I'd been going through one of my phases of not wanting to partake of the daily ritual of shaving, or perhaps I had an irresistible urge to look like Rasputin on one of his bad hair days.

I was transported back to the bad old days in Liverpool when few women were aware of the discomfort involved in shaving, preferring instead to conceal their hairy legs inside heavy stockings, or alternatively, pursue a career in a circus. It was left to us brave chaps to test out each advance in hair removal technology.

By the 1960s, we had come some way from the days when men scraped their faces with sea shells or flakes of flint, although, in truth, not all that far, as razor manufacturers were still working with materials and methods which were rendered obsolete about the time of the battle of Stalingrad. Stainless steel blades were still a distant dream, which men indulged in when faced with nightmare of razors, which rusted at the mere sight of a moist shaving brush.

My grandfather's preferred razor was made by Gillette and was called a 'Seven O'clock'. To me, the name clearly indicated that if one shaved at seven in the morning then one would need to scrape one's chin exactly twelve hours later – a sort of sharp-edged *aide memoire*. A cut from the easily-blunted blade meant a minute scrap of paper had to be applied immediately to stem the bleeding. There is no medical research to say how many men died of heavy metal poisoning from the news-print, but I'm sure there must have been some because many victims of a dull blade preferred newspaper to, say, Izal toilet paper (although how they managed to call it 'paper' and keep a straight face is beyond me – it was so stiff and shiny it could have been used to build artificial ski slopes).

I had only been shaving, or rather decapitating my acne for about a year when a techno-miracle arrived in the form of Wilkinson's sword edged blades. At last, someone had perfected a blade which glided over the skin and removed hair rather than digging into one's chin like an obdurate ploughshare bent on sowing a harvest of pain.

Those blades were so sought after by hordes of paper-festooned men that our local chemist in Lodge Lane rationed customers to two blades apiece! However, by dint of making a few trips to different chemists, one could amass razors aplenty and so be able to lose one's unwanted facial hair without spoiling the look of one's acne.

It was also at about that time that men were persuaded that women, for some inexplicable reason, preferred men who didn't smell as if they'd anointed their bodies with a week's supply of discarded socks. It transpired that women had been deceiving men since the dawn of time that they actually *enjoyed* the manly aroma which indicated that their lover hadn't even heard of soap, much less used the damn stuff. Those same fickle females, apparently, secretly hankered for men who smelled … well … funny.

I remember the first time I encountered the winds of change; winds that carried a strong whiff of the future. It was called Old Spice, which name was singularly apt, as it was more pungent than a day-old chicken vindaloo. Any man brave enough to wear it was instantly identifiable, as he alone smelled sweetly among the acrid aroma of stale bitter, *eau de building site* and Woodbine smoke. The merest scent of Old Spice caused grown men to quiver and sniff the air as if detecting the presence of a wild animal. Offenders were tracked down and, before a baying crowd, hounded with accusations of being … well … funny. Cruel epithets were muttered as the unfortunate quarry took to his heels and fled to the relative safety of the snug.

In truth it wasn't as violent as that, but the seismic shift in male scents caused profound grief among the older drinkers who, from their lofty age of twenty-five or so, were convinced that it was 'all a fad' and would disappear quickly. I see those men sometimes, especially if I'm passing an HIM (hostel for ignored males).

As for myself, a social conformist and erstwhile ladies' man, Old Spice rapidly became passé and so I moved on – so much so that by the eighties I was *au fait* with the merits of *Madame Gres pour L'homme* over say, *Armani*. I am nipping to the shops and have just applied a spray of D&G Masculine, a Christmas present from my teenage boys.

The ironic thing is that they think that buying perfume for a man is as natural as the smell of a baby's skin.

78. Get Off of My Cloud

When I was a kid I was brimful of optimism. I used to wake up in the morning and the first thought to enter my mind was, 'What nice thing will happen to me today?' Some days it was simply that the calendar had run down and a birthday was looming. At other times just the thought of going to town with my mother and possibly ending up in Paddy's Market or my great aunt Alice's was enough to make me want to wave to the sky.

Paddy's Market was a sprawl of stall and tables containing heaps of second hand clothes that propped up rusty sit-up-and-beg bicycles much prized by poor Lascar seamen, whose tired faces seemed to have survived either the ravages of ocean storm or smallpox, or both. A trip to Paddy's, or more properly, Saint Martin's Market, usually meant that we would walk back toward Great Homer's Street where, during the summer's glut, we would buy our fill of Canary tomatoes – paper-swaddled rubies nestled in a flimsy wooden treasure chest decorated with smiling Spanish ladies coyly twirling black fans. We would eat them as if they were cherries and my lips would pucker at the tart kiss of their acid sweetness.

In those days Cuba was just an island and a 'missile crisis' simply meant being outnumbered in a snowball fight. But at about that time I saw, at the Granada cinema, a documentary about a nuclear weapons test on a Pacific Island. I was too young to glimpse the irony of the event taking place at that location, but I understood what was happening when, after the rose gold palette of the sky had blistered and boiled until all the colours ran, several dummies, which had been bound to chairs three hundred feet underground, lay twisted and broken on the floor of the cavern.

The fiery hell on the silver screen eventually subsided and as the last of the atomic light flickered in the darkened cinema, so my own spirit began to gutter and wane. As if piling up terror on terror it was only a few months later, in the same cinema, that I was privy to a Walt Disney short film that demonstrated the speed of nuclear fission.

It was as ingenious as it was terrifying. On a billiard table a man laid scores of mousetraps, side by side, until the green baize was completely covered. Then the traps were set and ping-pong balls were placed where the cheese would normally go. At a given signal the man then tossed a ping-pong ball onto the table, whereupon it triggered the first trap, which in turn released its ball, and then there were two in the air. Two became four and four became eight and so on until all of the balls, hundreds in all, were bouncing everywhere. The whole event from first ball to last was over in precisely one second.

Disney then took pains to ensure we had seen exactly what had happened by re-running the spectacle in agonisingly slow motion. Even at slow speed the snowstorm above the leaping twisting traps created horror in me.

Thanks for that, Uncle Walt! Only you could transform ping-pong balls and a billiard table into a model of mass extinction

… and not just for the mice.

79. Tossin' and Turnin'

The first time I ever heard the term 'amphetamine' was sometime in the sixties, which is not to say that they weren't around long before then. Doctors throughout the fifties had often prescribed highly-addictive 'purple hearts' to housewives as 'slimming' tablets but within a decade those same housewives would be deemed lawbreakers if they should attempt to renew their earlier acquaintance with the very same drug, because by 1970 this particular creation of the pharmaceutical companies was perceived as a Frankenstein, an ogre to be destroyed, regardless of the wishes of the monster's victims.

The abuse of amphetamine wasn't solely restricted to those people who popped pills as if they were eating popcorn. I once came across a more subtle and infinitely more sinister misuse of the drug concerning a Mrs O'Casey and her beautiful but gullible niece, Sally. Every summer, Sally, who was about fourteen and hailed from a small village near Wigan, would make an appearance at her aunt's house and take up residence for the duration of her school holidays. Perhaps she thought Liverpool was an exciting change from her village, which was by all accounts so dull that the Parish council issued visitors' passes to the multitude wanting to view the recently installed Laundromat.

It was in the summer of 1954 when I first became aware that the red haired Sally, apart from being gorgeous, was quite the most hard-working and industrious young woman I'd ever seen. All through the glorious months of June and July Sally could be seen toiling away, cleaning and washing in her aunt's house like a Trojan on piece-work. Sally's obsessive approach to domestic chores meant that her aunt's usually dingy house sparkled – from its polished windows to its crisp bed linen. She almost never had time to talk, probably because that would have meant keeping still.

One day I heard my mother telling my father that she suspected Mrs O'Casey of slipping 'slimming pills' into Sally's tea. If it was true, and most of the neighbourhood were convinced it was, then the pills certainly worked, because Sally invariably returned to her village a damned sight thinner than when she arrived! I have sometimes wondered if that sweet girl ever became addicted to the 'slimming pills' that caused her summer to fly swiftly by with the speed of a swallow.

Many years later, I myself suffered a similar abuse at the hands of a young man called Wesley, who despite sharing his name with the famed evangelical preacher was quite simply Satan in a shiny leather jacket. It all began one Friday evening in our local, a tiny pub on the corner of Yanwath Street in Lodge Lane. Every Friday a gang of my mates would meet up and play draw poker in the back room, prior to heading downtown to a club. Wesley was a somewhat peripheral acquaintance, as more often than not he was travelling the country engaged in one moneymaking scam or other. With his swarthy looks and dark curly hair it was easy to believe the rumour that he was a Romany who only lavished his gypsy charms on unwitting diddicoys so as to have an alibi should the need arise.

I had lost heavily at poker and was just about to head for home when Wesley, who had witnessed my losses, motioned to me to go over to him at the bar. When I got there he looked around furtively and asked, "D'yer fancy an all-night party?"

Given that the alternative was watching an episode of *Maverick*, I couldn't help but agree. When I asked him where the party was taking place he grew somewhat vague, but assured me that it would be a good party. So saying, he slipped something into my hand. When I opened my hand I saw three 'purple hearts' nestling in my palm. I looked at him in bewilderment but he put his fingers to his lips and whispered, "These will make sure you stay the distance. You don't wanna fall off the perch do yer?"

Hesitantly, I agreed.

"Just pop 'em now... in one," he urged.

I did, and a broad smile spread across his face.

"I'm just nippin' out..." mouthed my Bohemian benefactor, "I'll be about five minutes."

I spent the next five minutes conjuring images of wild scenes of youthful exuberance, until Wesley came back in. He was no longer smiling. He trudged over to me and, in a melancholy tone, said, "The party fell through!"

What could I say? Nothing ventured, nothing gained.

It was only after I had spent the worst night of my life, tossing and turning in the confines of my mute and uncomprehending bed, that I realised the bastard had planned my chemically induced insomnia right from the outset.

Still, it did inure me to 'speed' and I never bothered with it again – ever – so perhaps Wesley was of God's party after all!

80. Picture This

When I was a boy, comics were probably the most important medium in my life. They provided me with companionship, information and entertainment, often of a very high order.

I can recall many a Friday afternoon after school had finished and I was waiting for my mother to come home from work, lighting the coal fire and spreading out my copy of the *Topper* on the floor. The brightly coloured antics of Mickey the Monkey would give me as much pleasure as the general knowledge section, which was inevitably about the strange habits and habitats of exotic animals.

I've lost count of how many times my exposure to such encyclopaedic trivia has enabled me to answer a television quiz question, to the obvious amazement of my modern-day 'video children', whose information gathering is often stultified by the rigid binary classifications of their computers. No large gatherings of the anarchic and wildly exotic there! Unless, of course, there is a directory labelled 'anarchic and wildly exotic'. I still remember with affection the bower birds, weaver birds, and kookaburras which, in spite of Conrad Lorenz's vision of birds as being perpetually engaged in territorial aggression, mated, nested and raised their young together on the back page of my common-or-garden comic.

Winter evenings in all areas of Liverpool were sometimes spent in the pursuit of 'swaps' – the exchange of one's own comics for another's. Accompanied by a friend, to ensure fair dealing, we would knock on someone's door and ask, "Any swaps?" whereupon the boy would inevitably produce his own bundle and proceed to barter for those he had not read. A peculiarity of the system of exchange lay in the fact that English comics were deemed to be inferior to American comics; to such an extent that one 'Yank' was the equal of two 'English'. There seemed to be an ideological message in this, as fifties Britain, its currency subservient to the rampant dollar, was rapidly becoming a client state of America.

Among the despised 'English' comics was *Classics Illustrated,* which set out to introduce young readers to the great classic novels. It was thanks to these that I enjoyed such diverse works as *Last of the Mohicans, A Tale of Two Cities* and *Men Against the Sea.* They were easy to read as they were well drawn in finely detailed coloured pictures of differing sizes – the key passages represented by large close ups, while the less significant scenes were simply thumbnail sketches.

Odd that they were known as 'comics' because my abiding memories are of the insights they afforded me rather than the chuckles they triggered. The same could be said of my favourite adult comic, the late and much lamented Lenny Bruce.

81. All Things Must Pass

I was thinking the other day about the jobs that have disappeared in Liverpool due to the inexorable progress of technology, and, in some cases, parliamentary legislation. For instance, my mother told me that when she lived in Cambridge Street a woman who was paid to rouse people from their slumber would wake her up at an un-earthly hour.

The woman was known as a 'knocker-upper' and her presence alongside many other people similarly engaged in earning a pittance, by dint of thwarting the Sandman, speaks volumes about the poor peoples' lack of possessions. I mean, I have so many quartz clocks, mechanical clocks and even digital clocks around my house that if time really does fly I will need to employ an air traffic controller.

Now presumably the knocker-upper also woke the lamplighters who went around employing long poles to light the town's gaslights twice a day at dawn and dusk. The lamplighters were made redundant when the city fathers introduced electric street lighting. So, the knocker-uppers got the bullet, closely followed by the lamplighters, and I must assume that the job prospects of the pole makers also went down the spout as well.

Then again, there must have been repercussions when the food supplies to England improved to the point where Greengrocers could no longer sell fruit to people who were unable to afford the best apples and oranges and so bought 'fades', which were essentially partly rotten fruit. I can remember apples, which on one side resembled a brown-eyed Cyclops as the taint of corruption spread in an ever increasing circle. Some shopkeepers excised the rotten bit, but most left the job of cutting away the festering portion to small boys eager for a chance to employ their rusty penknives.

My mother, who at one time worked for a greengrocers called Waterworths, always told me never to buy fruit salad, as it was likely that the chunks of fruit had been salvaged from 'fades'. If that was really the case then when the advent of refrigerators rendered rotting produce a thing of the past, a veritable horde of men and women must have had to cash in their paring knives.

It was about that time when I first managed to insinuate my seventeen-year-old frame into a Lodge Lane pub, known locally as the 'Redbrick'; and it was in there that I once overheard a furious argument between a man and his wife concerning her household's lack of modern conveniences. Eventually her fusillade of insults blew apart the man's reserve and he jumped to his feet, exploding, "What more do you want...? I bought you a stove and a fucking mangle!"

As the hubbub died down I swear I heard the sound of wheels, as John Bloom's Rolls washing machine revolution unleashed fleets of tumbrels, ferrying mangles, dolly tubs and washboards to the gadget guillotine. Modernity had struck again. Apart from a few washboard manufacturers who survived, courtesy of Lonnie Donegan and other skifflers, thousands of time served dolly-tubbers, washboard technicians and mangle makers must have gone to the washhouse wall.

Of course, it wasn't just technological advances that spelled the end for old and honourable professions. The introduction of the Gaming Act in the 1960s signalled the end of a cherished institution, the 'bookie's runner'. These were the men who, in the absence of legalised betting, took punters' wagers in the street and then paid the accumulated takings to another man, who was probably a legitimate on course bookmaker. They were a bit like those Americans on street corners who operated the numbers rackets, but without the tommy guns, molls and gardenias.

My natural father was a sometime bookie's runner although it's truer to say that he was a 'bookie's biker' as he used to deliver his cash by bicycle. Once, when his balance was impaired by a session in the Oak Tree Public house, he fell off his bike in the middle of Twig Lane and refused point blank to get up when requested to do so by a similarly mounted policeman. I can still see the small entry in the *Echo* that noted his being drunk in charge of a bicycle. I mean, it was in the days when the Krays, with their Jaguars and Bentleys, were darkening the horizon and my dad was rat-arsed on a Raleigh!

One bookie's runner used to stand under one of the few remaining gas lights and was a source of fascination to me as he always wore a shirt and tie, pin-striped demob suit and plimsolls. It will come as no surprise to older Liverpudlians that after one heavily-backed Grand National Steeplechase the athletically inclined turf accountant simply took to his heels and was never seen again. Quite possibly he first took advantage of punters and then the Gaming Act by going on to open a legitimate betting shop. Do let me know if you hear of a wealthy bookmaker with a penchant for running shoes, as the fleet-footed swine still owes my mother her winnings for backing Free-booter in the 1950 Grand National Steeplechase.

82. Message in a Bottle

By late 1963 I'd had enough of the Merchant Navy. You could say I was well and truly seasick and so I had to find another job. Liverpool has historically been a port of transit for the industrial revolution and Scousers had, in the main, acted as the mules to carry the raw materials to fuel the manufacturing bases of Manchester, Birmingham and Sheffield. Very little of the huge amounts of the raw imports were actually turned into locally manufactured items. Notable exceptions included Tate & Lyle, Kraft and Dunlop. It wasn't until the sixties that Ford opened its Halewood plant, 40 years after it had opened a similar one in Dagenham.

That we Scousers were the coolies of the industrial age is borne out by the fact that the renowned humour of our dockers, or stevedores, is a major facet of our local culture. Good jobs, such as engineering apprentices, etc, were at a premium. I had left school without any formal qualifications other than a reference from a man I'd never met in the year I had attended his school, which noted that I was "intelligent, honest and trustworthy". In other words, I was only fit for menial tasks.

A well-meaning friend told me to try the bottle works in Garston. So I did, and after a perfunctory interview, designed to establish that I could walk and spit at the same time, I was told to start on the afternoon shift. I've had some jobs in my time, but working as a bottle sorter was probably the funniest of them. Nowadays it would be called 'quality control' but back then we were just the blokes who found flaws in the bottles and threw the rejects into 'collet' bins for recycling. The job was so simple it could be mastered in an hour. A huge conveyor slowly and inexorably carried the gradually cooling bottles directly from the furnaces to us, the sorters. We would grab a bottle in each hand, hold them up to the light, spin, twirl and then toss them, either into cartons if they were okay or into the bins if they were flawed. The flaws ranged from the poetically named 'birdcage', which meant that a slender bridge of glass had formed inside the neck of the bottle, to the more the more prosaic 'oily neck', which was a result of the mould not being hot enough to disperse the lubricant which prevented the glass sticking to it.

The ranks of moving bottles were never ending, but that didn't mean we worked non-stop. We worked in gangs of four and were supposed to stay abreast of each other, taking off the bottles at the front apron. Instead, two of us would work the 'wings'. That involved taking the bottles off further up the line and creating a kind of fire break while the two guys at the front worked furiously, taking off what was left that side of the breach. This concerted effort meant that we had earned a fifteen-minute break until the tide of bottles reached the front apron again. Our days and nights were punctuated by these flurries of maniacal effort followed by sweat-stained respites.

On the night shift we would smoke or eat our sandwiches during the breathing spaces gained by our Stakhonovite efforts and thus when the official break came we would be at liberty to play poker.

One of our number was a peculiar little man who was a curious mixture of irascibility and guile. He was forever boasting about his experiences in the war. He had allegedly manned a Bofors gun and he rambled on endlessly about something called a Sperry predictor, which could have been connected to the gun or equally, for all I knew, could have been some kind of pregnancy test. Another, older man called Bernie, was of the firm opinion that our gunner was a fraud. I don't know about that, but I do know he was a cheat. One night I saw him cheat in an unbelievably brazen fashion and get away with it.

It happened like this. After weeks of losing, the gunner turned up one night and demanded that we use a new and unopened deck of cards. The rest of the card school agreed, and he offered the deck to another player to be cut. He then shuffled and dealt. Now I wasn't playing that night and so I was able to *kibbitz*. As I ambled round, studying the various hands, I was astounded by what I saw. Every one of the six players had a fantastic hand. In ascending order of merit the hands went: three sevens, a straight run, a flush, a full house, four nines and a royal flush! Bernie was in possession of the four nines.

Go on … guess who had the royal flush, to the ace?[7] I was the only one in the Godhead position, and predictably everybody else bet heavily and lost heavily. That was the last card game we ever played. The gunner kept his money but his reputation was shot.

There were other more engaging characters working there. Three are worthy of mention. One guy, I can't recall his name, had spent ten years in Broadmoor for an unspecified crime. His incarceration in Broadmoor appeared to be justified in part by the fact that he had the most bizarre method of dealing with long hair that I have ever witnessed. Above our heads, at the apron of the conveyor, hung gas-fired heaters. The exile from Broadmoor would take a piece of newspaper, shove it into the gas flame and immediately apply the brand to his frizzy hair, whereupon it would explode like a brush fire before he extinguished the blaze by dint of slapping himself hard on the head! The first time I saw this I thought it was an attempt at self-immolation and screamed in the same way I did when I saw Janet Leigh being snuffed out in *Psycho*.

There was another remarkable eccentric who was almost completely bald and, in what can only be described as a ludicrous fit of vanity, had resorted to plastering black boot polish on his head! One night, when I was engaged in the usual practice of having the local publican fill twelve Gonzalez Byass sherry bottles with draught beer to accompany the fish and chips that we took turns in obtaining for our late supper, I saw him with his lady friend. Even at a distance of twenty feet it was obvious that the fierce glare of the light bulb was melting his 'hair' like tarmac in a heat wave. That was bad enough, but when he was working on the conveyor directly beneath the gas heaters there was enough polish running down his neck to shine the boots of the entire household cavalry!

The last character is now famous in a quiet sort of way, but back then he was just driving a forklift which carried the enamelled Pepsi

---

[7] According to Ray Liotta's character in the movie *Phoenix*, the odds against dealing a royal flush and four of kind in the same game is two billion to one! Imagine the odds against our former gunner's deal!

Cola bottles to the ovens to be baked. Remember those beautiful but ruinously expensive bottles? Well, Les, I think it was his name, used to help transport them, when he wasn't drumming for a group called 'The Silver Beetles'. Yes, the precursors of the Fab Four! When I met him the Beatles were just breaking into the charts with 'Love Me Do' and so I was a bit sceptical when this man, whose front teeth were missing, told me that he had played with Lennon and McCartney. Years later I was reading that despicable book about the Beatles called 'Shout' when I came across his story. Apparently the Silver Beatles needed a drummer and he was chosen. On the subsequent tour of Scotland the van crashed, leaving Les in hospital and bereft of his front teeth. That night Lennon and McCartney dragged him out of a hospital bed to play!

Several weeks later, and again in need of his percussion skills, the greatest song-writers in history called at his house, whereupon the drummer's wife promptly told them to "Fuck off!"

How did that lyric go?

"I'll get by with a little help from my friends..."

83. The Night Before

When I was a teenager in Liverpool men were often judged by the amount of alcohol they could imbibe whilst simultaneously retaining the ability to wend their way home without falling over more than three times in the same street. I was never in the running really; three drinks and I was anyone's. That is, if there was anyone who wanted to be associated with an inanely grinning green-gilled jellyfish.

Of course, when I first trod the grape-hop-barley trail I was blissfully unaware that my tolerance limit would roughly approximate that of a supplicant receiving a teaspoon of communion wine. It wasn't until my late teens that I was forced to recognise that I was to drinking bouts what Twiggy was to pie-eating contests.

It's not as if alcohol *per se* was a stranger to my palette, because as a child I sometimes broached my father's supply of over proof rum that he brought back from his sea voyages. Of course, a dribble in the bottom of a glass was no preparation for the harsh reality of my youthful indulgence in the vintner's art, which experience I obtained from that purveyor of fine wines and spirits, Bent's Brewery.

Off licences, which were small shops attached to pubs, were a sort of upgraded 'Jug & Bottle', where one could buy alcohol without having to enter the pub proper. My first purchase of fine wine was from the off licence attached to the Eagle and Child, a local inn that was noted for its discerning clientele and Olde English charm. I first tried *Esterlina*, described as a 'full-bodied ruby port' and which came in flask-shaped half bottles. It was quickly consumed as there were six of us connoisseurs eager to sample Portugal's finest and so I had to make another visit to the off licence.

I was all of fourteen and seemingly possessed of a worldly *je ne sais quoi*, or perhaps the assistant just didn't give a toss. Whatever, on my second visit I plumped for *Juanita*, a very sweet sherry. Those exotic sisters of the vine, *Juanita* and *Esterlina*, seduced me effortlessly. However, within an hour of sampling the wine my love affair with the sirens of the Porto was over. The liquid contents of my stomach were unceremoniously un-corked and the gutter was suddenly a foaming glass, as I made the first of many vows to the effect of 'never again'.

Since then I have broken that vow more times than Harold Shipman has broken the Hippocratic Oath. There have been many contenders for the worst bout of all, but on reflection the joint winner has to be the night I once again indulged in a product of Bent's brewery... It was in 1964 and I was in the company of a mate called Bobby. I can't remember his surname but he had sparse ginger hair and lips so full that could have served as a warning against the dangers of botched collagen implants. We were going to the Thursday night hop at the Locarno when Bobby suggested we steady our nerves with a drink or two. Copping off with girls, you understand, wasn't without its stressful aspect, even for two cuties like Bobby and myself, and so I readily agreed.

Now at that time Bents had introduced a wine which must have been specifically targeted at those men who left work and went straight to a bar where they drank heavily, on an empty stomach, because, believe it or not, the novel wine was enriched with beef extract and was labelled 'Bentox'. The suffix 'ox' possibly referred to the popular beef extract stock cube called Oxo, that almost all housewives used to flavour stews, although it's more likely that it simply denoted the essence from an Ox. It was as vile a concoction as you can possibly imagine – cheap red wine heavily laced with gravy browning. We had fourteen singles each in the space of an hour and when we emerged into the oxygen rich Liverpool air we promptly collapsed against the first wall we hit and stayed there for hours. I can still feel the shame of it now. I mean, fancy disappointing all those eager young women!

The other candidate for the title 'a night from Hell' was in 1972 when I first made the acquaintance of a man who would prove a good friend to me for many years. His name was Keith Bax and he was, for me, the original hippy. With his full beard and long hair he looked like a hip Karl Marx, and was in many ways as shrewd as the

German *meister*. I had just finished work in Bidston and was persuaded by a work-mate to go for a drink. Tony was, as I later discovered, an alcoholic, but that night he was just a funny guy whose mannerisms and whimsical humour made me laugh. We ended up in a pub called the Custom House near the Albert Dock where Keith Bax was drinking with friends. Like his companions, Keith was dressed in the latest Haight-Ashbury style, flared jeans and sheepskin jacket with hand-sewn motifs. Tony, a most un-hip ordinary man was fascinated by the assembly and promptly offered to buy them all a drink. Keith graciously declined the offer, quietly pointing out that one drink was enough as they were smoking marijuana. With that he offered us a toke of the supersized joint. It wasn't my first taste of marijuana but it was the first I'd had while almost falling over drunk … and its effect on me was catastrophic.

I vaguely remember Keith guiding me around the horseshoe shaped bar and pointing me in the direction of the gent's toilet-cum-vomitarium. The next thing I remember was the manager gently shaking me and asking me to get up from the floor. I pleaded with him, slurring that I just wanted to lay my face on the cold floor, but he insisted, as I was in the girl's toilets and the ladies were a wee bit agitated about having to step over my inert body. Seeing that I was incapable of standing up unaided the manager then picked me up and carried me to the gents, where he left me to recover!

When I did recover the kindly Keith took me outside and waited with me until a taxi came. The taxi drew close and I was uncomfortably aware of the alarm on the driver's face. He put his head out of the window and made me promise not to be sick. I solemnly agreed but I hadn't been in the immaculately maintained interior two minutes before I added to my life's list of broken vows.

Years later, Keith and I attended the same university, where he went on to become a professor. He was such a lovely man, and my favourite Hippy. He died in a car crash one Christmas in Austria, on his way back home to Liverpool. Rest in peace, old friend.